By This Sign

By This Sign

Battle of the Milvian Bridge

Constantine's troops, their shields freshly painted with the symbol of Christ, utterly crush their opponents. Enemy soldiers that escape the sword die by drowning in the murky waters of the Tiber River.

Details from the illustration by Greg Harlin, page 144.

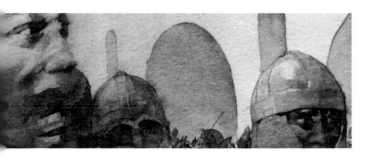

A.D. 250 to 350

From the Decian Persecution to the Constantine Era

The Christians

THEIR FIRST TWO THOUSAND YEARS

Third Volume

CHP

CHRISTIAN HISTORY PROJECT

THE EDITOR:

Ted Byfield has been a journalist for fifty-five years and a western Canadian magazine publisher since 1973, the founder of *Alberta Report* and *British Columbia Report* weekly newsmagazines, and founding editor of *Alberta in the Twentieth Century*, a twelve-volume history of Alberta. A columnist for Canada's *Sun* newspapers and sometime contributor to the *National Post* and *Globe and Mail* national newspapers, he is active in evangelical journalistic outreach. He was one of the founders of St. John's School of Alberta, an Anglican school for boys where he developed a new method of teaching history.

THE ASSOCIATE EDITOR:

Calvin Demmon of Marina, California, has worked as an editor of *Alberta Report* newsmagazine; as city editor of the *Huntington Park Daily Signal* and of the *Daily Southeast News* in Los Angeles County; and as a columnist and editor for the *Monterey County Herald*. He has contributed articles and short stories to a number of magazines and to several books.

COVER:

The painting by Greg Harlin of Wood Ronsaville Harlin, Inc. in Annapolis, Maryland, depicts the momentous vision given Constantine on his trek to Rome. A cross appeared in the sky accompanied by the words, "Conquer by this."

CHRISTIAN HISTORY PROJECT LIMITED PARTNERSHIP

President and CEO	Robert W. Doull
Controller	Beverly Arlow, CGA
Marketing Manager	Leanne Nash
Sales Promotion Manager	Brian Lehr
Contact Center Manager	Kathy Therrien
Contact Center Administrators	Grace De Guzman, Mark Dawson
Trainer	Keith Bennett
Distribution Manager	Lori Arndt
Information Systems Manager	Michael Keast

By This Sign A.D. 250 to 350 From the Decian Persecution to the Constantine Era

Writers	Charlotte Allen, Ted Byfield, Virginia Byfield, Vincent Carroll, Calvin Demmon, Mark Galli, Eleanor Gasparik, Ian Hunter, Eddie Keen, Frederica Mathewes-Greene, John Muggeridge, John David Powell, David Shiflett, Paul Sullivan, Steve Weatherbe, Joe Woodard
Art Director / Illustrations Editor	Jack Keaschuk
Page Production & Graphics	Dean Pickup
Illustrators	Richard Connor, Carlo Cosentino, Bob Crofut, Michael Dudash, Matthew Frey, Greg Harlin, Glenn Harrington, Jamie Holloway, Tom McNeely, John Rush, John Smith, Richard Sparks, Shannon Stirnweis, Rob Wood
Director of Research	Moira Calder
Researchers	Marilyn Bertsch, Erika Brown, Wendy de Candole, Ken Gee, Michelle Gee, Bruce Grant, Louise Henein, Gregory Kopchuk, Nathan Manning, Hope Martynuik, Ryan Roth, Dustin Tkachuk, Jared Tkachuk
Production Editor	Rev. David Edwards
Proofreaders	P.A. Colwell, Faith Farthing
Academic Consultants	Dr. Carnegie Samuel Calian, Dr. Kimberly Georgedes, Father Brian Hubka, Dr. Joseph H. Lynch, Dr. William McDonald, Dr. David T. Priestley, Dr. Douglas Sweeney, Dr. Eugene TeSelle

THE CHRISTIANS: Their First Two Thousand Years

Series Planner	Barrett Pashak
Assistant Planner	Louise Henein

© 2003 Christian History Project Inc.
© 2003 Christian History Project Limited Partnership.

Chairman	Gerald J. Maier

NATIONAL LIBRARY OF CANADA CATALOGUING IN PUBLICATION DATA

Main entry under title:

By this sign : A.D. 250 to 350 : from the Decian persecution to the Constantine era.

(The Christians : their first two thousand years ; 3)
Includes bibliographical references and index.
ISBN 0-9689873-2-X

1. Church history--Primitive and early church, ca. 30-600. 2. Persecution--History--Early church, ca. 30-600. 3. Constantine I, Emperor of Rome, d. 337. I. Christian History Project. II. Series: Christians : their first two thousand years ; 3.
BR165.B92 2003   270.1   C2002-911495-0

PRINTED IN CANADA BY FRIESENS CORPORATION

CONTENTS

ILLUSTRATIONS

(Artists)

For additional copies of this book or information on others in the series,
please contact us at:

The Christian History Project
10333 178 Street
Edmonton AB, Canada, T5S 1R5
www.christianhistoryproject.com

1-800-853-5402

FOREWORD

This volume, third of a projected fifteen, completes the first great era of Christianity. The three together—whose time frame runs from Pentecost to the Constantine era, a span of about three hundred years—tell how the Christians rose from their beginnings as a despised Jewish sect to become the dominant religious force in the Roman world.

Though the Christian triumph followed Constantine's military victory, it was in no sense a military achievement. Constantine did not bring the Christians to power. Much more truthfully, they brought him to power, for they were able to provide what Rome had lost, a sense of unity and purpose. However fitfully and imperfectly it was employed, that component was furnished by Jesus Christ, and Constantine's great city of Constantinople remained a Christian bastion for the next eleven hundred years.

Rather than a triumphal march, the rise of Christianity was a path of bitter pain and suffering, a prolonged ordeal that reached its apogee during the time span of this volume. Under Decius and Valerian, then some fifty years later under Diocletian, Galerius and Daia, the empire's officialdom launched vicious campaigns of torture, slavery and execution to stamp this movement out. Because of the staggering loyalty to their Lord of so many Christians, all these efforts failed. Then came Constantine, who in effect decided. If you can't beat them, join them—which he did.

How sincerely he joined them has been debated by Christians ever since. To many in the West, he was a mere opportunist who poisoned Christianity by making it an avenue to wealth and power. To eastern Christians, however, he is a revered saint. We have done our best in this volume to reflect the facts as they are known. Most will conclude, we think, that it is not at all an easy question. He was a man of striking contradictions.

But they will understand also why Christians of the age preferred Constantine's privileges to Diocletian's executioners. Our era has come to believe in a neutral middle position called "pluralism," in which the practice of all law-abiding religions is permitted. But that concept is scarcely a hundred years old, and already we see state authority increasingly invoked to inhibit Christian activity and the expression of Christian thought. Perhaps, therefore, a coming generation will discover that there is no middle position, that the painful choice must always lie between a Constantine and a Diocletian. Time will tell.

Ted Byfield

The year is 250, and at the door of one of North Africa's many Christian churches a soldier reads out the emperor Decius's solution for the failing Roman Empire. The loyalty of citizens is to be tested, with Christians marked for special attention. Leaders of the Church are to be surrendered for imprisonment and death. The rest of the faithful can survive only through oaths of fealty and offerings to the gods and to the emperor. Christianity, Decius declares, is to be eradicated.

CHAPTER 1

Give up the faith or die: the church's grim choice

The erudite emperor Decius sees in Christianity
a menace that must be wiped out once and for all,
and with brutal efficiency sets out to do just that

For Christians approaching the middle years of the third century, life in the Roman Empire had been remarkably tranquil. True, persecution had broken out from time to time in isolated areas over the past four decades. But Christian congregations could be found in all major centers and many smaller ones and, in the main, they had been free from the dreaded knock on the door at night, from harassment by the police, and from beating and mutilation at the hands of infuriated mobs. However, in the year 249, with the death of the emperor Philip the Arab, who some said was a Christian himself, Christians with long memories read ominous signs. Very dark days were ahead.

They had good reason to think so. Philip had died that year at the hands of the able and aggressive Decius, a man Christians spoke of in hushed tones, even dreading to mention his name. He was known to regard Christianity as a menace to the very existence of the empire. It must be scoured from the face of the earth by whatever means necessary, he had declared. So the accession of Decius caused Christians to tremble. Their long respite had ended, they feared. The horrors recalled by their parents and grandparents were about to begin again.

They didn't have long to wait. The trouble materialized full-blown with an edict against the practice of Christianity, issued by the new emperor in 250.

The response to it was instantaneous. Everywhere persecution and martyrdoms took place. In Sicily, a young Christian woman who would come to be known as St. Agatha caught the eye of the governor, who was so affected by her beauty that he pleaded with her to renounce her religion. Her refusal brought her death on hot coals. At Toulouse, Saturninus was tied to a wild bull and dragged to death. Bishop Babylas of Antioch (the man who, in fable if not in fact, had required the Emperor Philip to do penance) was martyred. In Caesarea, Origen was imprisoned and tortured, dying from his wounds three years later.

In Asia Minor, the frightened Bishop Gregory of Cappadocia fled his see while accepting the fact that most of his converts had fled their new faith. The bishop of Smyrna and other leading Christians of the city succumbed to the threat of persecution, and offered ceremonial sacrifices to the cult of the emperor. The persecution in Egypt is said to have taken sadistic forms as the authorities seemed eager to satisfy the blood lust of the mob. Women were beheaded. Many Christians were burned alive. Others died during a variety of tortures that inflicted pain beyond human endurance.

Desperate to escape such fates, some Christians bought certificates falsely documenting that they had worshiped the emperor as ordered, or they bribed their friends to obtain the documents. Others, in the larger cities, went into hiding, but whole congregations apostatized in smaller towns where hiding was impossible.

For Decius, the sudden crackdown merely confronted one of the many dangerous problems that beset his empire. It was showing signs of imminent collapse. There were worrisome doubts about the viability of its economy. Division was chronic at the highest level. Romans warred against Romans, soldiers proclaimed soldiers as emperors. Goths and a myriad of other German tribes crossed the frontier

The burden of returning the Roman Empire to its previous vigor is evident in the face of the emperor Decius (249–251). Among his strategies: Eliminate the Christians.

unchallenged to raid, pillage and destroy the towns and cities beyond. In the East, a new royal house in Persia laid claim to the whole Roman Empire east of the Aegean and Mediterranean.

What was needed, Decius concluded, was a resurgence of the ancient Roman purity and vigor by forcibly restoring the proper worship of the gods of the state, a practice that was in serious decline. But obstructing this, even jeering it, was this peculiar sect known as the Christians, with their roots in Palestine and Judaism, steadily growing and becoming more troublingly visible everywhere.

He had strong support for his edict, particularly among the ancient senatorial families at Rome. After killing Philip in battle near Verona in September 249, Decius was showered with accolades by a once hostile senate. It bestowed upon him the full title of Imperator Caesar, and gave him a multitude of other titles and names—Messius Quintus Trajanus Decius Pius Felix Invictus

As authorities sought to satisfy the blood lust of the mob, women were beheaded, many Christians burned alive, and other tortures delivered pain beyond endurance.

Augustus Pontifex Maximus Optimus Maximusque Princeps Tribuniciae Potestatis Pater Patriae and Consul.

He was an erudite man, even able to write his own speeches, an ability rare among soldiers. But then he really wasn't a soldier-emperor. Unlike his immediate predecessors, he was a son of the Roman aristocracy that had moved to the provinces. Born about 190 at Budalia (see map page 131, D3) in Lower Pannonia (the future Slovakia), he spent his formative years in the Danube region, where the military spirit and early Roman virtues were the strongest of anywhere in the empire.

In his youth, he had moved to Rome, a young man of lean and determined face, with thin lips and a narrow nose. He married into an old Italian family, as had his father. He advanced through a normal senatorial career, not as a soldier, but as a bureaucrat. His many years of public service saw him hold several important positions, including city prefect of Rome, and carry out his duties justly and well.

As emperor, he acted swiftly, launching a vast reorganization of government, laying out public works projects, and distributing money to the people, a custom for new emperors. He began immediately to strengthen the defenses against barbarian raids over the Danube. Much to the satisfaction of the Senate, he restored the senatorially appointed office of "censor," abolished some 270 years before. Not only did the censor keep the census, the official register of Roman citizens, he also determined who was not worthy or morally fit for citizenship; he could even remove a senator from office. The senators chose as the first censor the popular Licinius Valerianus, Valerian for short, a well-intended man of unfortunate omen for the Christians, and if anything, a worse omen for Rome itself.

But most determinedly, Decius reinforced the religious cult of the emperor, still regionally popular in the East, where cities kept temples dedicated to it. Solemn oaths were invoked in the emperor's name. His image, with a radiated crown symbolizing the sun god, was imprinted on Roman coinage. To worship the emperor was to worship Rome, and the prosperity of one seemed inextricably tied to the prosperity of the other. Much of the population supported Decius. They saw in the barbarian invasions, in the widespread poverty, in the outbreaks of plague and in every other illness and natural calamity, the anger of the gods toward a backsliding empire.

Christians, of course, participated neither in emperor worship nor in the worship of any of the empire's other deities. They shunned the myriad festivals and rituals for the gods. Their neighbors called them atheists because they dishonored the traditional deities, and accused them of conducting their own

Decius sought the acquiescence of Christians. If persuasion didn't work, the recalcitrant could be tortured, banished and relieved of personal property. Death was a last resort.

secret and despicable rites. For their part, Christians believed that pagans faced an eternity of fire and torment. They saw themselves as soldiers in the army of Jesus, an army they considered the best defense for the empire.

Christianity had grown relatively unabated between 212 and 249. Few Christians of the time had suffered for their belief, and even fewer had been forced to choose between life and their faith. Moreover, the large cities offered an unlimited buffet of temptations and had seduced many Christians through pride and ambition. Even bishops had succumbed to worldliness and gain.

It was a period, lamented Bishop Cyprian of Carthage, when men and women dishonored the image of God, oaths were taken and broken lightly, when Christian married non-Christian, when clergy engaged in questionable relationships with unmarried women, when rancor and hatred ran riot, and services were held in an atmosphere of gossip and frivolity.

Decius's edict was issued in the waning days of 249 or the first days of 250. It was the first imperial attempt to enforce religious conformity on people throughout the empire, and it came in two parts, one addressed to the public and the other addressed to imperial officials. The first decreed that between one and fifty days after the arrival of the edict, everyone must make sacrifice to the gods and to the emperor. Anyone refusing to pour a libation and taste sacrificial meat was presumed to be Christian and ordered tortured or banished. In addition, anyone professing Christianity, or assembling for Christian worship, was committing a crime.

Though the exact wording of the "loathsome edict," as the Christians called it, has not survived, historians have pieced together its provisions from documents associated with it—like the certificates, or *libelli*, issued in

Egypt, which stated that the person named had always sacrificed to the gods and was doing so now in the presence of commission members. One read, in part:

> To those superintending the sacrifices of the village of Theadelphia, from Aurelia Bellias, daughter of Peteres, and her daughter Capinis. We have sacrificed to the gods all along, and now in your presences according to orders I poured a libation and sacrificed and tasted of the sacred offerings, and I request you to subscribe this for us. [Signatures:] We, Aurelius Serenus and Aurelius Hermas, saw you sacrificing. Signed by me, Hermas.

Decius did not seek the death of Christians, but rather their acquiescence. If gentle persuasion didn't work, then the recalcitrant could be tortured, starved, banished, and relieved of all personal property. Death was a last resort. The second part of the edict established a bureaucracy to enforce it. It called for commissions of notable citizens who would preside over the sacrifices, issue libelli, and record the names of those who complied. They could impose the lesser penalties; only a proconsul after further investigation could impose death.

Events moved rapidly. On the theory that to kill the head was to kill the body, the primary target was the church's leadership. One of the first victims in Rome was Bishop Fabian, who met his death on January 20, 250. No details have been preserved of his trial or martyrdom.[1] Two of Fabian's presbyters and two subdeacons were jailed soon after, followed by other clergy and some members of the imperial household. Some died in prison, some were executed, some were sent to die a slow death in the awful mines (see sidebar page 122). Prisons in Decius's time were unspeakably vile hellholes, lacking air, light and

---

1. It is known that Fabian was not a member of the clergy prior to becoming bishop and had no aspirations of leading any church. He was visiting the city and watching the election of the next bishop when a dove landed on his head. This was seen as a divine sign that Fabian should lead the Roman church. During his tenure, Fabian established an elaborate organization for his diocese. He had forty-six presbyters, seven deacons, seven subdeacons, forty-two attendants, fifty exorcists and readers, and an unspecified number of doorkeepers.

Written in Greek and signed by the witnessing official Hermas, this libellus certifies that a woman and her daughter from the village of Theadelphia in Egypt were loyal citizens of the Roman Empire, having proved it by offering a sacrifice.

Birth of a great Christian nation

By the 300s, Spanish Christianity is booming, but its revered champion of
orthodoxy dismays the faithful by becoming a heretic near the age of 100

Although Spain would play a major and often decisive role in Christian history, surprisingly little is known of the faith's early years in that land. It is clear enough, however, that Christian evangelists reached Spain fairly quickly; the first of them was quite possibly Paul himself. Not only is there an enduring legend of a voyage to Spain by Paul, but Spanish Christians have long cherished the story of a visit to their land by the apostle James, with many communities named after him (Santiago or San Diego in Spanish). By the end of the second century, the Christian community on the Spanish peninsula appears to be so far-flung and well established that its roots must have been nourished by many decades of successful gospel preaching.

The evidence is, admittedly, scattered. Christian inscriptions in Spain are rare before the fourth century, and classical writers provide us with little help. As the historian H. V. Livermore observes, those writers "treat of Rome in the Iberian Peninsula rather than of the peninsula under Roman rule." By the time a chronicler who is interested in Spain itself arrives on the scene, in the person of Bishop Hydatius, it is the fifth century, and the barbarians are pouring into Spain from the north.

Nevertheless, in the early years of the third century, Tertullian wrote that "all the confines of Spain . . . have submitted themselves to Christ"—a vague but comprehensive description of Christianity's reach. Tertullian's report is confirmed in detail in the mid-third century, when Cyprian catalogs Christian communities in a variety of distant cities and includes north-central Leon, Merida in the west, and Saragossa in the northeast. Christianity was still the religion of a decided minority, of course, but in those areas that were most thoroughly Romanized—notably the Spanish south—it was a growing part of urban life.

Spain at this time was not quite the dank backwater that its distance from the great imperial cities would suggest. Roman troops invaded the peninsula some two hundred years before Christ, and more or less completed this conquest during Augustus's reign. In the first and second centuries, the city of Cordoba was considered a cosmopolitan "little Rome" that boasted resident communities of Greeks, Syrians, Egyptians, and Jews. It was also, in historian Victor C. de Clercq's phrase, "a much-desired assignment for proconsuls." The peninsula produced emperors (Trajan, Hadrian), literary giants (Seneca, Lucan, Quintillian), and first-rate exports such as olive oil. Given the times, it also produced its share of Christian martyrs, although details of their final tests of faith, including some dates, are often impossible to pin down.

The great Spanish Christian poet Prudentius, writing in the fourth century, contends that Spain boasted martyrs during every Roman persecution, and recounts the traditions of many of them. Among the most inspiring stories is that of Fructuosus, bishop of Tarragona, who perished during a persecution in 259, and whose composure and words of reassurance, as he was led to the amphitheater to be burnt alive, were noted with admiration by Augustine.

Twelve-year-old Eulalia of Merida was tortured and killed after refusing, probably in 304, to obey Diocletian's edicts to offer sacrifice to pagan gods. Vincent of Saragossa, another victim of the Diocletian crackdown, showed such legendary strength and serenity during his ordeal over a flaming gridiron that his fame rapidly spread far beyond his home peninsula.

Perhaps the most telling sign of Christianity's vitality in Roman Spain was the Council of Elvira, an early fourth-century gathering of bishops from around the peninsula in a now ruined town near Granada. Unfortunately, inscriptions on some of the surviving copies of the eighty-one canons approved at Elvira indicate the year 324—a wholly improbable date, according to the experts. For one thing, Bishop Hosius of Cordoba, who was certainly present at the council, was out of the country during that year. As a result, historians marshal a variety of arguments for a much earlier date—300 to 309, not long before or after the climax of the Diocletian persecution in Hispania.

The council's decisions address a staggering host of issues that illuminate early Christian life in Spain. They govern baptism, marriage, and the treatment of a variety of sexual transgressions (five years of penance for a first-time adulterer, for example). They lay out rules on fasting and usury; they stipulate prohibitions against idolatry and even toward such gambling games as thimbles. Most famously, the council approved the oldest command of its kind, that clergy abstain from sex. In their heavy emphasis on disciplinary matters, the acts reveal a community whose ethos appears, from a modern point of view, somewhat confining, but also one that took very seriously the all-encompassing nature of a Christian life.

This seriousness extended to contemporary struggles with heresies such as Arianism and Donatism. It was in the fight against them that Spain's Bishop Hosius rose to become the most influential champion of orthodoxy in the West. For a time, he exercised this influence from an enviable perch—as ecclesiastical adviser to Constantine the Great after that emperor's conversion to the faith. It was Hosius who reportedly presided at the Council of Nicea in 325, which began the development of the famous Nicene Creed.

Hosius maintained his impressive fidelity to orthodoxy during most of a life that spanned more than one hundred years (c. 256 to 358). Even after Constantine's son and successor, Constantius, embraced the heretical Arian view, Hosius remained steadfast in the face of imperial pressure. "Remember that you are a mortal man," he thundered in a bracing rebuke of the emperor. "Fear the day of judgment. . . . Do not interfere in ecclesiastical affairs, or dictate anything about them to us, but rather learn from us what you ought to believe concerning them."

Then, incredibly, Hosius capitulated. In his nineties and still under official pressure, Hosius signed his own name to heresy, forever sullying the reputation of one of the great Western defenders of the faith. It seems that he simply had lived too long; at least that is how many Christians have interpreted it, although according to Athanasius, he did return to orthodoxy just before his death.

It wasn't long, however, before the faithful in Spain had much more alarming events to cope with than an apostate bishop. The barbarians were on the march; the Suevi were the first of the pagans into Spain, a mere three years after they crashed the borders of the empire on the last day of 406. An era was ending; and at the time, Christianity's future on the peninsula seemed doubtful. Instead, when the dust had finally settled more than a century later, the barbarian kingdoms would become some of the greatest champions of the faith the world has ever known. ∎

Since the ninth century, Spanish Christians have claimed that the site of the inspiring cathedral of Santiago de Compostela (left) marks the tomb of the apostle James "the Great." The twelfth-century shrine was a favorite goal of pilgrims in the Middle Ages. In the early fourth century the sarcophagus of Layos (below), south of Toledo, was carved with exquisite scenes from the Old and New Testaments.

living space. The guards were brutal. What little food was available was usually contaminated or spoiled, and drinking water was polluted. Many Christians spent long months in these appalling conditions awaiting their fate. Death sentences were rarely carried out quickly. The condemned were made to endure lengthy and agonizing torture to terrify others. Simple beheading was considered an act of mercy.

The edict reached Carthage in the first months of 250. Some ignored it and suffered. Some fled. A large number rushed out to sacrifice and to obtain libelli. "At the very first publication of the (edict)," wrote Carthage's Bishop Cyprian, "the greater part of the brethren fell away and betrayed their faith. . . . They did not even wait to be summoned, much less refuse to obey the command. Before the battle began, many were conquered and overthrown without meeting the shock, not even delaying long enough to give the appearance of sacrificing against their will."

The red peaks of the Roman gold mines at Las Medulas in northwest Spain (see map page 130, A2) are now a designated UNESCO world heritage site. Slaves who worked the mines in the first two centuries A.D. were part of an advanced technology that used hydraulic power, tearing down the mountains to get at the gold buried in them.

A capitulation of faith was made easy. The government's demands seemed simple, straightforward, even reasonable. After all, good citizenship required obedience, and all a worshiper had to do was approach the altar in the morning with an animal and sacrifice it. Or if the person could not afford an animal, a pinch of incense thrown onto the altar would suffice. It was all neat and clean, and merely an outward appearance. Surely God knew what was really in the heart, and the emperor did not really want them to cease being Christians, merely to respect the empire's traditions as well. Such was the rationalization.

Still, for some of the *lapsi*, the "lapsed," as they came to be known, apostasy came with a price. Cyprian described one person who was "seized with dumbness immediately after he had done the deed." A woman was said to have bitten her tongue, "which had tasted and uttered the evil thing," and died after suffering unspecified "internal agonies." A husband dragged his wife to the altar, where her hands were forcibly held during the sacrifice. "It is not I, but you who sacrificed!" she exclaimed before she was sentenced to banishment. Others were led to recant, even by their clergy.

As the edict reached out into the empire, so too did the instances of defiant heroism.

Pionius, a priest from Smyrna, was well known in that great Asian port city on the Aegean for his straightforward eloquence, lively banter, and sheer goodness. Upon arrest, Pionius was determined to testify forthrightly for his faith. To show everyone who watched, as he was marched through the streets, that he was not going to participate in a pagan sacrifice, he put a rope around his neck and the necks of his companions. He was taken to the temple, where he addressed the loud and insulting crowd in the languages of the city. He quoted Homer to the Greeks, reminding them that the poet had declared that it was a sacrilege to taunt those who were about to die. The Jews he confronted with the words of Solomon and Moses. He also warned that punishment would befall those who killed Christians.

His eloquence was so moving that members of the crowd cried out to him, urging him to make the sacrifice and save his life. "Don't be obstinate," they implored. "Life is sweet, Pionius, and the light of day is good!"

'Your task is to conquer or to punish,' Pionius told his faltering inquisitor. 'You cannot conquer me, so get on with the punishment.'

To which he replied: "Yes, life is sweet, I know, but another life is waiting for us! And the light here is good, but it is the true light that we dream of possessing!"

"Your task is to conquer or to punish," he told a faltering inquisitor. "You cannot conquer me, so get on with the punishment!"

Pionius was sent to prison to await his execution, but he was not left long in his foul and dark dungeon to pray in peace and to prepare for death. Soon he was taken from his cell, placed on the rack, and torn with iron vises. Though urged by his bishop to save himself and sacrifice to the gods, through it all he did not waver. And when he was led into the arena, torn and bloodied, to be burned alive in front of the clamorous spectators, Pionius removed his clothes by himself, leaned against the stake, and ordered the executioners to nail him to it. As the flames were about to engulf him, Pionius cried out: "I hasten to my death so that I may awaken all the earlier in the Resurrection."

Pionius was not alone. There was Nestor, bishop of Magydus, who was so well respected that after being tortured and hanged, dying upon a cross, he exhorted the crowd to pray, and Christians and non-Christians knelt and prayed while he breathed his last breath. There was Alexander, bishop of Jerusalem and a friend of Origen, whom the beasts refused to attack, and who instead died in chains, in prison. There was Polyeuctus of Cappadocia, who was executed summarily after defiantly tearing up the imperial edict in the public square. Then there were Pergentinus and Laurentinus, two brothers who were still attending school at Arezzo in Umbria when they were brought before the court. Although they admitted to being Christians, they were released because of their youth and their nobility. They immediately set out on a successful evangelistic campaign, converting many before being arrested again and beheaded. Her youth did not save Agnes of Rome, aged twelve or thirteen, who was also beheaded. There were Mappalicus and his seventeen companions in Carthage who joined him in death—one under torture, another in the mines, and fifteen of starvation in two filthy, foul-smelling cells.

Though the Decian persecution lasted less than two years, it engulfed the entire Christian world in chaos. Parents and children no longer trusted one another, particularly if they were from households where Christians and non-Christians lived together as family. Those weak in conviction looked to their leaders for guidance and strength, but many bishops and members of the clergy took the easy road themselves. Some paid for their certificates with bribes. Still others fled into the wilderness or to other hiding places. Others held fast for a while, but sacrificed after suffering tortures. But some sustained their faith through every manner of ordeal. "Proof was given," wrote Cyprian, "when your brethren entered the proud fight, for they showed all the others how to overcome torture, and gave an example of valor and faith. They fought in the forefront of the battle until the enemy retired vanquished before them."

By 251, the fires of the persecutions were failing. Whatever damage the edict inflicted on the Christians, it did not notably restore the rectitude of ancient Rome. As months went by, the edict appealed only to the baser instincts of the

Valerian's second edict was the most vicious ever. It called for the execution of bishops, presbyters and deacons. Any aristocrat belonging to the church was to be executed.

eastern rabble, which is why many non-Christians, disgusted at the mob's enjoyment of blood and suffering, breathed a general sigh of relief when Rome, in the absence of the emperor, refused to continue the persecutions.

Decius's personal attention had been diverted by far more pressing issues—a civil war in Gaul, the outbreak of a plague that was to last twenty years, and a major barbarian breakthrough into Greece. He left Rome to confront the Goth chieftain Kniva near Nicopolis on the Adriatic coast. Kniva was defeated, losing more than thirty thousand men, but was not himself killed. Instead he took up with a second Gothic force, surprised Decius's army as it rested at Beroea, 150 miles to the northeast, and slaughtered it. Decius escaped to the north with what was left of his army into Moesia on the Danube, where the governor Gallus still had an army intact.

In June 251, Kniva lured Decius and his son, along with their troops, into the marshes near Abrittus, south of the Danube, in the future Bulgaria. His son perished first. No one must mourn, ordered Decius in a memorable line. "The death of one soldier is not a great loss to the republic." He then heroically led his troops into the bogs, where they were butchered as they floundered to gain their footing. The bodies of the emperor and his son were never recovered.

The Senate declared them gods, but it was the first time a Roman emperor was to die in battle at the hands of an enemy of Rome, a defeat from which, in the view of some historians, Roman fortunes on the Danube would never fully recover. Gallus then compounded the disaster by bribing the Goths into retiring back across the frontier to help defend the empire from other barbarian invaders. In September 251, the army proclaimed Gallus emperor, while rumor spread that he had plotted Decius's defeat, either by conspiring with the Goths or by holding back reinforcements.

The tomb of Decius's second son, Hostilianus, glorifies his exploits among the barbarians. Hostilianus's father and brother had both died at the hands of barbarians in the marshes south of the Danube.

Decius's short-lived attempt to revive the empire's majesty had miserably failed, and Gallus now faced a crisis on every front. Barbarians were attacking Italy from the north, the Persians were invading Syria to the east, and the Christians were growing again.

Worst of all, the plague's toll was mounting. By the spring of 252, it had claimed the life of the only surviving son of Decius, whom Gallus had made co-ruler in an attempt to dispel the rumors that he'd betrayed his father. The plague was killing five thousand people in Rome every day. Panic had seized the people of Africa, where half the population of Alexandria was to die. Homes were abandoned, and sick friends and family were tossed into the streets with the dead and the dying who pleaded for pity. No pity was found except from Christians who tended the sick regardless of their religious beliefs. Gallus was called upon to do something to stop the pestilence, and so he ordered all persons to sacrifice to the gods on behalf of the entire empire.

This gave him the opportunity to rid the empire of the remaining Christian bishops, but he took little advantage of it. Cornelius, the new bishop of Rome, was arrested and died in prison in 253. The next bishop, Lucius, was exiled, but was allowed to return after several months. By then Gallus had far more weighty problems to contend with. The Persian king, Shapur, had taken Armenia, Rome's buffer against the Persian Empire, then had invaded and looted Syria virtually unopposed.

On the Danube, Gallus's bribe-purchased peace did not long restrain the Goths. Those not subject to Kniva stormed over the river, where they were blocked by Aemilian, the new governor of Moesia. Victorious against the Goths, Aemilian now marched on Rome to challenge Gallus. The two armies met about fifty miles north of the city, but no battle ensued. Gallus's men, discerning inevitable defeat, killed Gallus and his son, then joined Aemilian. Aemilian now faced Valerian, the man the Senate had named censor, who was currently in command of Roman forces on the Rhine and was marching south to restore senatorial control of the army. His men had already named him emperor. Aemilian's troops promptly switched their allegiance, murdered Aemilian after a reign of three months, and prepared to welcome Valerian to the capital.

Valerian—Publius Licinius Valerianus was born about 195 into a distinguished Etrurian family. Loyalty to constituted authority was his marked trait,

Recent scholarship concludes that Agnes was martyred at Rome during the persecutions of the third century. This gilded glass platter, in the catacomb of Panfilo in Rome, was crafted shortly after her death.

though it was the dubiously legitimate Gallus who had put him in charge of the formidable legions of the Upper Rhine. The Senate gave Valerian a hearty reception and granted him imperial titles when he entered Rome in August. Among his first official acts was the elevation of his thirty-five-year-old son, Gallienus, to the position of co-emperor. At last, said the senators, Rome had a ruler with no trace of provincial barbarism. Valerian's background lay deep in an ancient Roman family. The empire would again have at its head a true Roman, a man who was magnanimous, urbane, closely connected to the ancient city, and devoted to a way of life that must not fail.

It was now the late summer of 253 and turmoil prevailed everywhere. Goths and Persians ran rampant on the frontiers. Brigands roamed the countryside. Pirates plundered merchant ships on the Black Sea. The plague continued unabated. Inflation spiraled upward. Inscriptions were no longer being carved on imperial monuments in the province of Dacia because invading Goths had destroyed them as fast as they rose, and Dacian cities were no longer able to strike coins for local use. As had Decius, Valerian needed to act promptly. He dispatched his son Gallienus to confront a new German incursion along the Rhine, while he moved east to meet the Goths, now raiding by sea along the eastern coasts. The Christians, meanwhile, took advantage of a four-year respite, grappled with the problems posed by the return of the lapsed, and added throngs to their numbers. Valerian, observed Alexandria's Bishop Dionysius, was kind and friendly to the Christians. So many Christians worked in his household it was almost a church in itself. Indeed, Valerian's own daughter-in-law was believed to be Christian.

Quite suddenly, however, in August 257, Dionysius was given horrific reason to revise this enthusiastic estimate. The emperor issued the first of two edicts that renewed the Christian persecutions. The desperate Valerian had concluded, like Decius, that only the intervention of the pagan gods could restore the imperial fortunes.

The first edict, directed at the clergy, was designed to encourage Christians to join their neighbors in regaining the favor of the gods. The terms were mild and required only that anyone not observing the Roman religion show loyalty by giving a token recognition of the ceremonies. But it also banned all Christian services, including those in cemeteries where Christians traditionally gathered. Many bishops refused to obey, among them Cyprian and Dionysius. These were exiled.

Still the gods frowned, meaning that the problems remained. So the second edict in the summer of 258 was the most vicious ever. It called for the execution of bishops, presbyters and deacons. High-ranking laymen were to lose their civil status and their property. Any aristocrat in the church who did not renounce the faith was also to be executed. The intent of the edict was twofold: to force Christians to recant their faith and worship Roman gods, and to restore the depleting treasury with the confiscated property of the church and its wealthier members.

The first to die was Bishop Sixtus of Rome. One of his deacons, the young and virtuous Laurence, begged that Sixtus allow him to die with him. Alban Butler's *The Lives of the Saints* (first published in 1756) tells the cherished story: "Where are you going, O holy priest, without your deacon?" Laurence is reported to have said. "Wherein have I displeased you? Have you found me wanting to my duty?" Sixtus comforted him with this answer: "I do not leave you, my son, but a greater trial and a more glorious victory are reserved for you, who are stout and in the vigor of youth. . . . You shall follow me in three days." Sixtus told Laurence that in the limited time remaining to him he should immediately distribute the considerable treasury of the church at Rome to the poor—some fifteen hundred of them. Laurence set out immediately to sell the church's golden ornaments and jeweled ceremonial vessels.

When the prefect of Rome got wind that this wealth was available, he summoned Laurence and told him to produce the items, saying without cracking a smile, "I am told that according to your doctrine, you must render to Caesar the things that belong to him." Laurence promised to make an inventory of the church treasures and give it to the prefect. He spent the next three days going all over the city, gathering up at the church, writes Butler, "the decrepit, the

With the bishop of Rome dead, the prefect of the city had in mind to strip the church of the wealth he supposed it to have. Laurence, deacon of the martyred bishop Sixtus, was ordered to surrender the wealth, and he had agreed. On the appointed day, Laurence appears before the astounded bureaucrat with the church's treasures: the poor, the sick, widows and children. This earns the young zealot a martyr's death, roasted on a red-hot iron bed.

Laurence and the flaming iron bed upon which he was martyred are memorialized in the lavish fifth-century mosaics at the mausoleum of the empress Galla Placidia in Ravenna, Italy (above). A cupboard on the left of the mosaic contains the four books of the Gospels, a treasure that Laurence protected with his life. One of the most revered of martyrs, Laurence has no fewer than eight churches in Rome dedicated to his memory. Principal among these is St. Laurence Outside the Walls (right), which was constructed over his burial site. The present basilica replaces several earlier structures, the first built by Constantine.

blind, the lame, the maimed, the lepers, orphans, widows and virgins." He then invited the prefect to come and see the treasure of the church. The prefect, disappointed and appalled at what he saw, began ranting and raving. Responded Laurence: "What are you displeased at? The gold which you so eagerly desire is a vile metal, and serves to incite men to all manner of crimes. The light of heaven is the true gold which these poor objects enjoy. . . . These poor persons are . . . the church's crown, by which it is pleasing to Christ; it has no other riches."

The furious prefect ordered Laurence to be burned to death, slowly, on a red-hot gridiron. The deacon was seized and held while the coals were heated, then placed on the glowing metal. His eyes ablaze with divine love, Laurence gave no sign of feeling any pain, and at one point told his tormentors cheerfully,

"Let my body be now turned, one side is broiled enough."

Many who had gathered to watch, including several senators, were so moved by his heroism and faith that they declared themselves Christians as well. According to the poet Prudentius, Laurence's death marked the beginning of the end for idolatry in Rome. Later, during Constantine's reign, a magnificent church was built over Laurence's tomb. Hundreds of churches, schools, chapels, hospitals and other places throughout the world commemorate him. The broad, majestic river that drains North America's five Great Lakes, and most of eastern Canada to the sea, preserves his name.[2]

Among other martyrs from Rome were Saints Anastasia and Cyril, who would come to be venerated particularly in the East. Cyprian, bishop of Carthage, was also to be among the first North African martyrs under the new edict. In Carthage, the persecution intensified until the city was in bedlam. Christians were arrested, imprisoned and executed. In 258, on a hill overlooking a Roman garrison town in northeastern Gaul, the local bishop, Dionysius, was arrested for having aroused the ire of local pagans. He was imprisoned, tortured and beheaded, and his body thrown into the river. Because of a legend that he was later seen carrying his head to the top of the hill, it became known as Montmartre (Mount of the Martyr), the river was the Seine, the Roman town was called Paris, and Saint Denys (as the name would descend into French) would become the patron saint of France.

In Numidia, exiled bishops and priests were brought back to be executed along with other Christians. In the eastern part of the empire, where the persecution was less severe, three peasants were fed to the beasts. In the Spanish coastal city of Tarragon, the bishop and two deacons were tied to stakes and burned alive. The terror continued unabated through 259, when the futures of

2. The French name St. Laurent, taken, of course, from the name of Valerian's Roman victim, appears 1,049 times in the 2002 Montreal telephone book. One St. Laurent, Louis by name, was prime minister of Canada from 1949 to 1957. The Times *Atlas of the World* lists thirty-four towns or cities called San Lorenzo, thirty-three called St. Laurent, six called Sao Lourenço, and four named St. Lawrence.

The slopes of Montmartre (literally the Mount of the Martyr) and the distinctive domes of Sacré-Coeur (Sacred Heart) cathedral doze in the afternoon smog of Paris.

Christianity and the empire came to the proverbial historic crossroads.

While the latest persecution was creating further havoc for the church, the gods still were withholding their favor from Valerian. In 259, the ravages of the plague so weakened his army as he passed through Cappadocia on his way to fight the Goths that he was forced to turn back to the safety of Samosata (see map page 131, F3), the fortified city that guarded an important crossing point of the Euphrates River. Here, he hoped to rebuild his ruined army. It was

A sardonyx cameo (below) depicts Valerian and his arch-rival Shapur I, king of Persia, in valiant hand-to-hand combat. The Persians remember the battles slightly differently: in a third-century cliff carving at Bishapur, Iran (right), the emperors Philip and Valerian are humiliated (though defeated at different times) by the triumphant Shapur.

not to be. The Persian king Shapur was advancing to retake the city he had plundered three years earlier.

Details of what happened next are sketchy and conflicting. Some accounts say that Valerian realized he could not win a battle with the Persian king, and so, in the summer of 260, he offered a large sum of money in return for peace. Shapur declined the offer and asked for a personal meeting with Valerian, probably because he knew the emperor was negotiating out of desperation. The emperor agreed to the meeting, but he was taken prisoner shortly after his arrival. Nothing is known for sure about Valerian's fate, other than that his son offered no ransom and that he died in captivity.

According to some Persian sources, Valerian spent the remaining months of his life in chains, serving as a human step stool whenever King Shapur entered his carriage or mounted his horse.[3] Other accounts offer a variation. They say that upon his death, Valerian's body was stuffed with straw and used as a footstool. Regardless, Christians of the time saw the hated Valerian's demise as the will of God.

His son, Gallienus, acted quickly to consolidate his power. He realized that a continuing religious feud with the strong Christian minority was detrimental both to the empire and to his own future. After all, the Christians had never shown political disloyalty to Rome, but only to her gods. He saw that his father's fruitless persecutions in the name of tradition and religion had been mistakes he could not afford to continue. Therefore, in a move calculated to gain public support, he issued an edict of toleration that returned to the church its confiscated property, places of worship, and cemeteries. He also ordered his governors to permit all bishops to perform their duties in peace, and to allow full freedom to the practice of Christianity.

Whatever the rationale behind it, Gallienus's edict was a milestone. For the first time, Christians found their faith legally recognized by the empire. Within the church, however, peace was not to be found. Since the waning days of the Decian persecution, church leaders had grappled with the question of what to do about the lapsi, which was tied directly to the much larger question surrounding the authority of the bishop. Rather than confess their faith and face the consequent torment, thousands of Christians had simply apostatized. Were they to be allowed back in? If they were, didn't that suggest that those who had stood fast and lost their lives did so needlessly? But if the lapsi were not to be let back in, did it mean that any sin committed after baptism was beyond forgiveness?

These questions would in the long run do far more damage to the church than either the Decian or Valerian persecutions. They would divide the flock, pitting Christian against Christian and bishop against bishop. For it was division from within, far more than persecution from without, that would always pose the most lethal threat to the Christian body. ■

After the death of his father, Valerian, in 260, the emperor Gallienus ended the horrors of the recurring persecutions of the late third century—a move likely prompted more by political expediency than by compassion.

---

3. A rock carving of Shapur I of Persia, apparently crafted in about 260, shows him triumphantly displaying his defeat of three Roman emperors, but who the emperors are is a matter of great conjecture. According to R. Ghirshman's *Iran: Parthians and Sassanians*, a body shown in the carving being trampled by horses is that of Gordian III, while Philip the Arab is shown on his knees, begging Shapur for his life. Behind Shapur's horse comes the hapless Valerian, dragged along by the wrist as if he were a child. Of the three, only Valerian was captured by Shapur.

The sage who escaped Decius

Dionysius could talk atomic theory and was sharp in doctrinal debate, but it was his merciful policy to those who had failed the test that won the bishop bitter criticism

Christianity has never had a problem attracting the best and brightest, despite what anti-Christian propagandists habitually insist. The faith has held special appeal to those who sense a deeper reality beyond the conventional thinking of their day, which has made Christianity the most intellectually revolutionary force in history, forever challenging the status quo, often at high cost to believers. The exquisitely educated Paul was an early example of a powerful Christian intellect who changed the world; he was followed in the faith's formative years by the likes of Cyprian and Augustine—and also Dionysius, bishop of Alexandria from 247 to 265.

Dionysius's was a mind for the ages, one that should be better known in modern times. On one day, he would debate atomic theory with his era's most vibrant atheists; his arguments against randomness as the First Cause continue to resonate in our day. Another occasion might find him illuminating the most intricate theological minutiae or composing history's most searing first-person accounts of plague and persecution. He is the model of the fully engaged Christian intellectual—one who fought with his head against the insanity of persecution.

Dionysius is believed to have been born around 190 to a wealthy family. He was steeped in the wisdom of his day, and he saw straight through it. "I myself lived in the doctrines and traditions of the heretics," he explained, "and for some time soiled my soul with their impure inventions; but at least I have, as a result of my stay among them, the advantage of confounding them in myself, and of having a much greater distaste for them."

It was the Epistles of Paul that spoke directly to him and led to his conversion. He also, early on, experienced a vision that set him on his path as an intellectual combatant. A voice "gave me an explicit order: 'Take all that you find, for you are capable of setting to rights and examining each thing, and in your case this has been from the first the cause of your faith.'" He interpreted this as a divine directive to study the work of his opponents, so that he could better bring them to the truth. In that endeavor he was perhaps unparalleled.

Dionysius rose quickly. He studied under Origen, a one-man Harvard University, and became the leader of Alexandria's famed catechetical school at thirty; in 247, he was named bishop

DIONYSIUS ON FORGIVENESS

Let us not thrust from us those who seek a penitent return. Rather, let us receive them gladly and number them once more with the steadfast. Let us restore again what is defective in them.

of Alexandria, a city said to be the match of Rome itself. Like Cyprian, the brilliant bishop of Carthage, westward along the northern coast of Africa, he shared many situations and opinions. he would quickly face challenges of almost supernatural breadth, depth, and horror. It is against this dark backdrop that the brightness of his achievement should be considered.

Bishop Dionysius had been on the job less than a year when unrest erupted in 248, largely over taxes. In the following winter, pagan mobs, inspired by a frenzied prophet, went on an anti-Christian rampage, brutal even by the standards of his day. First seized was an old man named Metras, who was beaten with clubs after refusing to deny his Lord, then blinded and stoned.

The pumps were now primed; the mob found its next victim in a woman named Quinta, who received the same treatment. An old lady named Apollonia had her teeth knocked out and her jaw broken. She was ordered to recant her faith as her tormentors suggestively lit a bonfire, and she is said to have struck a pose suggesting her possible compliance. But when her captors loosened their grip, she leaped into the flames, denying them their odious pleasure.

This was only the beginning. The emperor Decius began a formal persecution in 250, rounding up church leaders throughout the empire. Dionysius was eventually arrested.

Great lives are often marked by bizarre events that may suggest divine intent, and so it was with Dionysius. A band of men from a wedding party, tipped off that their beloved bishop was being marched to prison, put down their wine, and intercepted the procession, putting Dionysius's captors to flight.

The prisoner bishop, confusing his rescuers with robbers, offered them his cloak. No, they assured him, they had come to set him free. Dionysius could make no sense of this, protesting that he was fully prepared to wear the crown of martyrdom. Indeed, perhaps they would like to do

DIONYSIUS ON WORLDLY CARES

In truth, to those who occupy their minds with the distractions of life, life becomes a painful thing, which wounds the heart with the lustful desires of increase. And sorrowful also is the solicitude connected with covetousness: it does not so much gratify those who are successful in it, as it pains those who are unsuccessful; while the day is spent in laborious anxieties, and the night puts sleep to flight from the eyes, with the cares of making gain.

him the honor of cutting off his head. One can guess a sense of growing consternation among his liberators, who placed Dionysius on a donkey and escorted him off to Libya. He might have desired the martyr's crown, but other events awaited him.

Dionysius's return in 251 brought its own troubles, including the charge that he had fled to avoid persecution. He found his chief accuser in Germanos, an Egyptian bishop, and so faced challenges from within his church nearly as daunting as the external threat.

The question of what to do with those who had lapsed during persecution was tearing the African church apart. On this matter, Dionysius and Cyprian were relatively moderate, at least compared with those who would cast the lapsed into utter hopelessness while gaining for themselves control of the church. Dionysius and Cyprian built a solid intellectual bulwark against this merciless position, as was soon discovered by Novatian, whose ferocity toward the lapsed went to the extreme of denying them reunion to the church even at the time of death, and whose personal ambition led him to have himself improperly elected bishop of Rome.

Novatian made the error of asking Dionysius's blessing. The response was direct and to the point: "You ought to have suffered all things rather than have caused a schism in the Church. To die in defense of its unity would be as glorious as laying down one's life for its faith; in my opinion, more glorious: because here the safety of the whole Church is concerned."

To fellow bishops, he warned that if Novatian's position were to be adopted, "We shall do the contrary of what was done by Christ. He was good, he went out to the mountains to seek for the lost sheep; if the sheep fled away, he called it; if he found it he brought it back with difficulty on his shoulders. We see the sheep coming, and harshly repel it with kicks." Though his prose was highly polemical, it was employed in the service of advancing a Christlike mercy.

He was similarly direct with his outside accusers. During renewed persecution in 257, Dionysius was ordered to embrace the pagan deities. Not possible, he replied; that would be "contrary to nature." He then offered a short tutorial. "Not all people worship all gods, but each one those whom he approves. We therefore reverence and worship the One God, the Maker of all, who hath given the empire to the divinely favored and august Valerian and Gallienus; and we pray to him continually for their empire, that it may remain unshaken."

It is worth recalling who was holding the sword during this conversation, and that similar words were voiced by Cyprian during his confrontation with the authorities. In Cyprian's case, they led to an appointment with the headsman.

Dionysius brought his powers to bear on a vast number of subjects, including what was the proper length of fasting (he favored short fasts because they were easier for people to observe), when to celebrate Easter, and what could and could not transpire in the marital bedroom (he left this to the conscience of husband and wife).

He was at no time more brilliant, however, than when describing the darkest episodes in human physical experience. During a period when plague and civil war beset his city, his writing could sear like the best in literature. At times, the killings in his beloved city stained the waterways

with blood, he observed. "For often from the slaughters there committed they appear like the Red Sea," he wrote in one letter. "When can the air, poisoned by these noxious exhalations, become pure? For such vapors arise from the earth, and winds from the sea, and breezes from the river, and mists from the harbors, that the dews are, as it were, discharges from dead bodies putrefying in all the elements around us."

He was not seeking literary recognition, of course, but sought to inspire fidelity in the face of death, either by sword or by pestilence. This was no small assignment, but the power of his words brought a large measure of success. During plague time, the pagans

"pushed the sufferers away and fled from their dearest, throwing them into the roads before they were dead, and treating unburied corpses as dirt."

Dionysius's flock, however, heeded his call to take the opposite approach. "Most of our brother Christians showed unbounded love and loyalty, never sparing themselves, and thinking only of one another. Heedless of danger, they took charge of the sick, attending to their every need and ministering to them in Christ, and with them departed this life serenely happy; for they were infected by others with the disease, drawing on themselves the sickness of their neighbors and cheerfully accepting their pains."

It is noteworthy that Dionysius's

Plague followed pestilence in the Roman Empire of the late third century. According to Dionysius, bishop of Alexandria, the Christians became known for the care they gave victims of the plagues that decimated that great city's population. Attending to those not yet dead and burying those who were, Christians showed a courage and compassion that earned them grudging respect.

policy toward the stricken had results he could hardly have guessed. Historian Rodney Stark believes that the care offered by Christians may have cut the mortality rate by two-thirds or more and eventually led to a large number of conversions to this merciful creed. That, in turn, further secured Christianity's place in society and history. Thus his church, under his direction, prospered in the face of an almost unspeakable calamity.

There were calmer times, during which Dionysius would turn his mind to other challenges, often with great success. When an Egyptian bishop named Nepos began arguing that believers should expect a one thousand-year reign of Christ marked by vast corporal delights, he gained an instant following. That is not hard to understand. The Lord's imminent return was widely assumed, and the promise that privation and persecution would be replaced by peace, joy, and rivers flowing with wine had obvious and immediate appeal.

Yet this doctrine was contrary to church teaching, which Dionysius restated, gently yet persuasively, in his *Book of Promises*. Like many authors, he went on tour, in this case in the erring bishop's district, where he held a series of discussions with village priests. Within three days he had brought them around to his way of thinking, thus single-handedly heading off a schism that might have roiled and weakened the church for hundreds of years.

He was also very much at home with subjects of truly cosmic proportion.

While many in the modern age assume that atomic theory is of recent vintage, it was a matter of great discussion among the intellectual elite of Dionysius's day. The atomists argued that life was the accidental result of the collision of random atoms, a position heavy with philosophical implications.

Dionysius, who gave serious and respectful attention to his opponents' position, responded with his most enduring book, *On Nature*. Dionysius looked into the heavens and saw a Guiding Hand at work. It was his devout hope that he could bring his atheistic opponents to see this hand as well. "But who, then, is the sagacious discriminator, that brings certain atoms into collocation, and separates others, and marshals some in such wise as to form the sun, and others in such a way to originate the moon?" That "discriminator," of course, is God. This same hand created glories much closer to home, he added. "And whence came the soul, and the intelligence, and the reason, which are born with the philosopher? Has he gathered these from those atoms which are destitute alike of soul, and intelligence, and reason?"

Dionysius was spared the executioner's sword, living until the age of seventy-five or thereabouts, his mind active to the end. Indeed, like the soul in which he so devoutly believed, his mind sought the eternal, and in the fullness of time, achieved a distinct immortality. ■

CHAPTER 2

A disenchanted lawyer is drafted as a bishop

Witty, wealthy, and much admired, Cyprian abandons Carthage's hollow society to brilliantly lead his flock against Roman officialdom and Christian dissidents

Thascius Caecilianus Cyprianus seemed to have it all: wealth, health, status, intelligence, and the prospect of even greater days ahead. What could stop him? He excelled in law, rhetoric and business. He was widely admired throughout third-century Carthage. He had a penetrating wit and a wide circle of friends, he lived in an ornate house, and he was by any worldly measure a rising star in one of the world's most dynamic cities.

However, Cyprian knew his life was a sham—just as he knew that beneath its glittering surface, Carthage was a sinkhole of corruption. Its amphitheaters were drenched in blood. Sexual license was rampant in daily life and in popular culture. Judges lined their own pockets with bribes while breaking innocent citizens on the wheel, if that was what "order" required. The pagan religion, which had once held promise for Cyprian, had turned out to be as hollow as the society it served. Perhaps the skeptics were right. Perhaps life was a meaningless dance beneath the stars, followed only by eternal darkness.

But Cyprian could not accept such a bleak view of existence. He sensed a deeper reality beyond the marble walls, painted eyes, and empty whirl of Carthaginian life. He sensed a spark of eternity within himself, one desperately seeking communion with its source. And with the help of a Christian priest, he

At the present site of Carthage in Tunisia, there are few hints of that ancient city's greatness—a splendor that rivaled Rome itself. A weedy track (top), formerly a bustling commercial thoroughfare, passes between plain brick walls. Flowering meadows (above) cover the spot once occupied by the magnificent Antonine Baths. The columns of the Baths were long ago scavenged for use elsewhere, leaving only their white Corinthian capitals.

encountered that source: Christ Jesus, who had been raised from the dead two centuries before. Now Cyprian finally knew his life's true course: He would withdraw from the rat race to pursue a tranquil life of worship, study and meditation. In splendid solitude, he would find the fullest communion with his Savior—while escaping the slow death of a thousand empty accomplishments.

Or so Cyprian thought. Within a few years of his conversion to Christianity, he discovered, much to his dismay and discomfort, that God had very different ideas for his life. God wanted him back in the rat race, but in a very different role, one that would tax to their limits all the skills, determination, intelligence and toughness he had acquired in his earlier life. In fact, God would place him at the center of one of the most divisive struggles, up to that time, in Christian history.

At the heart of it was a single question: Was Christ's church to become a small, elite group of holy people, characterized by their willingness to sacrifice all for God? Or would it become "a school for repentant sinners" that could make room even for those who had denied and betrayed him? Would the Christians remain in the catacombs, or would they become the light of the world?

Cyprian would soon face ferocious opposition within the church, and deadly persecution from without. There would, no doubt, be many times when he concluded that the rat race he had left behind was a mere stroll in the park, compared to the race God had set before him. None of this could have been foreseen.

Cyprian was born around 200, apparently into a successful family, and took full advantage of a superior education. His mind naturally sought order and unity, and his talent for self-discipline was legendary. "With a powerful memory," notes biographer Edward White Benson, "and methodic, classificatory mind, Cyprian had pursued the highest literary culture."

Success followed success, and by his early forties, the world lay at Cyprian's feet. His villa was noted for its "Pompeian richness, frescoed walls, gilded ceilings and marble-lined salons." He dined with Carthage's "A-list," and was widely admired as a skilled rhetorician. He was, quite simply, a celebrity with a sterling reputation for probity. Cyprian "despaired of improvement," and indeed considered his shortcomings not only "natural" but "even favored them," as he himself would later put it.

Yet there was a growing tension within. While he was very much in the world, part of him stood outside it. As his fame and accomplishments grew, worldly society lost its glitter. Yes, he had risen high, but was that really so great an achievement? Was it not true that behind the elegant salons and imperial offices stretched a vast and soul-crushing corruption? Cyprian knew firsthand that the legal profession did a heavy traffic in bribes. Then there were the games. In one of the most chilling descriptions of the amphitheater culture ever recorded, Cyprian noted the "manly health and grace of the youths trained to mutual murder under the eyes of their own fathers; the brother waits his turn in the den, above which sits the expectant sister; the mother pays a higher price for the ticket to witness her child's death-wound on a gala day, and there is not the faintest sense of guilt on any conscience." The celebration of moral depravity, indeed, was seen as a mark of artistic sophistication.

Even twenty-first-century entertainment, whatever its iniquities, would be hard put to match the degradations of Cyprian's era. Here is the recollection of a third-century actor who was required to have intercourse on stage with a condemned woman, who would subsequently be eaten by a lion: "I was not only appalled at the disgraceful part I was expected to play: I was in terror of death. It occurred to me that when she and I were locked in what was supposed to be a passionate embrace, and the wild beast, whose part in the drama would be to eat her, came bounding into our bridal cage, I could not count on the creature's being so naturally sagacious, or well trained, or so abstemious, as to tear her to pieces as she cuddled close to me, but nevertheless leave me alone."

Of such as this, Cyprian could finally stand no more. He realized that the lions were not only devouring bodies; they were devouring souls. He had risen to distinction in a society where no decent man should want to succeed at all. But where to turn? He had earlier noted at least a hint of grandeur and transcendence in the pagan religions. But now, the closer he looked, the more barren their appeal. Their gods and priesthood did nothing to stem society's cruelty and squalor. At best, they were ambivalent; indeed, by their silence they endorsed the status quo.

Cyprian stood before his own time and place as if before a wall. Like countless Christians before him and countless Christians since, he discovered that this wall contained a window—a way out. In his case, that window had a name: It was Caecilius, a Christian priest, member of a faith that of late was gaining stature and converts all across northern Africa. Caecilius was animated by what he called "the Gospel." It meant "good news," and it conveyed a startling message: Jesus Christ, who had been crucified two centuries earlier, was very much alive today. He was not only alive but accessible. And he was not only accessible but dedicated to saving Cyprian's soul. He had paid the ultimate price in order to rescue men and women who found themselves in Cyprian's position. He had indeed died on Cyprian's behalf. Such was Caecilius's testimony.

Cyprian no doubt saw the contrast between that astonishing life of Jesus and his own life. Jesus had come into the world as an awaited messiah and king. Like Cyprian, he had been offered all the world's glories, glitter, and baubles. Unlike Cyprian, he rejected them. He was shown cruelty, and responded with love. He was shown depravity, and responded with sacrifice. He had made himself a servant to man. His promise to Cyprian, and to all humanity, was simple and profound. Those who believed in him would find everlasting life, beginning in this world and continuing in the world to come, a life of inexpressible peace. These were not mere words. This was Truth. Indeed, Jesus had called

It came down to one question: Was Christ's church to become a coterie of holy people or 'a school for repentant sinners' that could include even those who had denied him?

himself "the Truth" (John 14:6), and had certified it by his Resurrection.

Cyprian's conversion was total. His date of baptism is given as Easter 246, some time after which Caecilius died, apparently leaving his family in Cyprian's care. But for Cyprian, this was no mere "lifestyle change." He sold most of his property and possessions to the benefit of his new faith and the poor. He embraced a "perfect chastity"—a vow similar to that made by frontline Roman soldiers. His life was made anew. "I had wandered blindly in the darkness, tossed by the tempestuous sea," Cyprian later recalled. "I had floated at the mercy of the waves, ignorant of my life." Yet "after the strain of early years had been washed away with the help of the water of new birth, a light from above, serene and pure, had been poured into my forgiven heart. After a second birth had remade me a new man by means of the spirit breathed from heaven, then in a wonderful way what had been doubtful became sure, what had been hidden was revealed, what had been dark was illumined, what had seemed difficult before could now be attempted, what had been thought impossible was now able to be done."

Cyprian's sense of satisfaction was complete. He would now enter his study, shut the doors, and train his considerable intellect on larger matters. One can easily imagine him rubbing his hands in anticipation of this exquisite life of the mind that lay ahead. He had ample cause to believe that his will and his Lord's were one and the same, indeed that the Lord delighted in rubber-stamping Cyprian's own wise choice.

And so it went, but not for long. Soon his dream began coming apart. Less than three years after Cyprian's conversion, Bishop Donatus of Carthage died. This was a great loss, but God no doubt would provide a suitable replacement.

Cyprian, a wealthy and influential citizen of Carthage, held lavish gatherings for the city's elite at his splendid villa. But when Cyprian decided to dedicate his life to Jesus Christ and his Gospel, he realized a change was necessary. The new convert opened the doors of his house and his rooms again and oversaw the dispersal of his accumulated possessions, selling or giving away everything.

These were dynamic times for the church. Conversions were increasing, among both the masses and the elite. There were several capable candidates to fill Donatus's shoes, each qualified and experienced—and each adamant that he was the man for the job. Yet a troubling consensus was forming among the Carthaginian Christians, troubling at least from Cyprian's perspective. Many saw their church as stagnant in the face of unparalleled opportunity. Fresh blood was needed: The times required someone old enough to possess wisdom but still in possession of youthful energy. An organizer. A speaker. Increasingly, there was one name on the lips of the faithful. That name was Cyprian.

Not me! Cyprian earnestly protested. The other would-be bishops wholeheartedly agreed with him. How could anyone even think that so new a Christian could be considered worthy? After all, Carthage was equal to Rome itself, many Carthaginians thought. Of all the choices, Cyprian would be the worst. What had gotten into the masses? What forces, Cyprian no doubt wondered, were at work to turn his newfound life upside down? These were undoubtedly his thoughts that day when, less than three years after his conversion, a large group of believers marched to his residence. The consensus, they said, was overwhelming. Cyprian had the skills and vigor the church required. Besides that, there was just something about him—a presence the other candidates could not hope to match. Pontius, a deacon in the African church and later Cyprian's biographer, described it well:

> So much sanctity and grace beamed from his face that it confounded the minds of the beholders. His countenance was grave and yet joyous. Neither was his severity gloomy, nor his affability excessive, but a mingled tempering of both; so that it might be doubted whether he most deserved to be revered or to be loved. . . . And his dress was not out of harmony with his countenance, being itself also subdued to a fitting mean. The pride of the world did not inflame him, nor yet did an excessively affected penury make him sordid.

Then the crowd called on Cyprian to come forward and present himself to them. According to custom, the presiding bishop from a nearby diocese asked the crowd three times: "Is this the man whom ye decide for a ruler? Is he blameless, and is he worthy?" The crowd shouted its assent: "Axios! Axios! Axios!"[1] If

Even in ruins, the grand basilicas of North Africa still speak of the Christian devotion there. The basilicas were large, architecturally complex and wonderfully decorated, with spacious areas for teaching and, in some cases, for providing hospitality to the Christians who were already turning the graves of martyrs into places of pilgrimage. Virtually all the ancient Roman cities of what is now Tunisia had Christian communities that constructed churches ranging from the humble to the opulent: (1) in the old olive-growing city of Sbeitla (see map page 130, C4), about 130 miles south of Carthage; (2) at Bulla Regia, nearer the coast; (3) in the spa center of Thuburbo Majus, known for its winter baths.

there was a discordant voice among them, it has escaped the record.

Suddenly, Cyprian was bishop of Carthage. Bishop! Just a few years ago he was a burned-out lawyer seeking respite from the world. Could Cyprian have been blamed for wondering, "Why me, Lord?" Just yesterday he was a Christian believer, a man devoted to his study. Now he had been pushed by forces beyond his control into a job for which he had no training and no desire. And those were the least of his problems. Imperial Rome was once again turning its baleful eye on a familiar scapegoat: the Christian church.

Cyprian nevertheless assumed his new duties with obedient enthusiasm. There must, after all, be a good reason for so unexpected a development. "Where better, where more happily might I be, than in the place where God willed me to believe and grow?" he would later reflect. There was no doubting that his organizational skills were sorely needed. Paganism resonated with fewer and fewer Africans. Christianity was becoming the faith of the future. It not only promised eternal life, but its moral teachings were far more profound. Moreover, there had been no serious persecution of Christians for half a century. No longer did the Christians consist of a small, tightly bound, fiercely dedicated core of believers whose faith had been gravely tested. Even in areas once militantly hostile to Christianity, such as neighboring Numidia, the faith was rapidly taking root unopposed.

None of this was lost on the Roman authorities, however. They sensed, too, that these Christians seemed to be growing more hostile toward Roman institutions, and that the Christians were not alone in this. The wild tribesmen to the south and west were harassing the African frontier and occasionally raiding the emperor's North African olive groves, which were vital not only for trade but also to keep the lights burning in Rome itself. It seemed time for Rome to gain a tighter grip there. On the home front, a fresh round of persecutions was very much in order. That possibility was already a preoccupation with Cyprian. One

CYPRIAN ON HEALING OF SOULS

How can the medicine of permissiveness profit anyone? What if a physician hides the wound and does not allow the necessary remedy of time to heal the scar? To not require repentance makes the way for new dangers. To do that is not curing someone. If we are honest, it is slaying him.

---

1. To this day, at the ordination of deacons, priests and bishops in the Eastern Orthodox Churches, the people repeatedly shout *"Axios!"* ("He is worthy!") as the candidate is garbed in the vestments of the church.

night he had a vivid dream: A father and his family faced a menacing opponent, one who sought their destruction. On waking, Cyprian was filled with the greatest foreboding. Trouble clearly lay ahead for the church. He would not have to wait long to see his nightmare become reality.

Cyprian was therefore hardly surprised when, in 249, Emperor Decius concluded that Rome's problems were, at least in part, due to the displeasure of the gods. The remedy was simple enough. An imperial edict was forthwith produced: All who live under Roman rule must sacrifice to Rome's gods, and all must offer tangible evidence of compliance, a signed certificate (*libellus*) documenting the fact that the individual had performed the rite. There were to be no exceptions. Since those who refused were threatening the health of the empire, the refusal would be taken as sedition, a capital offense.

By 250, all-out persecution was under way. In some cities, including Alexandria, Christians were chased down by mobs and burned at the stake. Decius meant business. In Rome, Bishop Fabian was arrested and executed. Later that year, the new proconsul arrived in Carthage. Cyprian knew he would

Cyprian knew he would be next. 'You must flee,' he was told. Yet how could he flee while the faithful were slaughtered? He'd be damned if he fled, and killed if he didn't.

be next. So did his closest associates. "You must flee," he was warned. Tertullus, whose devotion to prisoners and martyrs was unquestioned, quickly became adamant. Cyprian must conceal himself for the church's good. Without constant government, the church would disintegrate under these pressures. Tertullus had heard the chants in the streets: "Cyprian to the lions!"

Yet there were other considerations. If Cyprian appeared to choose personal safety over staying with his flock, there would certainly be critics. He could imagine the taunts. What sort of leader goes into hiding while the faithful are slaughtered like sheep? The church had long taught that martyrdom is the highest honor a Christian can achieve. In martyrdom, then, it was seen that God revealed his full glory. Why would Cyprian decline this golden crown? Perhaps he did not truly believe these things.

His dilemma was brutally simple: He would be damned if he took flight, and killed if he didn't. And so the question became: What did God want? Had he raised Cyprian to this position, so rapidly and unexpectedly, in order to have him killed so soon? Cyprian could not believe that. He would flee—not far, but to an undisclosed location near Carthage. This "evil time," he wrote colleagues, has "laid low our people in very great part." His mind was made up. He would avoid his enemies, but continue serving his flock. So he fled.

Of his retreat into the wilderness, he later wrote: "As the Lord gave commandment, immediately on the appearance of trouble, when the people had fiercely and repeatedly clamored for my blood, I withdrew, taking thought rather for the tranquility of the church than for my own safety, to prevent a further outbreak of the animosity which had been fired by my unwelcome presence."

But he did not disappear. Instead, Cyprian quickly established his "government in exile," dispatching priests to care for victims of persecution, providing funds to Christians sentenced to hard labor in the mines, and exhorting the faithful to stand fast and await better days. "Although absent in body," he wrote, "I have not been absent in spirit, or in action, or in my admonitions, so that I might at least, with what moderate ability I could, look out for our brethren according to the precepts of our Lord."

Tertullus had been correct: Cyprian was providing vital cohesion to the

The mysterious St. George

A man about whom very little is known became a worldwide hero stirring such fabulous stories that even a pope couldn't rein in

"Cry God for Harry, England and St. George!" shouts the English king at the siege of Harfleur in Shakespeare's play, *Henry V*. Harry is, of course, the nickname of King Henry himself. England is England. But who is St. George? That question cannot be easily answered, any more than the astounding celebrity of this fourth-century saint can be easily explained.

Historians seem to accept only two facts about St. George as reasonably reliable. He was a Christian and he was martyred, probably at Lydda on the coast of Palestine, during the Diocletian persecution. There are reasonable grounds to believe, though there is no compelling evidence, that he was also a Roman soldier, who put his faith before his life.

Historians regard as myth and legend the many other ostensible facts about George that proliferated across Europe in the centuries following his death. The church does not believe, says the *Catholic Encyclopedia*, that George was put to death three times—once chopped into small pieces, once buried deep in the earth, and once consumed by fire—each time to be reassembled and then to declare his faith. Neither do they believe that he habitually brought dead men to life and baptized them; that he converted people by the tens of thousands, one of them an empress; that he instantaneously destroyed armies of idols or caused beams of

The most familiar image of St. George depicts him freeing a distressed maiden from a dragon, a dramatic story but one with no historical basis.

timber to burst into leaf; or that when he was finally beheaded, milk rather than blood flowed from his body.

Finally, they do not believe that George slew a dragon—an act forever linked with his image in paintings, statues, stained-glass windows, and British coins—to rescue a damsel that had been turned over to the beast (in some versions, merely a large lizard or other reptile) to save her town from dragonish destruction—if only because the story was not told until he had been dead for nine hundred years.

Having made all these disclaimers, however, historians concede that a puzzle remains. George, whoever he was, must have been an astonishing man. There's evidence that great pilgrimages were being made to his supposed burial site before the end of the fourth century. Pilgrims spread such astonishing accounts of his miraculous powers that in 495, Pope Gelasius decreed that no more than three miracles could be attributed to him. The stories were straining the credulity of the faithful, he said.

The tales continued to grow, nevertheless. Then, with the Crusades early in the second millennium, devotion to St. George suddenly exploded. The crusaders reported visions of St. George during their sieges of Antioch and Jerusalem. Richard the Lionheart returned to church at a time of horrendous external pressure. The Romans recognized exactly why he had taken this step, and made public demands for his capture. This must have been of some comfort. But Cyprian's expectations of criticism were also realized. A letter from church officials in Rome carried a particularly stinging rebuke. After praising Fabian's martyrdom, it exhorted clergy who had not fled Carthage to fill the void created by the "lapse of some eminent and timorous persons."

The word "lapsed" was increasingly on the lips of Cyprian's critics, and indeed on his own lips as well. By 251, the persecution was waning, and a

England urging the Cross of St. George as the English flag. Combined with the Cross of St. Andrew and the Cross of St. Patrick, it now forms the Union Jack.

In his book, *St. George: The Saint With Three Faces*, author David Scott Fox attributes this burst of medieval interest to the growing devotion to the Christian Code of Chivalry, which sought to bring warfare within agreed-upon bounds and adopted St. George as an outstanding model. New orders of knights were created all over Europe, many of them with St. George as their patron.

He was the patron saint of Austria, Burgundy, Holland and Spain, and of the emperors of the Holy Roman Empire. As special protector for travelers by sea, Venice, Genoa and Barcelona have him as their patron. The Portuguese and the Spanish both claimed George's patronage in their wars with each other. He championed the Spaniards against the Muslim Moors, and figured prominently in the seven-hundred-year war to expel the Muslims from Spain.

An even greater devotion to St. George developed in Russia and Greece, the former not even evangelized until seven hundred years after his martyrdom. In Russian lore, the saint's foes were the Mongols, and the shout, "St. George for Holy Russia," became the dominant battle cry. In Greece, St. George has the title *megalomartyr*, martyr of the highest order, while his April 23 feast ranks highest after Christmas and Easter, and is still an occasion for games, feasting and dancing. There are sixty churches of St. George on Cyprus. No Greek or Russian church is complete without an icon of St. George.

St. George is also the patron saint of Lebanese and Palestinian Christians. In Egypt, he is the principal patron of the Coptic Christians, and forty Coptic churches and three monasteries bear his name. In Ethiopia, he is known as "the King of Saints." He and the dragon often appear on gorgeous embroidered Ethiopian saddlecloths. And all this for a man about whom almost nothing is known. It is, some historians admit, a mystery. ∎

Centuries and worlds apart, two churches attest to the popularity of the mysterious martyr George. The church of St. George at Lalibela in Ethiopia (left), like others in the area, was constructed in the tenth century by digging down into solid rock. The fifteenth-century Gothic turrets of St. George's Chapel at Windsor Castle in England (above) offer a more conventional tribute to the saint.

debate about what to do with the lapsed—that is, those Christians who had submitted in one form or another to the Decian edict—had moved to center stage. The issue: Under what circumstances would those who had denied Christ be allowed back into the church? Should these lapsed Christians be readmitted at all? What about clergy who had sacrificed to the Roman gods? Indeed, what about clergy who had fled persecution?

As Cyprian made his way back to Carthage, he knew the future of the church was at stake. His critics had already formed hard opinions, and bolstered their positions by pointing out that it was not they who had gone into hiding. Why should anyone listen to Cyprian? The lions were back in their cages, but other claws were out for Cyprian.

The first fact confronting Cyprian was the massive size of the problem he confronted. Softened by nearly a half century without persecution, many had easily capitulated. Enormous numbers of Christians had chosen apostasy over persecution. On the other hand, Cyprian noted, some had held fast with unbecoming

Cyprian must act swiftly but not rashly. If the standards for return were too stark, mass defection would result. Yet the families of martyrs must not feel betrayed.

enthusiasm. "They ran voluntarily to the forum; they rushed spontaneously to death, as if this were a thing that they had yearned for beforehand, as if they were seizing an opportunity given which they had always wanted."

"To many, their own destruction was not enough," he wrote. "Encouraging each other, the people were urged to ruination. They drank to each other's death in the fatal cup." Bishop Dionysius of Alexandria, whose bonds with Cyprian had been strong (though there is no record of correspondence between them), filed a similar report from his post. Christians "cowered with fear," he wrote, and while some held out, "others ran eagerly towards the altars, affirming by their forwardness that they had not been Christians even formerly."

The degree of apostasy was perhaps breathtaking, but it could not be considered a surprise. Many of the apostates had been new converts when persecution began; their faith was shallow and untested. Many had not made a clean break with paganism and so reversion to the old gods not only was expedient but seemed the sensible thing to do. Historian W. H. C. Frend notes: "No one disobeyed an imperial edict lightly. When confronted with the choice of empire or Christian church in 250, the great majority of Christians played safe and sacrificed."

The number of the lapsed was not the only problem, however. Some clergy, most notably Donatus, Novatus, and Felicissimus, were already freely readmitting apostates and thus polluting the church, at least in Cyprian's eyes. These men rejected Cyprian's protests. After all, they had stuck it out in Carthage during persecution, and now Cyprian, who had left Carthage, had the nerve to exclude Felicissimus. There was a further problem. Some

There was only one way to escape the fate that awaited Christians under the emperor Decius: obtain an official certificate (a libellus) declaring that one had offered the imperial sacrifice. There were, however, two ways to procure that certificate: by publicly recanting the Christian faith and actually offering sacrifice, or by paying for a forged certificate declaring the sacrifice had occurred when it had not. As this wealthy woman realizes, the danger of the imperial authorities discovering the forgery, along with the shame of being found out by members of the Christian community, made even the latter a miserable option.

Christians who had withstood persecution and torture, now called "confessors," were assumed by many to have the authority to provide letters of readmission for the lapsed. Entire families were being pardoned by the good-hearted yet indiscriminate confessors.

Cyprian must act quickly, but not rashly. As he saw it, the stakes could not be overstated. If the standards for readmission were too stark, wholesale defection would result. Christianity's recent gains would be lost. The church would return to its status as a cult, one characterized by the willingness of its members to die for their faith—and also by its minute size. Or perhaps Christianity would splinter into various sects, then disappear as so many cults had before. And this exodus would occur just at the time when Christ's "great commission" to go forth, teach, and baptize, was bearing real fruit, when huge numbers of people from all levels of society were acknowledging him. That, Cyprian reasoned, could not possibly be what God desired.

Yet at the same time, the integrity of the faith must be maintained. Many Christians had withstood torture without relenting. Many had died, and surviving family members would feel betrayed should those sacrifices be mocked by a policy that accepted apostasy without recrimination.

There was also the matter of lapsed clergy. The flight from faith was common at all levels, including the clerical one. "In the bishops, there was no religious devotion," Cyprian observed. "In the ministry, there was no sound faith. In works, there was no mercy. In morals, there was no discipline."

Modern-day Christians can imagine the pressures Cyprian faced, at least to a degree. Should a pacifist congregation with members imprisoned during wartime readmit those who submitted to conscription? Should congregations strongly dedicated to stopping abortions or capital punishment reprove members who avoided taking a stance out of fear of ridicule or worse? At the same time, the immensity of the challenge must be kept in mind. Cyprian could either lead Christianity into the future or preside over its possible dissolution.

To resolve these questions, he quickly convened his bishops, and together they devised a reasonable policy—or so Cyprian believed. Both needs had to be served, the integrity of the church and its role as a hospital for repentant sinners. Therefore, those who had fraudulently purchased a *libellus*, but who had not offered sacrifice, were guilty of denying Christ, but not to the same degree as those who had actually sacrificed and drunk a libation. After review on a case-by-case basis, the former could be restored to the church at once. Those who had sacrificed, however, must be demonstrably penitent, and must undertake a specific penance before being readmitted. Even then, reunion would be withheld until the time of death.

This was no easy route, and it was not meant to be. It reflected the seriousness with which Cyprian and his allies took apostasy, while simultaneously reflecting a Christlike mercy toward the lapsed who would not be stripped of all hope. Cyprian made it clear that penance was not to be lightly undertaken. "You must pray more eagerly," he instructed. "You must spend the day in grief;

wear out nights in watching and weeping, occupy all your time in wailing and lamentations, lying stretched on the ground. You must cling close to the ashes, be surrounded with sackcloth and filth. After losing the raiment of Christ, you must be willing now to have no clothing."

He would not be fooled by empty displays of contrition, said Cyprian. "Do we believe that a man is lamenting with his whole heart, that he is entreating the Lord with fasting, and with weeping, and with mourning, who from the first day of his sin daily frequents the bathing-places with women? Or who, feeding at rich banquets, and puffed out with fuller dainties, belches forth on the next day his indigestions, and does not dispense of this meat and drink to aid the necessity of the poor?"

Thus was the line drawn, and many were without doubt excluded. Those who found penance too difficult were left without reason for hope. Lapsed clergy, meanwhile, were permanently barred from the priesthood. Indeed, Cyprian warned, congregations that readmitted fallen priests became complicit in their sin. "Flee from the pestilential contact of these men," he warned. This particular teaching met with wide approval among the faithful. The Italian bishops, meeting a few months later, agreed these guidelines were fair and just. Yet there were critics as well, some in very high places, and these now declared total war on Cyprian.

The attack came from both directions—those who considered his formula too severe, and those who considered it not severe enough. In Carthage, the fallen were already being readmitted by Cyprian's critics. One of them was Privatus, the deposed bishop of Lambaesis, who organized a whole college of fallen bishops. His churches offered instant forgiveness without mention of penance at all.

The second line of attack developed in Rome and began soon after the martyred Fabian was replaced, in March 251, by Bishop Cornelius. The election of Cornelius was challenged by a presbyter named Novatian (not to be confused with Novatus, one of those opposing Cyprian at Carthage). Novatian not only rejected Cornelius but arranged to have himself appointed bishop of Rome by a group of supporters. So in Rome, there were now two rival bishops.

Cyprian saw the danger. The Roman state had not succeeded in destroying the church, but internal disunity just might. He reconvened his bishops, and declared Cornelius the duly chosen bishop of Rome. This alienated Novatian, who responded by attacking Cyprian's policy with the lapsed. It was far too lenient, he said. Those who lapsed were not to be reconciled to the church even at the time of death, no matter how penitent they might now be. Only God could forgive them, should that be his will. Clemency was beyond the power of the earthly church. Then, in 252, Novatian took a further step. He consecrated a former presbyter named Maximus as the new bishop of Carthage, and dispatched him there to serve as a thorn in Cyprian's side. While Maximus attacked Cyprian for his leniency, the Privatus group denounced him for being far too severe and meanwhile consecrated Fortunatus, one of Cyprian's former presbyters, as bishop of Carthage. So where Rome had two rival bishops, Carthage now had three.

Chaos reigned, or so it seemed. But now, at least, Cyprian could see why he had been denied the tranquil Christian life he had once envisioned. The most devastating toll of the Decian persecution had been its disruptive effect on the church. God had endowed Cyprian with immense abilities. He possessed an unshakable assurance that he commanded the high ground. His energy was unflagging, and he could wage fierce intellectual warfare. All his rhetorical and literary powers he now trained on those he saw as the agents of disunity.

Novatus, one of those who had condemned him at Carthage for being too harsh, had by now traveled to Rome, where he joined Novatian in condemning Cyprian as not harsh enough, an inconsistency which drew a full salvo of Cyprianic invective: "Eager for novelties, raging with the rapacity of an insatiable

Though obviously a reference to Jesus the Good Shepherd, this carving might also symbolize the pastoral labors of bishops such as Cyprian of Carthage. Discovered in the basilica of Damous el-Karita in Cyprian's city, it was carved in white marble at about the time Cyprian was caring for his embattled flock.

avarice, inflated with the arrogance and stupidity of a haughty pride . . . a flatterer to deceive, never faithful to love, a torch and a fire to kindle the flames of sedition, a whirlwind and tempest to make shipwrecks of faith . . . a foe of peace."

About Novatian, the would-be bishop of Rome, Cyprian wrote that he "has sundered the church and drawn some of the brethren into impiety and blasphemy, and has introduced impious teaching concerning God, and has calumniated our most compassionate Lord Jesus Christ as unmerciful. And besides all this, he rejects the holy baptism, and overturns the faith and confession which precede it, and entirely banishes from them the Holy Ghost, if indeed there was any hope that he would remain or return to them."

But bashing his critics wouldn't heal the fractured church, and Cyprian knew it. A cohesive vision of the church must be advanced as well, and his essay on the ultimate unity of the church became an ageless testament to the church's permanence, made remarkable by the fact it was written in the midst of fierce ecclesiastical strife.

"There is one church," he wrote, "which outspreads itself into a multitude, wider and wider in ever increasing faithfulness; just as the sun has many rays but one only light, and a tree many branches yet only one heart, based in the clinging root; and while many rills flow off from a single fountainhead, although a multiplicity of waters is seen streaming away in diverse directions from the bounty of its abundant overflow, yet unity is preserved in the head-spring. Pluck a ray away from the sun's body! Unity admits no division of light.

Indoor baptism

Pools and basins served early Christians as the sacramental spring became a 'font'

When Christians first began to designate specific buildings for worship, baptismal facilities became an important feature. In the East, the earliest were pools or cisterns in which a new Christian could be totally immersed. In the West, shallower pools were hewn from the stone within the Roman catacombs, and a neophyte stood with feet immersed while another person poured water over him or her, or water was released from an overhead stream or passageway. Such a basin was often called a *fons*, a spring of water, eventually yielding the word "font" to describe any such sacramental vessel no matter what size or how elaborate.

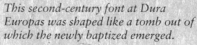
This second-century font at Dura Europas was shaped like a tomb out of which the newly baptized emerged.

Break a bough off a tree! Once broken it will bud no more. Cut a rill off from the spring! The rill cut off dries up. So too the church, flooded with the light of the Lord, flings rays over the whole world. Yet it is one light which diffuses itself everywhere; the unity of the body knows no partition."

Squarely in the midst of this internal church strife, the empire struck at the Christians again. In 253, the new emperor, Valerian, made it clear that fresh persecutions were to be expected. That same year, a new proconsul, Galerius, arrived in Carthage, giving rise to yet another wave of arrests, torture and executions, and another ecclesiastical struggle.

Cyprian immediately recognized the devastating effect a new round of persecution would have on the church, and convened a council of his bishops to revise their policies. The council feared, quite reasonably, that lapsed Christians, still outside the church but seeking readmission through penance, would fall away in great numbers in the face of renewed pressure. In what might be called an act of faithful pragmatism, he and his bishops declared that penitent sacrificers would be reunited with their beloved church immediately, instead of being forced to wait until the time of their death.

For many, however, the time of death was advancing hard upon them. Rome, turning to its task with typical vigor, slaughtered the humble and exalted alike. In June 253, Rome's Bishop Cornelius was arrested and marched to prison. In an act of defiance, a huge number of his congregation walked with him to his cell. He lasted only a few weeks. His successor, Lucius, survived into the following year, and was succeeded by Bishop Stephen. The latter, by repudiating a long-standing practice in the African church, posed a new kind of threat to church unity, Cyprian was soon to find.

The ancient church on the Greek island of Paros has an early fourth-century, cross-shaped font (left), as does that at Shivta in Israel (right).

Cyprian's issue with Rome's Bishop Stephen was only obliquely related to the persecution. It had to do with the acceptance into the faith of those baptized by schismatic clergy, meaning those who had severed themselves, or been severed, from the main body of the Christian church. This, of course, would include people baptized by lapsed clergy. To Cyprian, there was no issue here. If a bishop or presbyter wasn't part of the Christian community, then any baptisms he conducted were not valid. Bishop Stephen disagreed. He had, in fact, supported the reinstatement of two fallen Spanish bishops. But so far as Cyprian was concerned, the matter had long been settled. "We decided long ago . . . that the ancient practice against heretics should be maintained and held firm," he wrote. "We have decided that all baptism administered outside the church must be rejected."

Bishops who operated outside the church had absolutely no standing, he said, and their baptisms were at best meaningless rituals. "Who, moreover, is able to give what he himself does not possess?" he wrote to his allies in Numidia. "Or how can he who has lost the Holy Spirit perform spiritual functions? And therefore, he who comes untrained to the church must be baptized and renewed in order that he may be sanctified within by those who are holy, since it is written, 'Be ye holy, for I am holy, said the Lord.' Therefore, he who has been seduced into error and been discolored outside, ought to lay aside this very thing in the true baptism of the church—that he, a man coming to God, while he seeks for a bishop, fell by the deceit of error upon a profane one."

In this issue, Cyprian found himself opposed by *both* of Rome's bishops— Stephen, whom despite their disagreement Cyprian considered the legitimate one,

Some interpret the shape of the font at Sbeitla in Tunisia as representing a womb from which Christians are reborn to a new life.

and Novatian. Cyprian was characteristically dismissive of Novatian who, after all, had come to power by rejecting the duly chosen and now martyred Cornelius.

Stephen, like Cyprian not lacking in self-assurance, denounced Cyprian as a "false Christ." Rebaptism, he argued, was not necessary. Anyone baptized in the name of the Father, Son and Holy Spirit could be received into the church by a simple laying on of hands. Cyprian's reply reads red hot: "An excellent and lawful tradition is indeed put forward by our brother Stephen's teaching! He supplies us with a sufficient authority. . . . To this depth of evil has God's church, Christ's spouse, sunk, that she must follow the example of heretics; that light must borrow its order for celebrating the heavenly sacraments from darkness; and Christians must copy Antichrists."[2]

Yet there was to be no meeting of the minds on this issue, as with many others that divided the church during this decade of upheaval. A third Council of Carthage, in 256, unanimously declared that heretics must be rebaptized, and so that policy remained. But the debate was cut short, at least from Stephen's end, in August of 257, when Stephen died a martyr. Cyprian knew the circle was closing. He had just over a year to live himself.

Against this backdrop of ecclesiastical turmoil and mass persecution, the fuller picture of Cyprian is easily obscured. He was, at his heart, a pastor—a calling he came to delight in. Nothing seemed to please him more than the ordinary tasks he undertook as a shepherd of Christ. His dedication to the poor and afflicted was unstinting. He regularly implored his wealthier congregants for donations, with which he augmented a monthly tax for the relief of widows, orphans, and the destitute. When Christians were enslaved by rebel tribesmen in 253, he raised funds for their ransom and forwarded the collection to the church in Numidia. And when plague ravaged Africa, he mustered the faithful who, under his leadership, provided relief to Christians and non-Christians alike.

Round fonts at Heraclea Lynkestis (center) and Stobi (right), both in Macedonia, are of late fourth-century construction.

The devastation wrought by that plague in full fury is all but unimaginable in the developed world of the twenty-first century, although it would hardly surprise those living on the continent of Africa at the beginning of the twenty-first century, when the population was being decimated by AIDS. One notorious third-century plague outbreak began in Egypt's slums, sometime around 251. By some estimates, half the population of Alexandria fell. When the disaster struck Carthage, Cyprian's biographer Pontius would later write, the horror "invaded every house of the trembling populace, carrying off day by day with abrupt attack numberless people, every one from his own house. All were shuddering, fleeing, shunning the contagion, impiously exposing their own friends, as if with the exclusion of the person who was sure to die of the plague, one could exclude death itself also."

Before considering Cyprian's response, it should be remembered that there was no knowledge in the third century of the actual causes of disease; the discovery of germs was to come far in the future. The civil authorities took what steps they could—a demand for more sacrifices to the gods, and perhaps the minting of a new line of coins in honor of Apollo. These were unsuccessful strategies; the dead packed the streets and warehouses, while

2. Though the North African churches continued for some time to require the rebaptism of those previously baptized by heretical clergy, both Western and Eastern churches abandoned the requirement, provided that the original baptism had been made in the name of the Father, Son and Holy Spirit.

the survivors filled the days and nights with wailing.

Cyprian, seeing his duty in no uncertain terms, exhorted Christians to stand firm in the face of this rampaging pestilence. This scourge, he said, "examines the minds of the human race, to see whether they who are in health tend the sick; whether people truly love their kindred; whether masters pity their languishing servants; whether physicians do not forsake their beseeching patients; whether the fierce suppress their violence; whether the rapacious can quench the ever insatiable ardor of their raging avarice even by the fear of death." As he knew better than most, God is most devoutly served in times of upheaval and uncertainty, and even death.

Indeed, dying for Christ became a constant theme in his writings, including a series of letters, probably written in the last year of his life, arguing for a uniform policy in Rome and Carthage on matters great and small. In one of these letters, he tells the story of a priest named in a will to be a tutor. The priest should demur, Cyprian argued, because clergy should not be distracted from their holy mission by secular business concerns. In another letter, a deacon's sexual encounter with a virgin is discussed. Cyprian urged instant excommunication for the deacon, and reconciliation for the woman.

Death was very much on his mind, perhaps because he increasingly sensed

Role models for the ages

Saints like Christopher, Barbara, Catherine and Christina left sparse records, but their deaths in the persecutions flowered in Christian lore

The mid-third and early fourth centuries furnished the Christians with a broad inventory of saints, most of them martyrs, who would serve as role models and a focus for devotion for centuries to come. The Decian persecution and those that followed immediately were responsible, along with the Diocletian persecution that took place some fifty years later, and then the vicious crackdowns of Galerius and Daia.

It was during this period that some of the most cherished names in Christian history made their appearance. Their lives and deeds are sometimes documented, but frequently so little is known about them that their stories are little more than legends.

Dangling from the rearview mirrors or attached to the dashboards of countless automobiles in the twenty-first century, for instance, are "Christopher medals," representing the motorist's unspoken prayer to St. Christopher, long the patron saint of travelers. The real St. Christopher is believed to have suffered martyrdom under Decius, somewhere in Asia Minor. Almost nothing of historical credibility is recorded of him.

In the legend that grew up around him, he was a huge man who earned his living by carrying travelers across a river. Once he was called upon to carry a little boy, and found himself bent double under enormous weight. The name "Christopher" means "Christ-bearer;" the boy turned out to be Christ, who was himself bearing the weight of the world.

Similar permanent popularity attaches to St. Barbara, listed as virgin and martyr, indicating that she must have died in the Diocletian era or earlier. However, there is no mention of her whatever in the ancient records. By the seventh century, legends about her had accumulated, and large numbers of Christians had developed a devotion to her. An account of her martyrdom, dating from the ninth century, describes a young woman who becomes Christian. Her wealthy pagan father has her tortured and condemned, then carries out the death sentence himself and beheads her. The father is thereafter struck by lightning and dies. The eighteenth-century Franciscan mission on the California coast, and the graceful city that grew from it, preserve her name.

The history of St. Catherine of Alexandria is also obscure. She, too, is among the most widely venerated of women saints, and tradition dates her martyrdom to the early fourth century. The first account of it does not appear until the tenth century. It tells of a bright young woman of noble birth, highly educated, who rebukes the that his initial hopes of living to old age were not in keeping with his Lord's will. There was no need to fear it, however. He knew that the man or woman who dies for Christ achieves a glory beyond comprehension. The very presence of such martyrs, in fact, transforms places of persecution into holy altars, as he explained in a letter to prisoners in the Roman mines: "Oh, blessed prison which your presence has illuminated! Oh, blessed prison which sends men of God to heaven!" Those who see death in these places miss the point, for "let no one think of death, but of immortality, nor of punishment in time, but in glory everlasting."

The time for Cyprian's final showdown with the imperial authorities had come. In 257, Cyprian was summoned before the proconsul and warned that "conventions"—meetings—of any type were forbidden. This included the Christian practice of meeting in cemeteries. They were being instructed, in effect, to renounce their faith.

"Do what you are ordered," Cyprian responded. "I am a Christian and a bishop; I know no other gods but the one true God." He added, in an echo of Christ, that he recognized the prerequisites of temporal power. "We Christians render service to this God, and we pray for the safety of the emperors."

He was shuttled off to an "assigned residence" at Curubis, some fifty miles

In a detail from a sixth-century mosaic (Sant'Apollinare Nuovo, Ravenna, Italy), a group of saints processes to the altar bearing crowns of varied design, symbols of martyrdom.

emperor Maximian for his persecution of Christians. To dissuade her from her faith, he pits her against some of the best logicians in the court, whom she bests in one dialectical contest after another. Maximian has her thrashed and imprisoned. The Catherine wheel, which has spikes projecting from the rim, is named for the way she was tortured. When she successfully converts her jailers, he has them executed with her.

Tradition ascribes a particularly gruesome death to another female saint from the period, Christina of Tyre, who refuses her mother's pleas to apostatize and is, according to the legend, unsuccessfully burnt in a fire that instead kills hundreds of pagan onlookers. She bleeds milk instead of blood when her breasts are cut off; continues to preach after her tongue is cut out; throws the tongue at the judge, permanently blinding him; is tossed into the sea, where she is baptized by Jesus and returned safely to land by Michael the Archangel; and is finally killed by an arrow.

This was also the period of the famous Pantaleon or Panteleimon, whose ability to cure diseases has been called upon by devout believers for seventeen centuries. The existence of Pantaleon is certain, as is the fact he was martyred under Diocletian around 305. He was an unmercenary healer, treating people free of charge and thus winning people to Christianity.

Shakespeare's *Henry V* made famous Saints Crispin and Crispinian, by legend two Roman Christian brothers who fled to Soissons in Gaul during the Diocletian era. There, they became shoemakers, taking nothing for their work except what was freely offered. Finally caught, they were put to death. Shakespeare conflates the two names into "Crispian" and has Henry fire up his troops for the Battle of Agincourt, fought on "St. Crispin's Day," October 25, 1415. Henry's speech ("For he today that sheds his blood with me/Shall be my brother") serves as a memorial to veterans of all wars in all ages. ■

away, until final arrangements could be made. The first night in Curubis, he again saw his future in a dream, one that has been preserved for the Christians of future ages to contemplate. According to the account of Peter Hinchliff, one of Cyprian's biographers, "he saw himself led by a very tall young man into the Praetorium at Carthage. There he was made to appear before the judgment tribunal. The proconsul's court was in session. In the frustrating and terrifying way that dreams have, there was no sound, only action.

"The proconsul wrote on his wax tablet, as though formally recording a sentence. He has asked no questions, indicated no charge, established no guilt. . . . But the young man had placed himself behind the proconsul's back and was, therefore, in a position to see what was written. With a slicing gesture of his hand he signaled to Cyprian. The mimed sword stroke indicated that it was a sentence of death."

Was Cyprian again filled with foreboding? The man who had been ridiculed for fleeing Carthage earlier now expressed no fear for his fate. He certainly knew he was hardly the only marked man in this most dangerous neighborhood. The Romans had already sent a ghastly notification of what was coming to every Christian in North Africa. A roundup of Christians had been made at Utica, twenty-five miles from Carthage. The Christians, said to be about three hundred in number, were lined up around an industrial lime kiln that had been set afire. Nearby, a supply of incense was placed for them. "Choose whether you will offer incense to Jupiter or be thrown into the lime," they were told. In response, says the Christian record, all three hundred turned to the governor, confessed that Christ was the Son of God "and with one swift impulse hurled themselves into the fire."[3]

Now it was Cyprian's turn. On the thirteenth of September, 258, he was summoned to the home of the proconsul, Galerius, just outside Carthage. There was a formality to be disposed with. Christians and non-Christians assembled to watch the trial of a beloved bishop.

"The most sacred emperors have commanded you to conform to the Roman rites," said Galerius.

"I refuse."

"Take heed for yourself," Cyprian was advised.

"Do as you are bid; in so clear a case I may not take heed."

Galerius is reported to have been uncomfortable with the task his emperor had set before him. He, too, was a pawn in a much larger drama, and his health was so poor that he died just a few days later. With apparent reluctance, he said Cyprian had lived an "irreligious life" that was an affront to both the "gods and the religion of Rome," as well as its pious emperors. "You shall be made an example to those whom you have wickedly enlisted; the authority of

---

3. The exact date of the martyrdoms at Utica is usually given as August 24, 258, which would have put it just ahead of Cyprian's execution. However, the Utica date is uncertain. The *Catholic Encyclopedia* places the event as occurring between 253 and 260. The bodies of the Christians in the lime kiln at Utica would have been dissolved into the white lime powder. Their sacrifice was compared with that of Christ and termed the *Massa Candida*, "the White Mass."

law shall be ratified in your blood. It is the sentence of this court that Thascius Cyprianus be executed with the sword."

"Thanks be to God," he replied.

The crowd cried out and appeared to be attempting a rescue, which caused the guards to enclose Cyprian among them and move him to the place of execution, where he would be held overnight.

And so Cyprian's final hours had arrived. There seems little doubt that he had fully prepared himself. A passage from his *Exhortation to Martyrdom* is especially telling: "The brave and steadfast mind, founded upon religious meditation, stands firm and, against all the terrors of the devil and the threats of the world, the spirit persists unmoved, strengthened by a sure and solid faith in what will be. In persecutions, the earth is shut up but heaven is opened."

The next day, September 14, 258, Cyprian was marched to the place of execution. He wore a simple homespun coat. Witnesses say that the man himself

The radiant Cyprian was marched to the place of execution. When his executioner shrank from the job, he told his flock to give the man 25 gold pieces, then bound his own eyes.

was radiant, his demeanor providing for those who looked on an example of Christian courage. His executioner, arriving late, appeared unwilling to carry out the order to kill this great man. Cyprian, as was his habit, took mercy, ordering his followers to give the headsman twenty-five gold pieces. He then knelt in the dirt and bound his own eyes.

The crowd drew close, tossing their cloaks beneath their beloved bishop to catch his precious blood. He did not offer a last statement, but showed impatience at the executioner's slowness. A centurion standing by grabbed a sword and beheaded the bishop. As the final deed was done, some present may have recalled another passage from Cyprian's pen: "What an honor . . . to shut one's eyes for a moment, with which men and the world are seen, and to open them once to see God and Christ."

Cyprian's holy rat race had ended. The disputes that roiled his administration would continue for another two hundred years. His writings, however, remained popular throughout antiquity. His rivals could not always claim as much. Novatianists, increasingly marginalized, were held to be heretics until the time of Constantine, whose edict in 321 offered toleration and gave them the right to own buildings and burial places. In 439, their fortunes were reversed when Celestine, bishop of Rome, took away their buildings. However, the Novatian Church survived into the seventh century.

Cyprian's basic insight—that the church must both maintain the high calling of Christ, "Be ye perfect" (Matt. 5:48), while also accommodating the penitent fallen—would remain for the centuries to come the paradoxical double task of Christians. He left also the example of his own experience. Don't presume to know what God has in mind for you. There may be major surprises. ■

Steadfast to the end, asking only for a blindfold, Cyprian, the head of the church
in Carthage, goes to his death. As he awaits the blow of the sword that will end
his life, members of his flock allowed to witness the execution toss shawls and

The amazing underground city

The catacombs were far more than a cemetery: In mile after subterranean mile they preserve a detailed portrait of early Christian life

On May 31, 1578, some Italian vineyard workers made a significant discovery. Near Rome, they stumbled onto the entrance to a catacomb, an underground graveyard of the sort their ancestors had used twelve centuries earlier. "Wonderful to relate," gushed Cesare Baronius, a church historian and the runner-up in two sixteenth-century papal elections, it was nothing less than "a city beneath the earth." Rome, he added, "was astonished."

Particularly astonished was Antonio Bosio, an eighteen-year-old law graduate from Malta. Bosio's life was at an impasse. Law had lost its charm for him. From his uncle, he had inherited the job of agent for the Knights of Malta in Rome. But a lifetime stamping passports held little allure for a man with Bosio's intellectual and scholarly gifts. Then came news of the discovery: A window had reopened on ancient Christian Rome. Bosio determined to spend the rest of his life investigating what lay beyond it.

So he did, leaving at his death in 1629 two volumes of manuscript notes, each containing over a thousand pages in folio. This massive, handwritten data bank formed the basis for Bosio's magisterial *Roma Sotteranea* (Subterranean Rome), whose publication two years after he died justly

prompted his admirers to dub him "The Christopher Columbus of the Catacombs." Indeed, since Bosio's discoveries, Jewish and Christian catacombs have been found in many ancient Roman cities.

Bosio's first journey underground almost ended in disaster. In 1593 he and a group of friends set out on a tour of the catacomb, named for St. Flavia Domitilla, a noblewoman who had owned the site in the first century. "From central grottoes," he wrote in his journal, "there departed galleries in all directions of the wind, galleries that, in turn, seemed to divide themselves into thousands of new galleries." In the presence of such wonders, time ceased to matter. That is, until it dawned on him that their candles had run out. Around them lay miles of unlit, unmapped passages. No wonder, as Bosio wrote in his journal, that he and his friends fully expected to end up "polluting this holy monument with our impure bodies." That didn't happen of course. But what Bosio's near-death experience did do was lead him to take a scientific approach in exploring the catacombs.

In the first place, it made him resolve never again to venture below ground without ropes, shovels and, of course, plenty of candles. But another lesson the Domitilla Catacomb taught him was the vital importance of being

methodical. It is no coincidence that in the history of archaeology, Bosio is famous for attention to detail. Catacomb research in his day was spasmodic and haphazard. He turned it into a veritable science.

Knowing of an ancient Roman bylaw forbidding burials within the city walls, he looked for catacombs in the countryside. Reason convinced him that such extensive construction would most likely have taken place along highways. So he focused his attention on the main roads leading into Rome. He also studied the *Itinerari*, a series of early medieval tourist brochures for pilgrims visiting martyrs' shrines in Rome.

Thus he brought thirty catacombs to light, surveyed, sketched and measured them, and copied the inscriptions on their walls. Because some can no longer be found, scholars rely on Bosio's *Roma Sotteranea* as evidence that they once existed.

What, then, did Baronius's "city beneath the earth" actually consist of?

So far, sixty catacombs containing an estimated 750,000 graves and forming a 620-mile-long multilevel labyrinth have been unearthed. Archaeologists have good reasons for believing there are still more to come.

At a time when horsepower referred to horses, how was such extensive tunneling possible? One thing that helped was Rome's subsoil, which consists for the most part of tufa, a porous volcanic material ideally suited to subterranean construction. Then there were the expert *fossores*, or diggers. Far more than just pick-and-shovel men, they designed and engineered, and they may have had a hand in wall painting as well.

Fossores built catacombs in stages. A fossor would cut a vertical shaft, say, ten feet down, then a horizontal shaft at right angles, at the end of which he would hollow out a *cubiculum*, or bedroom, and line it with rows of *loculi* (rectangular indentations to put individual corpses in). As cubicula filled up, he would build others at the end of

Artwork in the richly decorated burial chamber on the Via Latina catacomb (top) has both pagan and Christian themes. This may be evidence of a shift in faith of the family interred there, or of the ease with which Rome's early Christians mixed both themes. Under the catacomb of Callistus is the more avowedly Christian "Crypt of the Popes" (lower photo), so named because many of the early bishops of the city were interred in it.

other passages. When the fossor found himself up against his employer's property line, he would dig vertically instead of horizontally before excavating another cubiculum. Some Roman cubicula are stacked seven stories high. And finally, the fossor would make the whole place habitable by digging shafts called *lucernaria* to let in light and air (which did not, however, prevent Bishop Gilbert Burnet, an eighteenth-century Briton, from grumbling about "the darkness and thick air" in the catacombs, and refusing to stay in them more than an hour at a time).

In the fourth century, after the triumph of the emperor Constantine and the end of the persecutions, the number of Christian converts increased and therefore the number of Christian dead. So the old haphazard arrangement of loculi gave way to efficiency. No space was wasted; the corners where two galleries met were divided into smaller plots for children, an arrangement that served not only to relieve the pressure on the morgue but also, no doubt, to sweeten the local fossor's commission.

As time passed and Christianity became fashionable and finally legal, loculi were made over into more elegant resting places. Graves of martyrs were refurbished, and pilgrims from outside Italy began visiting, eating a funereal meal called a *refrigerium* (the word still appears in Roman Catholic prayer books) near a martyr's tomb, and attending anniversary masses at his grave. What *didn't* happen in the catacombs were regular church services. Nowhere was there enough space to hold them. Nor, as Bosio mistakenly claims, did Christians take refuge in the catacombs during persecutions. Catacombs were cemeteries, known and maintained by the Roman government, and the authorities could as easily have found worshipers there as above ground.

In the years after Constantine's triumph, the catacombs enjoyed their golden age. Elegant inscriptions (archaeologists have so far counted forty thousand of them) began to appear, as did a distinctively Christian art. Perhaps because of the Romans' deeply held reverence for the dead, they seem to have made no attempt to interfere with Christian funereal art. But it evolved in a pagan setting. The sarcophagus of Marcus Aurelius Prosenes, dating from the end of the third century, is a pagan work of art in every respect but one. An inscription informs us that on March 3, 217, Prosenes was

"led back to God." In other words, he was Christianized, but his coffin retained elements of paganism.

Later Christians began adapting pagan symbols for their own purposes. As the theologian Alexander Schmemann writes, "In accepting any particular form [of natural religion, even of paganism], the church in its own mind has returned to God what rightly belongs to him, always and in every way restoring the fallen image." So an apparently pagan funerary inscription complete with acanthus leaves includes the unmistakably

The basilica of St. Sebastian (model, bottom), one of the earliest of the great churches of Rome, was built over smaller side chapels that themselves covered catacombs (below). The word "catacomb" itself comes from this site, which in ancient times was called "basilica catacumbas," from the Greek meaning "near the hollow." Originally dedicated as the Basilica of the Apostles, the church was renamed in the ninth century to honor the popular martyr Sebastian, buried there.

Among the earliest and most popular themes for the frescoes in Rome's catacombs was the Orans, a figure of a person (usually a woman) with hands raised in prayer. The meaning was clear: Prayer, to their God and for each other, lay at the heart of the Christians' experience (catacomb of Priscilla, second half of the third century).

Christian symbols of two fish and an anchor. Elsewhere, other pagan images received Christian interpretations. The pagan *kriophoros*, or ram-bearer, doubled as Christ the Good Shepherd; Venus, the goddess of love, did duty as the Virgin Mary; and Endymion, a young man put to sleep forever by the moon goddess Selene, is recycled as Jonah resting under his climbing gourd. And finally, the pagan symbol *becomes* a Christian one. Thus the addition of a bird to a representation of Deucalion, sole survivor of a mythological flood ordered up by Zeus, tells us that buyers of this picture were thinking not of Deucalion, but of Noah.

As striking as their art and architecture may have been, a visit to the "city beneath the earth" remained a chilling descent into the land of the dead. The fourth-century Christian scholar Saint Jerome offers a first-person view: "When I was a boy, receiving my education in Rome, I and my schoolfellows used, on Sundays, to make the circuit of the sepulchres of the apostles and martyrs. Many a time did we go down into the catacombs. These are excavated deep in the earth, and contain, on either hand as you enter, the bodies of the dead buried in the wall. It is all so dark there that the language of the prophet seems to be fulfilled, 'Let them go down quick into hell.' Only occasionally is light let in to mitigate the horror of the gloom, and then not so much through a window as through a hole. You take each step with caution, as, surrounded by deep night, you recall the words of Virgil: 'Horror on every side, and terrible even the silence.'"

After Constantine moved his capital to Byzantium (now Istanbul), Rome became prey to attacks by foreign invaders. The catacombs were particularly vulnerable to grave robbers, so in 817 Pope Pascal I brought above ground to the Church of St. Prasede the bodies of twenty-three hundred martyrs. Thus did the catacombs cease to be of interest to pilgrims, and the memory of them faded. But not the significance of their contribution to Christian history. ■

CHAPTER 3

The gradual evolution of the word 'Catholic'

It began as a Greek adjective meaning 'universal,' but by the 300s it became a noun and Christians disputed which beliefs were the Catholic ones

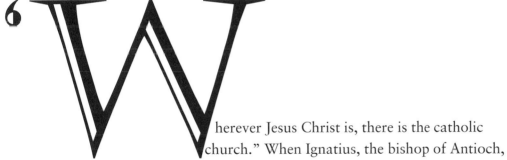

herever Jesus Christ is, there is the catholic church." When Ignatius, the bishop of Antioch, wrote that sentence in Greek to the Christians at Smyrna (now Izmir on the shores of the Aegean in western Turkey, see map page 131, E3), he did not know he was introducing into the Christian vocabulary a term that would be used for the next nineteen hundred years. Neither did he know that the adjective "catholic" would become a noun as well, in fact a proper noun in virtually every human language. Finally, he would certainly never have guessed that for the last four hundred of those nineteen hundred years, this noun would evoke scorn in some Christians, deep respect and affection in others.

To Ignatius, the Greek word *katholikos* simply meant "general" or "universal," originating from two other Greek words that together meant "whole" or "complete." Aristotle had spoken of a "catholic rule," meaning a general rule. Polybius wrote of a "catholic pronouncement," meaning one that was intended to apply universally. Ignatius, for the first time, had applied the term to the whole Christian community, no doubt to emphasize that the church was one, and the church was everywhere; it was "universal."

Ignatius wrote the sentence around the year 110, and thereafter the word *katholikos* gained ever-wider usage among Christians. In the mid-second century, Justin spoke of "the catholic resurrection" (meaning, the general resurrection), in the third, Tertullian had referred to "the catholic goodness of God" (meaning the universal goodness of God), while Irenaeus spoke of "the four catholic winds" (i.e., north, south, east and west). From the start, however, one problem had become both pressing and alarming. Christ's flock could withstand the full fury of the Roman persecutors. But its real danger came from within, the problem of maintaining its unity. By the third century, Christians spoke of a "catholic" or universal church. The problem lay in determining who was and who was not "catholic," and how Christians could decide.

In Alexandria, Carthage and Rome, there were periods of bitter division, with rival bishops each claiming to be the authentic one. Worse still, it was becoming more difficult to know what exactly a Christian was supposed to believe. He must believe in Jesus Christ, of course, all Christians replied. But then, who was Jesus Christ? The Son of God, just as it said in the Christian Gospels and Epistles, came the reply. But what did "Son of God" mean? How could God be both up in heaven and also a man on earth? Were there two Gods? Or three?

Here the answers conflicted. Most Christians insisted that Christ was one of the Three Divine Persons in whose name Christians were baptized. Wrong, said those who were called Modalists, God must be thought of as One Person, though he appeared in different "modes," sometimes as Father, sometimes as Son, sometimes as the Holy Spirit. Wrong, said the Adoptionists, there were Three Persons all right, but the Second Person had actually been "adopted" by

In this third-century stone inlay image, Jesus is portrayed as bearded, hand upraised in blessing. It is one of the earliest examples of the manner in which he would be depicted for the next eighteen centuries (Ostia Museum, Italy).

the First. Wrong, said the Subordinationists, there had been no such "adoption," so the Second Person must be considered "subordinate" to the First.

All these versions had arisen by the third century. Meanwhile, some of the groups that had sprung into being in the second century over other doctrinal questions were still active, though rapidly declining in the third—like the Marcionites, who rejected the God of the Old Testament because they believed in a "God of love" (see earlier volume, *A Pinch of Incense*, page 237); or the Docetists, who believed that Jesus merely reflected God and didn't suffer crucifixion, some contending that Simon of Cyrene had switched places with him at the last minute.

Egypt was the birthplace of many dissident theories, some about the nature of God, many about other issues. Not all the dissidents proved obstinate, however. One third-century Egyptian bishop, for instance, a certain Nepos, became

People of considerable education were seeing in Jesus Christ truths that satisfied the soul, but their honest inquiries met such a baffling array of answers that they were discouraged.

persuaded from the Book of Revelation that Jesus would imminently return and establish an earthly kingdom of sensual pleasures and luxury. After Nepos's death, his followers were persuaded to abandon the theory and return to the "catholic" tradition.

Other religious innovators would prove far less acquiescent. Out of Persia, for example, came the disciples of the prophet Mani early in the third century. From second-century Gnosticism and some of the teachings of Paul, Mani had constructed his own version of human salvation. Satan, he said, had stolen the particles of "light" with which God intended to illumine the world. He had imprisoned these particles in the minds of men. The mission of Buddha, the great prophets of Israel, Jesus, and Mani himself, was to liberate these particles, and the purpose of the whole physical universe was to enable this liberation to occur. By denying oneself the physical comforts of life, including the pleasure of eating meat, one could participate in this liberation process. By the fourth century, Manichaeanism, as it was called, had established a strong presence in Egypt, and was commanding much attention in Rome. It was viewed by the Christians as a serious threat and challenge.

To many Christians, this baffling diversity of theories and doctrines was inconsequential. They believed in Jesus, whoever he was, and that was enough for them. However, by the late third century, Christianity was beginning to intrigue people of considerable education. They saw in Jesus Christ truths that satisfied the soul. But their honest inquiries met with such a bewildering array of contradictory answers, that they were discouraged. The Christians realized that they could not refute these teachings unless there was some agreement on what Christians believed. In other words, there must be an agreed-upon "universal" Christian answer to the issues being raised. After all, Christ himself had

This magnificent mosaic was discovered beneath a field in the village of Hinton St. Mary, Dorset, England, in 1963. Likely the floor of a two-room chapel in a Roman villa of the early fourth century, it spreads through what appears to have been two connecting rooms, approximately fifteen by twenty-four feet in size. Designs in the smaller room show hunting scenes and images of pagan heroes. The floor of the larger room, however, features not only hunting scenes but the busts of five males. The central roundel (detail at right) is believed to be the earliest representation of Christ yet found in Britain: The familiar Chi-Rho, formed of the first two letters of "Christ," appears behind the clean-shaven, long-haired youth. Pomegranates on either side may have symbolized hope. The remaining four figures, placed in each corner, are thought to represent the four evangelists or the four winds, or both.

not evaded the crucial issues of his day—paying taxes to caesar, healing on the Sabbath, knowing who would be greatest in his kingdom. He had met these challenges with a response. God had given human beings minds. He presumably expected men to use them.

Something else was evident. Though these dissident groups might command much local attention, many tended to be short-lived, or to change radically, or to fragment into a diversity of quarrelsome subgroups. Meanwhile, there clearly existed an amazing consistency of belief among nearly all the bishops and the vast majority of Christians. In the late second century, the pagan writer Celsus referred to this huge and growing body of adherents as "the Great Church." To this "Great Church" the word "catholic" was increasingly applied. But catholic beliefs were specifically spelled out only in doctrinal statements adopted by

Something else was evident. Though dissident groups might command much local attention, many were short-lived, or changed radically, or split into quarrelsome subgroups.

churches regionally. There was no universal creed. The faithful recognized what was not Christian, even if they weren't quite sure what was.

They knew that every Christian community had a "bishop," which meant an "overseer." The office of bishop went back to New Testament times, when Paul advised Timothy of a bishop's qualifications—"blameless, the husband of one wife, vigilant, sober, given to hospitality, apt to teach" (1 Tim. 3:2)—and by the dawn of the fourth century, the number of Christian communities, and therefore of bishops, ran to well over one thousand. The *Didache*, a manual of Christian behavior that dates from the early third century, portrays the bishop as successor to the office of "prophet," a revered figure in early congregations, that survived in some up to the mid-third century.

The bishops saw themselves as the successors of the apostles. Upon the head of a bishop at his ordination had been laid the hands of other bishops, upon whose heads had been laid the hands of bishops earlier still. In this way, it was reasoned, there was a physical connection between themselves and the apostles, who had laid their hands on those they commissioned (Acts 13:3, and 1 Tim. 4:14). In the "consecration" of a bishop, not only was the Holy Spirit seen as conveyed from one generation to the next, but a body of teaching was viewed as similarly passed on.

While early bishops were chosen by the congregation, according to the *Didache*, a Christian bishop must also be "consecrated" by at least two other bishops, usually from the immediate area, all laying their hands on the head of the kneeling candidate and praying for the Holy Spirit to come upon him. This implied that the man chosen must have support from beyond his own community. One notable exception to this rule, however, was Alexandria, where the bishop was traditionally consecrated not by other bishops but by his own clergy, a custom that survived until the fourth century.

Within his diocese, the bishop's powers were virtually incontestable. His authority was "almost unchallengeable," writes historian W. H. C. Frend in *The Rise of Christianity*. "Being a representative of Christ, his authority was absolute," says historian Henri Daniel-Rops in *The Church of the Apostles and Martyrs*. While he might take highly controversial matters before his clergy and laity, the ultimate decision was his alone. It was he who admitted new Christians and could expel the deviant. He ordained his own clergy, and could depose them; he controlled the congregation's revenues and supervised the distribution of charitable funds. His flock, while they could elect him, could not depose him, though other bishops within his province, in extreme instances, had that power. The same Ignatius who introduced the word "catholic" to the Christian vocabulary also spelled out the monarchal role of the bishop. The bishop's authority was that of God, he said, so that "he who honors the bishop has been honored by God." However, as doctrinal and disciplinary questions arising from the persecutions became more pressing, bishops increasingly deferred to church synods and consultation with other bishops.[1]

Despite their heavy authority, the bishops were generally revered by their flocks, and the Oxford historian C. H. Turner, writing in *The Cambridge Medieval History*, makes a touching portrait of their relationship: "His flock was small enough for him to carry out to the letter the pastoral metaphor, and to 'call his sheep by name.' Even though the 'angel of the church' in the Book of Revelation may not have been, in the mind of the author, at all intended to refer to the bishop, yet this quasi-identification of

1. Not all historians would agree the monarchal role of the bishop went back to the New Testament. Some view the words "pastor" or "elder" or "bishop," as they appear in English translations of the New Testament, as synonyms, denoting a specifically pastoral responsibility, and see the "monarchal" bishop as a later development.

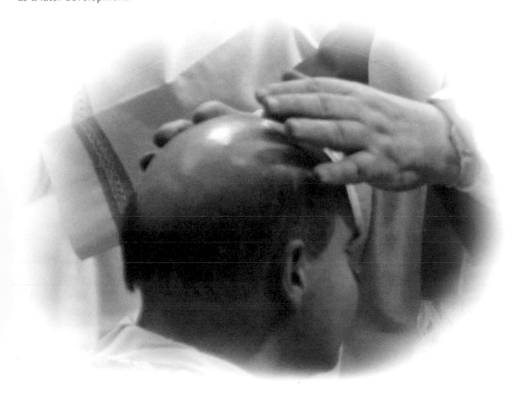

However it is understood by various groups, the laying-on of hands has since the earliest years of the church remained the most usual form of ordaining, investing and commissioning Christian ministries. As described in the New Testament, the practice showed that the one being ordained and the one doing the ordaining shared the same faith.

History preserved on coffin lids

The painters and carvers were often pagan, but their embellishments to Christian tombs and catacombs reveal a wealth of detail about the lives of early believers

The places and manner of their burials tell a great deal about the lives of the Christians at the end of the third and beginning of the fourth century. Christians embellished their tombs, coffins and catacombs in a manner that borrowed heavily on Roman tradition. The images found on them range from the deeply personal to the scriptural. *Clockwise from top:* (1) On a sarcophagus lid now at the Museo Nazionale Romano in Rome, a group of Christians is seen sharing a funeral banquet not unlike those that their pagan counterparts would have held. (2) The image of the Good Shepherd, like this one on a sarcophagus now in the Archeoloski Musej at Split, Croatia, was common to the tombs of many wealthy. (3) The tomb of a Christian named Seberus in Rome is decorated with a vat and an incorrectly designed Chi-Rho, indicating perhaps that the artisan who did the work was not familiar with the symbol. (4) Again like the burial practices of pagans of the era, an early fourth-century tomb slab from Spain bears the mosaic likeness of the deceased, this one in the familiar pose of the *orans*, a person praying. Such portraits are striking for the realism and apparent accuracy of the faces depicted. The merchant classes as well as the wealthy would engage the services of local (frequently pagan) artisans to decorate their burial vaults. ∎

the community with its representative exactly expresses the ideal."

The power of Christian worship lies in "the prayer of the bishop and the whole church," writes Ignatius. Justin Martyr depicts "the brethren" with "the president" (i.e., the bishop) as the Christian congregation. A special chair or throne, called in Greek and Latin a *cathedra*, was reserved in the church for the bishop.[2] On it was a white wool cushion, wool symbolizing the Earth and identifying the bishop as representing the church on Earth. Fourth-century Christian art often shows the bishop on a chair holding the Gospel book against his breast, his right hand stretched out in a gesture of blessing.

The territorial structure of the church naturally tended to follow that of the Roman Empire, so that a province of the empire came to be coterminous with a province of the church. Each bishop's jurisdiction was known as a diocese, a term derived from the Roman imperial administration, or as a "see," another term derived from the bishop's official "chair," this one from the Latin word for

The phenomenon of the 'parish priest' did not appear at Rome until the sixth century, because bishops feared independent parishes could too easily become independent churches.

a seat, *sedes*. The English word "bishop" comes from an ancient Anglo-Saxon corruption of the Greek word for "overseer," *episcopos*. The bishops, as a group, are known as "the episcopacy." An action approved by a bishop is said to have "episcopal" authority.

By the early fourth century, there might be many sees within a province, and the bishop whose see was the province's capital soon came to be regarded as holding senior rank, with the title of archbishop or metropolitan. Since by the fourth century there were 120 provinces in the empire, there were also a great many metropolitans. For bishops of the empire's major cities—Rome, Alexandria, Jerusalem, Antioch, and, from the late fourth century onward, Constantinople—the more advanced title of patriarch gradually emerged. Bishops in major cities were usually assisted by auxiliary bishops.[3] However, a diocese could also be very small. When Gregory the Wonderworker, biographer of Origen, became bishop of Neocaesarea, his diocese consisted of seventeen Christians.

Beneath the bishop there were, of course, other offices. Both bishops and deacons are mentioned in Paul's letter to Philippi (Phil. 1:1) and in the pastoral epistles, First Timothy and Titus. The Book of Acts mentions the office of presbyter or elder (Acts 20:17), a term sometimes applied to the bishop as well, but

---

2. The bishop's "chair" would often be the only chair in the church. The other clergy sat on benches. The laity stood, as they do to this day in many Orthodox churches and, until recently, the Roman basilicas.

3. An "auxiliary bishop" is a bishop who assists the diocesan bishop. An auxiliary bishop designated to automatically succeed the man he is assisting is a "coadjutor bishop." In the Roman Catholic Church the metropolitan of a province carries the title of archbishop. The other bishops within his province are said to be his "suffragan" bishops. In Anglican usage a suffragan bishop is the equivalent of an auxiliary bishop in the Roman Catholic Church. In the early centuries, however, the application of these titles was far less defined than it is today.

As did a number of Christian communities throughout the empire, this one constructed a building of substantial size for its assemblies. On this Lord's Day gathering, the Christians stand (following the usual practice) to
hear the homily or sermon of their bishop, seated at the ambo, a raised area. Though custom varied in local
churches, this congregation is arranged loosely according to ministry: presbyters and deacons around the
bishop, widows (in black) and virgins near the front of the church, and then the rest of the faithful

soon designating another office below the rank of bishop and above that of deacon. The word presbyter originated from *presbyteros*, the word Greek-speaking Jews used to describe an elder of the synagogue. By the third century, seven gradations of clergy had been established below the bishop—presbyters, deacons, subdeacons, acolytes, readers, exorcists and doorkeepers.

As congregations grew in size and number, the presbyters assumed some of the functions of the bishop, celebrating the Eucharist or Communion and performing baptisms. By Tertullian's time, mention is made of penitent Christians prostrating themselves before "confessors," meaning Christians who had once been incarcerated, as well as before presbyters, to receive God's forgiveness. Cyprian describes Christians approaching

death as confessing their sins to either a presbyter or a deacon.

By the second century other terms for the clergy appeared; the Latin word *sacerdos* and the Greek word *hiereus*. Both had been used to describe a pagan priest or a priest in the old Jewish Temple who ritually slew animals in atonement for man's sins. These new terms at first applied only to bishops, later to presbyters as well. They emphasized the bishop's and later the presbyter's role in the Communion, which is viewed by some as a recollection and by others as a more literal enactment of Christ's sacrifice on the cross. In English, French, Spanish and German the word for "priest" descends directly from the original term *presbyteros*.

As urban dioceses grew and became far too big for a bishop to administer, the Christians divided themselves into smaller assemblies, or parishes (from the Greek word *paroikia*, meaning a "district" or "neighborhood"). Eventually, each parish was under the care of a presbyter, or priest, who was responsible for the spiritual welfare of his flock and, on pain of excommunication, for the church's property. However, the phenomenon of the "parish priest," in existence at Alexandria by the late third century, was slow to develop elsewhere, and did not appear in Rome until the early sixth century, because bishops feared independent parishes could too easily become independent churches.

The office of deacon developed in a different way. The deacon began as the administrative assistant to the bishop, not to the presbyters. Where the presbyters

or priests became the bishop's assistants in spiritual matters, the deacons became his assistants in administrative affairs. The deacons were also responsible for the congregation's ministry to the poor, and for keeping order during religious meals. At first, the deacons took little part in the liturgical services of the church. They became the church officials most closely known to the members of the parish.[4]

Due to the precedent set forth in the first church at Jerusalem, where seven deacons were appointed to assist the apostles (Acts 6:5–6), the number of deacons in many dioceses was restricted to seven. This gave rise to two other developments. As Christian congregations rapidly grew, the office of subdeacon was created, to

Praying Christians line the walls of a Roman villa excavated at Lullingstone, Kent, England, in 1949. As in other house chapels at the turn of the fourth century, there is evidence in the villa that the owners themselves became Christians during the time that the house was being decorated.

permit the appointment of a greater number of men to the job, and also that of archdeacon, who reported directly to the bishop on behalf of them all.

Like the deacon, the deaconess makes her debut very early in the Christian story. In the earliest appearance of Christians in secular history, the Roman proconsul of Bithynia reports his torturing two deaconesses to get to the truth about this strange sect called Christian (see earlier volume, *A Pinch of Incense*, page 45). Some biblical scholars believe that New Testament references to deacons apply to deaconesses as well, and that Clement of Alexandria and Origen drew the same conclusion. The *Didache* plainly regards the deacon as being either male or female.[5]

The deaconess was responsible for the care of the sick and infirm in the congregation, and was expected to report instances of illness and need to the bishop. She would also anoint women for baptism. The office was widely used in the Eastern church, where a form of ordination for deaconesses survives. In the West, it declined rapidly, and a church council at Nimes in 394 forbade further ordination of deaconesses.

The other offices of the church varied from century to century. Cornelius, bishop of Rome, writing in the mid-third century, shows the office of acolyte already in existence in the West, but it will not appear in the writings of the

An intriguing church office was that of exorcist, who performed a common task among early Christians. The devil, screaming abuse through the mouth of the possessed, was thrust out.

East for another 250 years. The duties of acolytes are obscure, though they seem to include attending to the lights of the church and procuring wine for the Communion service. Readers or lectors also appear first in North Africa as men designated to read the Scriptures before the celebration of the Eucharist. Cyprian speaks of the office as an apprenticeship to the clergy. Today, door-keepers would be called janitors, men whose chief responsibility was maintaining the church's property.

An intriguing office is that of exorcist, usually listed at or near the bottom of the hierarchy. Its rank, however, does not reflect the attention paid to its activity, which was fascinating. The Gospels report at least six instances in which Jesus performed exorcisms, and driving devils from people was a common task among the first Christians. The historian Eusebius calls it "an office of special

4. The direct connection between the bishop and the deacons would survive in the Western church in a curious way. Although at the ordination of a priest the bishop and several other priests lay their hands on the head of the ordinand, at the ordination of a deacon in the West, only the bishop's hands are placed on the man's head. In the East, the bishop alone conducts all ordinations.

5. The *Didache*, defining the duties of a bishop, declares: "Wherefore, O Bishop, thou shalt appoint unto thee laborers of righteousness, helpers with thee unto life. Those that seem good to thee out of all the people thou shalt choose and appoint deacons, a man for the doing of many things that are needed, and a woman for the ministration to the women. For there are houses where thou canst not send the deacon unto women because of the heathen; but thou shalt send the deaconess. For as in many other things, the office of a woman is required."

labor," conducted before the congregation, in which the devil, screaming abuse through the mouth of the possessed, is thrust out.

As the fourth century unfolded, all these orders began separating themselves from the laity (the "lay" people, from the Greek *laos*, "the people"—the worshipers, as distinguished from the clergy). A clerical career became a matter of climbing the clerical hierarchy. Typically, a man would start in his youth as a reader, then become an acolyte or subdeacon. At age thirty, says the historian Henri Daniel-Rops, he could become a deacon, at age thirty-five a priest, and at forty-five a bishop. Clerical garb came to be either black or white. The vestments that Christian clergy would use for the next seventeen hundred years were simply the dress-up clothing of late Roman aristocrats.

Such was the structure of the church that emerged from the Decian and Valerian persecutions in the mid-third century. Notwithstanding the imperial disfavor, Christian numbers grew steadily over the next forty years, while officialdom looked on alarmed. In Cyprian's time, there were between 130 and 150 dioceses in North Africa. By the century's end, this had grown to more than two hundred. Every church seemed to be acquiring property, and church buildings became common all over the empire, many of them packed and overflowing for the Sunday services. Large Christian centers became common on the outskirts of the major cities.

Biggest of all the Christian congregations was the one at Rome, where the bishop in 251 could count forty-six presbyters, seven deacons, seven subdeacons, forty-two acolytes, fifty exorcists and readers, several doorkeepers, and fifteen hundred widows and sick people being supported by the church, all numbers that would be dwarfed by the church in the imperial capital a century later.

"Mother church is strong in peace," declares this mosaic, at least in one translation. Discovered at Tabarka in Tunisia, it dates from the latter half of the fourth century and is unusual in its subject matter. It appears to depict a church of a symbolic form common to those of North Africa: a three-aisled basilica with a curtained entrance, the altar near the center.

However, while the church at Rome was flourishing, Christianity in the Latin-speaking Western world still accounted for as little as a tenth of the population by the early fourth century. In the Greek-speaking East, the Christian proportion was much higher, though specific percentages are difficult to establish. This was due to the fact that Christian evangelism moved from East to West, from the Greek-speaking part of the empire, then to the Latin-speaking, so that the Eastern church had a full hundred-year head start.

In both East and West, soaring numbers of Christians made necessary greater administrative activity. Matters left to the grace of God in an earlier era must now be institutionalized, not necessarily because people prayed and believed less fervently, but as the inevitable consequence of growth. If the Christians did not competently count the money, maintain the properties, instruct the converts, organize the divine services, admonish the errant, and systematize the care of the needy, the result would be not greater holiness, but utter chaos. As with every human endeavor, whether economic, governmental, military or spiritual, the price of sustained success was bureaucracy. The "heroic age" must yield to the "administrative age."

Historian Frend, a professor of archaeology at the University of Glasgow, views negatively what he sees as the emergence of a church in the fourth and fifth centuries, run almost totally by clergy. The losers, he writes in *The Church of the Roman Empire, 313–600* (included in *Town and Country in the Early Christian Centuries)*, were the laity, whose role in the church was severely

Songs that fan a spark into a fire

The first Christian music was drawn from the Bible; then came the first hymns, one of the earliest sung by a martyr as he walked into the flames

The oldest Christian hymn sounded forth in the first century, when angel voices sang "Glory to God in the highest, and upon Earth peace, goodwill to men" (*Gloria in Excelsis Deo*) to announce the birth of Jesus. These ancient words have been sung, especially at Christmastime, for two millennia.

Among the earliest hymns were the psalms, found in the Old Testament. They were central to Jewish worship, and the tradition of singing in the synagogue was one that early Christians appropriated. Singing unites people in praise and worship, and in dark times, a song to God can lift the spirits. It was almost certainly the singing of hymns that prisoners in the jail cells of Philippi overheard from their fellow captives Paul and Silas on that momentous night, recorded in Acts 16.

When he was Roman governor of Bithynia early in the second century, Pliny reported to the emperor Trajan that Christians sang together ". . . in honor of Christ as if to God." Another second-century writer, Clement of Alexandria, remarks how often Christians sang at mealtimes (saying "grace," perhaps). And in his early fourth-century history, Eusebius comments: "How many psalms and hymns . . . celebrate Christ, the Word of God!"

The most universal canticles—songs derived directly from the words of Old and New Testament—were drawn from Luke's Gospel, and three of them especially, are still sung today in Catholic, Anglican and Orthodox worship (see earlier volume, *The Veil Is Torn*, chapter 3).

The *Magnificat* ("My soul doth magnify the Lord") is a song from the words of the Virgin Mary after learning that she has been chosen to bear the Savior of the world. The words of the *Benedictus* ("Blessed be the Lord God of Israel/For he hath visited and redeemed his people") were proclaimed by Zacharias on the eighth day after the birth of his son, John the Baptist. The *Nunc Dimittis* was spoken by the old prophet

Simeon as he beheld the child Jesus when Mary and Joseph brought him to the Temple: "Lord, now lettest thou thy servant depart in peace."[1]

These and other canticles have three common features: First, they use actual words of Scripture. Second, they are given a regular, fixed place in worship. Third, and most important, they enable the singer to participate in a *universal* act of worship; the best canticles transcend all particularities of geography, culture or race.

The *Sanctus* ("Holy, holy, holy, is the Lord of hosts") comes from Isaiah 6:3; St. Clement of Rome, who died in about A.D. 104, testified that the Sanctus was regularly sung at Christian gatherings. In the West during the Middle Ages, the tradition of ringing church bells during the Sanctus began.

The *Benedicite* ("Bless the Lord all you works," from the song of the three young men tossed into the fiery furnace) calls upon every created thing—sun and moon, wind and fire, rain and dew, lightning and cloud, river and sea, the whole round Earth and all its inhabitants—to bless the name of the Lord, "to sing his praise and exalt him forever."

The *Venite* ("O come, let us sing unto the Lord" Psalm 95), by contrast, is a song of triumph; it rejoices in "the strength of our salvation." It renders God personal, by referring to the sovereign Creator as "our" God, and by confirming that "we are the people of his pasture and the sheep of his hand."

In addition to sung canticles, early Christian congregations joined in brief affirmations or responses, spoken or sung at particular times during worship, such as the *Gloria Patri* ("Glory be to the Father and to the Son and to the Holy Ghost"), familiar to Catholics and

---

1. The titles of these and other familiar canticles are usually taken from the first line of the hymn in the Latin version of the Scriptures.

diminished, so that the church appeared to outsiders more as an institution than as a way of life.

But historian Turner in the *Cambridge Medieval History* presents a different picture. To him, the losers were the bishops. He writes: "The necessity for new organization had to be met in some way which would preserve at all costs the oneness of the body and its head. It followed that the work and duties which the individual bishop could no longer perform in person, must be shared with, or deputed to, subordinate officials. As a result, new offices came into being in the course of the third century. This produced the *clerus*, or clergy, which gradually acquired during the fourth and fifth centuries the character of a hierarchy,

Protestants alike, and later the Greek *Kyrie Eleison*: "Lord, have mercy."[2]

While canticles derive directly from Scripture, hymns allow room for creativity and artistic imagination, elaborating upon Scripture with poetry and music.

Clement of Alexandria's "Fisher of men, whom thou to life does bring," one of the earliest complete and explicitly Christian hymns, is believed to have been written about 170. Clement also preserved another early hymn, "Bridle of colts untamed."

Still in use is "O Gladsome Light" (*Phos Hilaron*) usually attributed to St. Athenogenes, martyred about 305 under the emperor Diocletian. According to tradition, Athenogenes sang the second stanza of this hymn as he entered the flames that consumed him. In 1899, Robert Bridges, poet laureate of England, undertook a translation from the Greek of that second stanza:

> Now, ere day fadeth quite,
> We see the evening light,
> Our wonted hymn outpouring,
> Father of might unknown,
> Thee, his incarnate Son,
> And Holy Ghost adoring.

In the 1920s, a fragment of papyrus was found at Oxyrhynchus in Egypt; on one side it had jottings of Egyptian corn accounts, on the other, five lines, complete with musical notation, of a Christian hymn predating the Council of Nicea in 325. These ancient words affirm that, at all times, the Christian message is "good news":

> Might and worship and majesty belong always to God,
> The giver alone of all that is good.

The three Old Testament youths, Shadrach, Meshach and Abednego, raise their hands in song amid the flames of the fiery furnace (Catacomb of Priscilla, Rome).

By the end of the fourth century, hymn writing was flourishing, laying down for future generations a treasure trove of Christian insight and inspiration. Hymns created in the intervening seventeen centuries continue to fulfill St. Paul's charge that Christians should "admonish one another in psalms and hymns and spiritual songs, singing with grace in your heart to the Lord" (Colossians 3:16).

St. Theophan the Recluse, a nineteenth-century Russian monk, understood the powerful appeal of church hymns, ancient and modern: They "make the spark of grace that is hidden within us burn bright and with greater warmth . . . Psalms, hymns and spiritual songs are introduced to fan the spark and transform it to flame." ■

---

2. In ancient Christianity, no musical instruments were used in worship. Pagan religious rituals were usually accompanied by flutes or other instruments; the Old Testament describes Temple worship as accompanied by instruments. However, after the destruction of the Temple (and perhaps even before), no instruments were used in synagogue worship, and the Christians followed this practice.

nicely ordered by steps and degrees." However, the origins of some of these offices went all the way back to the New Testament.

The bishop, particularly in the larger centers, soon lost immediate touch with his flock. When it consisted of several hundred he could know them all. When it became several thousand, this became impossible. Even his hitherto indispensable contact with his deacons was lost, for now they often reported not to him but to a single "archdeacon" who in turn reported to the bishop.

Much of the bishop's former pastoral function was conferred upon the presbyters or priests. The priest became the celebrant of the Eucharist in the bishop's stead. Historian Turner observes another subtle change. This priest's role as the celebrant of the Eucharist was seen no longer as derived from the bishop, but rather from his priesthood. Another link had been broken. The deacons, meanwhile, usurped from the readers the role of lector, reading the Gospel in the church. Less and less was the deacon the bishop's administrative assistant; more and more he was an assistant to the priest in the church's liturgical services.

Most notable of all was the innovation of regular clerical salaries. The notion of fixed salaries for the clergy was considered an outrage in Rome and in Asia Minor as late as 200, writes the Oxford historian Robin Lane Fox in his *Pagans and Christians*. Fifty years later, however, we find Cyprian at Carthage concerned that his clergy be adequately paid. By then, the bishop of Rome had a salary of seventy-two hundred sesterces a year. Hardly munificent, notes Frend in *The Rise of Christianity*, since a mid-range governmental official or a professor of rhetoric in that day would have earned about one hundred thousand sesterces a year.

One loss to the laity was their role in electing the bishop. In the third century, it was the people who chose Cyprian over the voluble objection of the presbyters. In some instances, however, this lay voice continued to be heard. Ambrose of Milan in 373 and Nectarius of Constantinople in 384, both with strong popular support, were elevated from layman to bishop in less than a week. But again, the vast numbers made change necessary. A few score clergy could be easily assembled and their votes counted; a few thousand laity could not. So very soon, the choice of the bishop became a clerical prerogative.

As the clergy gained in responsibility and power, there developed a parallel movement to preclude them from marriage. The respect paid to celibacy went back a long way. The Princeton University historian Peter Brown notes in his *The Body and Society: Men, Women and Sexual Renunciation in Early Christianity* that near the Dead Sea in the first century, "the wilderness of Judea harbored sizeable settlements of disaffected males." The Jews of the Essene community near Jerusalem were admired for resisting "the seductive wiles of women" by embracing celibacy. The Jewish philosopher Philo and the historian

Josephus portray the Essenes as an all-male utopia, their denial of sexual inclination as embodying a "singleness of heart" toward God.

While several of the Christian apostles were almost certainly married, Paul declared celibacy a preferable condition in the strained circumstances of a world that many saw as soon to end. It was also true, of course, that the same Paul warns Timothy not to be deceived by teachings given by "men who are lying hypocrites," men "who forbid marriage and command abstinence from foods—good things which God created to be thankfully enjoyed" (1 Tim. 4:1–5). Tertullian, happily married himself, nevertheless recommended celibacy as a mark of holiness. On the other hand, some senior bishops, like Demetrian of Antioch (251–261) were married. In fact, Demetrian was succeeded in that office by his son. Bishop Phileas of Thmuis in Egypt was urged by a judge to consider his family responsibilities before committing himself to martyrdom around 307. A century later, Hilary, an adult convert and married, was nevertheless made bishop of Poitiers in France, and a century after that, the Christian author Sidonius Apollinaris, likewise married, became bishop of Clermont.

Only the bottom of this gilded wedding bowl remains, but the message is still clear. Surrounded by saints, the Christian couple for whom it was made is being crowned by Christ. They were to understand the sanctity of their marriage and its significance as a way of witnessing their faith, equal in honor to that of martyrs (see page 55).

Even so, pressure mounted at church councils from the early fourth century onward for a celibate clergy. The early fourth-century Spanish Council of Elvira (see map page 130, A3) imposed celibacy on all Spanish bishops, priests and deacons, and warned that if they continued to live with their wives and children, they would be deposed. In 314, the Council of Ancyra, held in the city that would one day become the capital of Turkey, ordered that deacons must choose between marriage and celibacy before they could be ordained. The Council of Neocaesarea, early in the fourth century, ruled that presbyters who marry after ordination must be deposed, while a council at Rome in 386 forbade married clergy to have intercourse with their wives, and a council in France in the fifth century required married clergy and their wives to swear they would refrain from sexual relations.

At the great Council of Nicea in 325, a resolution was advanced imposing celibacy on clergy throughout the church. It was defeated. However, says the *Catholic Encyclopedia*, a celibate clergy was the rule throughout the West from the time of Pope Leo the Great onward. Leo died in 461. In ensuing years, the

Coded artwork in the catacombs

At first, cautious Christians decorated tombs mainly with signs or symbols, but by the fourth century many catacombs included unmistakable scenes from Jesus' life

It's the second of the Ten Commandments: "You must not make a carved image for yourself, nor the likeness of anything in the heavens above, or on the earth below, or in the waters under the earth" (Exod. 20:4 REB). To some Christians in the first three centuries, that admonition seemed clear: Any kind of image was forbidden in the exercise of faith.

Most saw the commandment as prohibiting the worship of images, not their use for decoration or instruction. Given the tension between the two camps, if there was Christian art it was initially symbolic, purposefully not an easy object for worship.

Early in the catacombs, overtly Christian themes were rarely painted or carved on the sarcophagi of the faithful, and depictions of Jesus himself omitted such powerful, explicit events as the Crucifixion or Resurrection. Instead, some paintings used Old Testament themes to illustrate Christian tenets: Christ's triumph over death was echoed in Jonah's escape from the fish or in Daniel's survival in the lion's den. There were more subtle hints: Christians would recognize an ordinary man carrying a sheep as a reminder of Jesus the Good Shepherd.

By the fourth century, catacomb art had grown to include more representational forms. Illustrations clearly portrayed events from the Gospels and central themes such as the Incarnation. There were depictions of the angel Gabriel announcing to Mary that she would give birth to "Immanuel" and of the visit of the Magi to the Holy Child. Images of the Virgin and Child also began appearing on Christian tombs in the catacombs.

Walls and ceilings of the later catacombs in Rome abound with frescoes of Gospel events. Miracles such as the healing of the woman with the hemorrhage (left) were frequent subjects for encouraging the faithful by reminding them of the power of their Savior. Other frescoes, such as this of the exchange between Christ and the Samaritan woman at the well (above), carried theological messages—in this case, the "living waters" Jesus promises her would sustain the woman and, by extension, all believers (Catacomb of Marcellinus and Peter).

The resurrection of Jesus Christ was an obvious theme for artists decorating the Christian catacombs of Rome. However, the message was delivered indirectly, by depictions of scriptural events that implied or symbolized the resurrection that all could anticipate. Christians would have understood that the painting of Jonah being thrown to the sea creature (left) was an Old Testament prefiguration of the sacrifice and resurrection of Christ (Catacomb of Marcellinus and Peter). In the catacombs on the Via Latina, a fresco of Jesus raising Lazarus from the dead was painted over the loculi of one believer, the implication being that the deceased saw in it the hope of his own resurrection.

By the fourth century, artwork in the catacombs was dealing squarely with the other central tenet of Christian faith, the Incarnation. Numerous examples can be found of the scene described in Luke, when Gabriel announces to Mary that she will give birth to "Immanuel" (left, in the Catacomb of Priscilla). Elsewhere, the visit of the Magi is featured. And other works, though not as numerous, illustrate the now-familiar image of the Virgin and Child (below, fourth-century catacombs of the Cimitero Maggiore).

rule would create numerous problems. At various periods, many clergy persistently cohabited with women who were not their wives. In other instances, men abandoned their families to offer themselves to the priesthood, a phenomenon so common that a Roman law was passed in 420 expressly prohibiting this.

In the East, however, married clergy continue to be permitted to the present day, though candidates must declare an intention to either marry or remain celibate before they're ordained, and if they choose marriage, they must find a wife prior to their ordination. Eastern bishops are drawn only from the celibate clergy and are usually monks, though occasionally a widower will become a bishop.

While the development of clerical regulations enabled the Christians to cope much more effectively with the vast numbers now joining their ranks, it did not solve another problem, and even may have made it worse. That was the problem of belief. What exactly were Christians to believe as true? What rules should they

A natural and ancient instinct

Venerating the remains and artifacts of the martyrs became a Christian practice early on. Was it superstition? If it was, its biblical origins lie in both the Old and New Testaments

The veneration of relics—treating with reverence the bodily remains of a saint after his or her death—spread both east and west during persecutions in the third and early fourth centuries, with the numerous bodies of martyrs providing both the opportunity and the material. Indeed, during the Diocletian persecution, the bodies of martyrs were thrown into the ocean in order to prevent their veneration.

Veneration of relics is found in many religions, particularly Buddhism, says the *Oxford Dictionary of the Christian Church*, because "it is the natural instinct of men to treat with reverence what is left of the dead they love."

Thus, in the Old Testament, miracles are worked through the bones of Elisha (2 Kings 13:21). Material that made contact with the body of a holy person is similarly revered and miraculous powers are attributed to it. The mantle of Elijah worked miracles (2 Kings 2:14). In the New Testament, a woman is healed by touching the hem of Jesus' garment (Luke 8:43–44), healing is attributed to Peter's shadow (Acts 5:15), and handkerchiefs and an apron that had touched Paul were used as instruments of healing (Acts 19:11–12).

Martyrs' bodies were venerated from the earliest post-biblical times. The relics of Polycarp, bishop of Smyrna (see earlier volume, *A Pinch of Incense*, chapter 2), were carefully collected, and miracles were later attributed to them. In the catacombs, thanksgiving services were held over the tombs of saints.

Other practices included the building of martyria that sometimes rivaled church buildings, the burial of the pious near the saints, and the bringing of martyrs' bodies into urban churches despite Roman law and religious taboo that kept the dead outside the sacred city.

By the end of the fourth century, the practice of veneration had become so widespread that Vigilantus, a presbyter from Gaul, initiated a movement to stop it. He was opposed by St. Jerome, who held that "the relics are honored for the sake of him whose martyrs they are." While they lived, the bodies served the saints as organs of the Holy Spirit, concurred St. Augustine, and they should therefore remain dear to Christians. ∎

This gilt and silver reliquary containing the remains of the soldier-martyr Maurice is in the abbey and city in Switzerland bearing his name, St. Moritz.

observe concerning sex, marriage, military service, and heeding the religious requirements of a pagan government? And most important of all, who exactly did they believe Jesus to be? Was he God? Was he man? Was he both, and if so, how?

Questions like these would arise in different ways in different places, and the method that developed to deal with them was that of the regional synod or council. Like so much else in Christianity, the holding of a synod or council (the words in the early church meant the same thing)[6] called by a bishop or several bishops from the same province to resolve a doctrinal or moral question, was not invented at any particular point. It simply evolved.

The first recorded council held by the Christians was the meeting of the apostles at Jerusalem, described in Acts 15, to authorize Paul's mission to the Gentiles. A second-century synod was held in Asia Minor to deal with the Montanist question. Tertullian mentions a council that was called in Carthage to discuss whether the book called *The Shepherd of Hermas* should be included in the emerging New Testament. A series of councils was held at the end of the second century in the Eastern churches to discuss the conflict that had developed with the bishop of Rome over the date of Easter (see earlier volume, *A Pinch of Incense*, page 280). Cyprian used the device of North African councils to resolve the host of problems that confronted his church.

But there had never been a council intended to represent the "civilized world" (meaning in that day the Roman Empire, from Britain to the Sahara, from the Atlantic to the Euphrates). If any really serious issue divided the Christians everywhere, it would have to be decided by such a council. However, in the years when Christianity was illegal, suspect and subject to periodic persecution, such a council was a practical impossibility.

There was a further problem with the councils. They represented, in fact, a federal system of government, and presented therefore, the usual problem of representation. If the formula of equality were adopted—one bishop, one vote—then huge dioceses with thousands of Christians would carry no more weight than tiny dioceses with only several hundred. This was

Early reverence for the saints and embellishment of their lives in popular legends is evident in these two fourth-century carvings. Peter and Paul exchange a brotherly kiss (lower photo) in a bas-relief fragment (Paleochristian Museum, Rome). The sarcophagus in Arles, France (upper photo), depicts a legend that while a prisoner in Rome's Mamertine jail, Peter miraculously made water flow from a previously nonexistent spring.

6. The term "synod," derived from the Greek word *synodos*, was used to describe these church meetings in the East; the term "council," from the Latin *concilium*, to describe them in the West; and they were used interchangeably. Later, however, "council" would refer to broader meetings of the whole church, while "synod" came to be applied to local or provincial meetings.

to cause difficulties, though not as grave and enduring as one final problem.

If the power to decide doctrine and discipline was to lie with the councils, then what exactly was the authority of the bishop of Rome? From the earliest days, the other bishops had recognized Rome's bishop as preeminent, because he was the successor of Peter and Paul. The reference to Paul was soon omitted, and the case founded solely upon Peter. For had not Jesus himself said, "Thou art Peter (a Greek word meaning a stone or rock), and upon this Rock I will build my church" (Matt. 16:18)? Had he not conferred upon Peter the "keys of the kingdom of heaven"? Had he not endowed Peter with special authority— "whatever thou shalt bind on earth shall be bound in heaven, and whatever thou shalt loose on earth shall be loosed in heaven" (Matt. 16:19)?

Had not Clement, bishop of Rome,[7] as early as the late first century, written to the Christians in Corinth, admonishing them for their misconduct, much as Paul had, and did this not early on give evidence of the Roman bishop's exercise of Peter's authority? Did not the great Irenaeus of Lyons describe Rome as the church to which all Christians must "conform"? Even dissidents like the Adoptionists had sought ratification of their views by contending they had once been the view of the church at Rome. And did not the record of Rome's bishops testify to their faith? In the first three Christian centuries, in which Rome counted twenty-nine bishops in all, thirteen had assuredly been martyred, while deaths of six others could arguably be described as martyrdoms.

That the bishop of Rome was the successor of Peter, few fourth-century bishops would have questioned. But what precisely was Peter's authority? Had he ever attempted to order the other apostles around? Indeed, it was Paul who had admonished Peter's hesitation in approving the mission to the Gentiles. Some saw Rome's bishop as "first among equals." Some saw him as one of the great "patriarchs," Eastern bishops describing him as "the patriarch of the West."[8]

Had not Bishop Victor of Rome, in the late second century, attempted to impose a date for Easter on the churches in the East, and had they not successfully defied him (see earlier volume, *A Pinch of Incense*, page 280)? And though Cyprian had affirmed Rome's preeminence, he had also said that every bishop's see was "the see of Peter," and he had battled stubbornly against Rome's Stephen over the question of rebaptism.

However, the concept of a supreme pontiff[9] over all the other bishops was not specifically and determinedly advanced, observes the noted church historian Henry Chadwick in *The Pelican History of the Church*, until late in the fourth century. Even then, it was not universally accepted in the East, and never would be accepted there right through to the twentieth-first century. At that point, 455 million Protestant Christians did not accept the authority of the bishop of

7. The Roman list identifies Clement as the third bishop of Rome in line after Peter. However, many twentieth-century scholars describe him as a sort of "corresponding secretary" for the Roman presbyters. Clement does not, in his letter to Corinthians, identify himself as bishop.

8. "Because of its great antiquity," wrote the sainted Irenaeus of Lyon in describing the church at Rome, "it is with this church in which the tradition of the apostles has always been preserved by the faithful from everywhere, that every church, consisting of the faithful who bare from everywhere, must conform." The historian Robert M. Grant writes in his *Augustine to Constantine* that the meaning of at least nine key terms in Irenaeus's celebrated testimony to Rome "offers matter for debate."

MCNEELY

Rome, 130 million Eastern Orthodox Christians would still view Rome's bishop as merely "the patriarch of the West," while 890 million Roman Catholics view him and revere him as the "supreme pontiff" of Christianity.

As the fourth century unfolded, however, the issue of church authority did not lie between the councils and the bishop of Rome. A new and massive factor would soon be introduced, notably, the influence of the emperor. As long as the

Early Christians took seriously the call of their Lord to practice love toward neighbor in the form of acts of charity. Daily distributions of food, provided from donations of the faithful, allowed churches to assuage the crushing poverty of many in an empire in decline. Such acts were viewed by authorities and nonbelievers with a sullen mixture of respect and resentment.

9. The title *Pontifex Maximus* ("Supreme Pontiff") was originally a pagan title, designating the chief priest at Rome. F. L. Cross in his authoritative *Oxford Dictionary of the Christian Church* notes that from the fifth century on it became a title of honor for the bishops of Rome and was occasionally used by other bishops as well. In later times it was confined to the Roman pontiff. The title "the Pope" is taken from the Latin *papa* ("father"), says the *Dictionary*. Now restricted to the Bishop of Rome, it was in early times used of any bishop in the West, and in the East confined to the Bishop of Alexandria who still uses the title in the Coptic Church. At the Synod of Pavia in 998, the Archbishop of Milan was rebuked for calling himself Pope, and at a council held at Rome, Pope Gregory VII in 1073 formally prohibited its use by any other bishop but Rome's.

emperor was pagan, his dealings with the Christians were entirely centered on the question of whether he would tolerate them. But what would happen if the emperor himself became Christian? In the days of Decius and Valerian, such a prospect would have seemed too absurd to contemplate. However, that was soon to change.

Something else would change. In the late third century, what chiefly brought people into Christianity was neither its hierarchy nor its institutional structure, which some in the imperial bureaucracy envied. Rather, it was the recurrent instances of miracle, particularly miracles of healing, reported among its members. Almost as compelling were the unstinting works of charity in which the Christians engaged. By the third century, Christian charity extended well beyond the Christian community to those around it. Impoverished widows, wounded soldiers, the jobless and the chronically ill came to find help from the Christians that was available nowhere else. Philanthropy must be practiced generously and selflessly, wrote Dionysius the Great, and dispensing material goods was not enough. Personal service to the needy was also required. Even the distant and dreaded barbarians, frequently left starving on the fringes of the empire, became recipients of Christian food, clothing and money. Ancient society had never seen anything quite like this.

Should the emperor become Christian, however, there would emerge another reason for conversion. It could become a path to prestige and power. And that in turn would present the Christians with a very different set of problems. ∎

Countdown to the twenty-seven

As the New Testament evolved, James, Hebrews and Revelation were challenged, but what ultimately selected all the books was the usage of Christian worshipers

In the year 303, the question of which Christian writings would go into the New Testament took on a sudden urgency. Indeed, for many of the faithful it became a matter of life and death. An imperial decree ordered them to surrender their sacred texts to authorities so they could be burned.

Those Christians willing to comply with such a demand, and risk the contempt of the Christian community, could simply give up every suspect work in their possession. (The English word "traitors" comes to us from a Latin word, *traditores*, which meant "handers-over.") But what of those who wished to evade the edict but could not credibly deny that they owned banned books? For example, what if they were readers in their church? Could they satisfy the book-burners and still maintain their Christian reverence by turning over, say, a work of secondary importance, such as *The Shepherd of Hermas*, or the *Letter of Barnabas*, without being labeled as apostate? Rarely has there been such a practical need to distinguish the sacred from the merely religious.

The book-burning of 303 was only one of many events in the early history of Christianity that nudged believers toward adoption of a canon of Scripture—a catalog or list of writings acceptable for use in worship. A previous volume in this series, *A Pinch of Incense*, describes the bewildering array of works that vied for Christians' attention by the late second century— more than fifty gospels alone, including five documents attributed to the apostle Thomas. Yet by the end of the fourth century, the effort to prune this profusion of writings down to the twenty-seven that came to comprise the New Testament would essentially be complete.

Yet the idea of a New Testament as we conceive of it today simply did not exist in the early decades after Jesus' Crucifixion. Not every book that eventually appeared in the New Testament had necessarily even been written by the end of the first century, or so some historians maintain. And once the notion of a single corpus of texts did begin to take hold, Christians naturally examined the writings in their possession to cull all but those that represented the genuine apostolic tradition and the authentic teachings of Christ. That process, a messy one, would take time.

Paul's letters were almost certainly collected and considered as a group some time within the first century. By the end of the second century, they were being copied and circulated as a single set. Christians were also quick to recognize the synoptic Gospels of Matthew, Mark and Luke as a related body of uniquely sacred writing. The Fourth Gospel, John's, the last to be written, was the only one to spark resistance in some quarters—in part because of its popularity among the gnostics. Yet skepticism toward John never really took hold, either. By the mid-second century, for example, when Tatian decided to harmonize the Gospels into a single hybrid known as the *Diatessaron*, he chose the work of all four evangelists. Not long afterward, Irenaeus insisted that the same four Gospels, and only those four, should be included in a sacred canon.

Irenaeus, whose life was described in an earlier volume of this series (see earlier volume, *A Pinch of Incense*, chapter 5), was a practical fellow, whose interest in a canon was spurred in part by the religious heresies he sought to combat. These had their own sometimes-exotic ideas about which works to emphasize. The gnostics may have admired John, for example, but they also favored books such as the *Gospel of Thomas* and the *Gospel of Peter*. The mid-second-century heretic Marcion, on the other hand, was a pruner: He embraced ten Epistles of Paul and only one Gospel—Luke's— which he then proceeded to edit ("mutilate" is how one historian describes it). The sect founded by Montanus, meanwhile, drifted the other way, adopting a more open-ended attitude toward sacred writings while accepting new and controversial prophecies. The historian Hans von Campenhausen argued that the challenge

The Codex Vaticanus is one of the oldest editions of the complete Bible as it was known in the early fourth century.

of Montanism, above all else, "brought about the concentration of the canon in a 'New Testament.'"

Heresy, persecution, and the growing confidence of the Christian community in its own mature insight into the faith all goaded Christians into defining a canon. Yet not every decision turned out to be as straightforward as those involving the Gospels and Paul's Epistles. Most of the remaining books were not as well known or as broadly used, or they had at least some influential objections that had to be overcome. Those books were:

The Pastoral Epistles (1 Timothy, 2 Timothy, Philemon, and

The devil chained in the abyss is vividly illustrated in this tenth-century Spanish commentary on the Book of the Revelation, now in the possession of the Pierpont Morgan Library, New York.

Titus): These were among the thirteen letters of Paul that were embraced almost universally once they achieved wide distribution, but the pastorals nevertheless did generate mild controversy on two fronts. Since they targeted heresy, heretics themselves bitterly denounced them. More significantly, Second Timothy was attacked even by some orthodox Christians for its reference to nonscriptural books; Origen demolished this concern by pointing out that First Corinthians did the same thing, yet no one had sought to banish it from the core of sacred texts. The pastorals easily survived the storm.

The Acts of the Apostles: Written by Luke along with his Gospel, Acts was never really disputed, but it still didn't come into its own as acknowledged Scripture until late in the second century. It may be that finally recognizing Acts was a powerful way for mainstream Christians to reinforce the importance of the apostolic tradition against the contrary claims of heretics.

The Epistle to the Hebrews: Doubts about authorship have dogged the Epistle to the Hebrews almost from the beginning, while delaying its entry into the Western canon until the fourth century. To some readers, Hebrews seemed to radiate a more elegant, literary style than the rest of Paul's letters. Even more suspicious from the orthodox point of view, the heretical Montanists seemed partial to chapter 6. However, the Greek East had no hesitation regarding Hebrews, attributing it all along to Paul, and as time passed, the Eastern view prevailed over that of the dubious West. By the time of Eusebius, the great church historian of the early fourth century, Hebrews was firmly back in the fold, listed as one of the New Testament books universally considered sacred. Yet its life of controversy was hardly over: More than a thousand years later, Luther and Calvin would resurrect questions about its authorship, though not its canonicity—Luther postulating that it was written by Paul's trusty colleague Apollos. Such questions persist to this day.

The Catholic Epistles (James, 1 Peter, 2 Peter; 1 John, 2 John, 3 John and Jude): Dubbed catholic, meaning "general," because they are not addressed to any specific community, these seven epistles include several that were not accepted without reservation until well into the fourth century. First Peter and First John were the exceptions; they were widely embraced, even in the second century. Jude's movement into the canon appears to have been relatively uneventful too: It was written very early, it achieved wide distribution by the second century, and it was recognized as Scripture by the so-called Muratorian Canon, an early Christian Scripture list published around 200. Yet Jude's acceptance must have been fragile: The book also found its way onto a list of disputed texts that the historian Eusebius of Caesarea compiled more than one hundred years later, as did James, 2 Peter, and 2 and 3 John.

The Epistle of James: C. F. Evans, in *The Cambridge History of the Bible*, calls James "perhaps the biggest riddle of the New Testament." Scholars dispute who wrote it, when it was written, for whom, and for what purpose. It is first mentioned by Irenaeus, and while Origen seemed to consider it Scripture, he admits that his view was not the dominant one in the third century. The fourth century was the turning point, the key date being 367, when Athanasius confirmed the apostolic status of the letter. Jerome accepted this opinion when he began his seminal translation of the Bible a few years later, while St. Augustine's writings also reveal the greatest respect for the Epistle of James. Thus the die was cast.

> *The Epistle of James has been called "perhaps the biggest riddle of the New Testament."*

Second Peter: Not only was 2 Peter one of the last books to gain entry into the New Testament canon, it was also, in the opinion of a number of modern scholars, quite possibly the last New Testament text to be written—although at the absolute latest by 125. Origen is the first writer we know to mention it, and it apparently remained obscure and neglected well into the third century.

Revelation: This was the final book to enter the New Testament canon, but it was delayed because of resistance by leaders of the Eastern churches. In the West, the Book of Revelation was prized steadily from the second century on—as were, to a lesser degree, two other apocalyptic books: *The Shepherd of Hermas* and the *Apocalypse of Peter*. To many Eastern ears, however, apocalyptic writings had too much in common with extravagant claims by the Montanist sect of a "new prophecy"—and it didn't help matters that the Montanists themselves admired the Book of Revelation to no end. It is still not read in the worship services of the Eastern church.

In addition, there was the nagging question of who wrote it. Eusebius tells us that Bishop Dionysius of Alexandria, midway through the third century, produced a sophisticated analysis of Revelation's style, and concluded that the author could not possibly have been John the Evangelist. Nor was Eusebius himself an enthusiast of Revelation. He lists it among the New Testament books, but grudgingly adds, "should it seem right." It did seem right in the West, where Revelation would appear in Jerome's Vulgate translation of the Bible.

Christians, of course, believe that the New Testament books are the Word of God, and so they naturally balk at the possibility of an arbitrary or haphazard selection of their sacred canon. But Christians of the early church did not believe they were making arbitrary selections, either. They saw the guidance of the Holy Spirit behind the formal and informal processes that eventually settled on a closed body of New Testament Scripture, just as the Holy Spirit had inspired those who wrote the Word in the first place.

What is remarkable, in any case, is how little high-level debate was even necessary, given the scope of the possible wrangling and the circumstances of the time. After all, Jesus himself did not author any text. His early followers relied on oral accounts of his mission and its meaning. Meanwhile, the books that came to comprise the New Testament were written independently, usually for a specific purpose, and often for a specific audience. They were not easy nor inexpensive to copy, let alone to combine into a unitary text the size of the New Testament, so that even the concept of a canon did not readily spring to mind. For that matter, the Jews at the time of Christ had not yet set limits on their Scripture, either.

The wonder is not that Christians took many years to define a canon, but that they managed to do so largely by reaching a grassroots consensus based upon common usage. Various church councils—in Rome in 382, in Hippo in 393 and in Carthage in 397, for example—approved the New Testament canon as we accept it today, but they were mainly ratifying with formal action what the body of the faithful already had established in practice.

It was the Christian community as a whole, by and large, that decided what was true to the tradition of their faith, and faithful to the message of their Savior. And the durability of their decision, nearly two millennia later, is testimony itself to their inspired wisdom. ■

The Christians

Their First Two Thousand Years

A unique new series of books about the real people and events of 2000 years of Christian faith

From the Media:

stellar cast of writers

...you'll find this book a good read. In the hands of a stellar cast of professional writers, academic consultants and designers, this book lands in the best traditions of journalism.
— *Edmonton Journal*

succeeds admirably

Keeping it lively, conversational and relevant ... The Veil Is Torn succeeds admirably.
— *Monterey County Herald*

From our Readers:

beautiful book

This is a beautiful book — indicative of a well-researched and excellently presented history of Christianity!

abundance of information

This volume is excellent and contains an abundance of information on both the Holy Bible and Christian History.

The Christians

Their First Two Thousand Years

The opening volume of *The Christians: Their First Two Thousand Years* has been receiving superior reviews. *The Veil Is Torn* draws the reader in with a dramatic retelling of the Pentecost experience. It goes on to describe the conversion of Paul—the most vehement anti-Christian—into its greatest proponent. The events described in the Acts of Matthew, Mark, and Luke are vividly brought to life. The volume ends with the horrific siege and destruction of Jerusalem by the Romans in A.D. 70.

But the story continues. Volume two, *A Pinch of Incense*, maintains the intensity and drama as the faith grows in spite of profound and relentless persecution in the years up until A.D. 250. *A Pinch of Incense* will move readers to learn of the incredible strength of conviction our fore-bearers had as they boldly faced hideous deaths in torture chambers and arenas. Inspiring stories of conversion and love are supported by the words of Jesus as recorded by the Apostles.

More from the media:

nothing compares

For sheer scale, ambition and audacity, nothing in recent memory compares with the illustrated series, *The Christians*.
— *Montreal Gazette*

informative, entertaining

The Veil Is Torn is well written, informative, entertaining, and educational, a must for all who want to further their understanding of the Christian faith.
— *Living Light News*

More from our readers:

masterful treatment

The Veil Is Torn is a masterful treatment of the first generation of the Christian Church, filled with information that indicates careful, conservative scholarship.

wonderful book

Thanks for introducing me to this wonderful book!

can't wait for Volume 2!

Very nice book. Read it all and can't wait for Volume 2!

CHAPTER 4

Diocletian: the worst persecutor of them all

His deft reforms gave the empire one more century, but his sudden late-in-life turn against Christianity launched a decade of horror for the faithful

I t was a trial by the army; and even for the year 284, it was brief. The charge was murder of an emperor; and the verdict, announced in a raucous roar by the thousands of assembled troops, was guilty. All eyes now turned toward the judge, a tall, somber, intense man of forty, in the dress uniform of a top-ranking Roman officer. He rose, drew his sword, and raised it high. Swearing an oath to the god of the sun, he advanced upon the prisoner. With one thrust, he plunged the weapon deep into the man's chest. Blood spewing with the last few spasms of his failing heart, the prisoner collapsed in a heap at the judge's feet.

The cheer of the legions was deafening. "*DIOCLES!*" they thundered. "*AUGUSTUS! AUGUSTUS!*" And Diocles, or Diocletian as he restyled himself, dated his ascendancy to the imperial throne from that moment. He would be known to the Romans as the man who halted the disintegration of the imperial order, a disintegration that had been in process for fifty years. He would be known to history as the man who extended the life of that empire for another century. But he would be known to the Christians as the instigator and fastidious administrator of the worst persecution they would endure until the twentieth century.

Diocletian's first rival now lay dead at his feet. The accused, Aper, had been prefect of the Praetorian Guard, charged with murdering the emperor Numerian—hardly remarkable, as it happened, since twenty-two of the last twenty-eight emperors had been killed by their own troops. But Aper had badly miscalculated. The troops preferred Diocletian. And anyway, had not the fate of the Praetorian prefect been foretold? *Aper* was the Latin word for "wild boar"; and had not a Druid priestess in Gaul prophesied years before that Diocletian would become emperor after spearing a wild boar? Why contest such inevitability?

Diocletian would give the empire a new constitution, revamp its civil service, reorganize its army, begin stabilizing its frontiers, and briefly rejuvenate its economy. Then, even more astonishing, having given the empire twenty years of stable government, he would leave office neither murdered nor killed in battle,

A new generation of Christians had grown up unconcerned about their safety; then the blood-soaked crackdown struck the church like a tornado on a sunny day.

nor even dead from natural causes. He would instead offer the unprecedented spectacle of a peaceful retirement, a retreat to his estate at Spalatum (modern Split in Croatia, see map page 131, D3), in his home province of Illyricum on the east coast of the Adriatic to content himself with raising prize cabbages.

But to the Christians, his name is blood-soaked. The Diocletian Persecution would strike the church like a tornado on a sunny day. Christians had enjoyed over forty years of official, if not social acceptance, ever since Gallienus's Decree of Toleration in 261.

Saxons and Franks might sack the towns of Britain and Gaul, and Persians might annihilate Valerian's army and plunder Antioch. But for at least a generation, Christians had been busy spreading the gospel, organizing charities, erecting beautiful churches, gradually penetrating society, and sometimes rising high in the army and civil service. In this process, they had largely acclimatized themselves to the pagan jungle in which they lived. A new generation of Christians grew up unmolested, arriving in the Diocletian era unconcerned about their safety. For the first eighteen or nineteen years of his twenty-one-year reign, he by and large left them alone, reflecting little or no hostility. Indeed, they saw him, as did most of his subjects, as Providence's gift to their security and comfort. And with good reason. The boar-killer who became emperor was born, like most of the Christians, a man of humble beginnings, the son of a freedman, a former slave, on December 22, 244 (give or take a year), at Spalatum. He received little or no formal education, and like many of his fellow Illyrians, he early sought a career in the army. A bust found at his capital of Nicomedia (see map page 131, E3) shows a vigorous, wide-faced man, large-skulled, eyes set wide apart and watchful.

Illyricum was the Appalachia of the empire: rough and uncultured, but also the last repository of old-fashioned values—discipline, ambition, patriotism

More than just natural aging registers in these two likenesses of the emperor Diocletian. The cares of nearly two decades at the helm of the Roman empire changed the vigorous, laurel-wreathed, idealistic, robust man (lower left) into a sad, perhaps disillusioned, version of himself (right).

and traditional piety. During the third century, the Roman army had begun relying on the new mobile tactics of its cavalry. With this came the growth of a new corps of professional officers, the *protectores*, gradually taking over from the military amateurs of Rome's senatorial class who had long provided the officer cadre. This caste was soon dominated by Illyrians, and that gave the rustics access to power. In 268, Emperor Gallienus was murdered by his cavalry officers, and a succession of short-lived, mostly Illyrian soldier emperors took over: Claudius, Aurelian, Probus and Carus. Each in his turn beat back new barbarian incursions, only to fall victim to his own officers.

Nothing is known of Diocletian's career before 284, aside from his early posting as *Dux Moesiae*, commander of the major garrison on the lower Danube. But his subsequent career reveals his character: Though bold, restless and ruthless, he was no lover of war and violence. At work he was tireless, self-controlled though observably edgy. He was truly pious in a traditional, unquestioning way. Most important, he was ceaselessly wary, observant, ready to question supposed expertise, inexhaustible in deliberation, and a chronic planner. He mastered both the broad concept and all the details, especially the scope and workings of the diaphanous web of spies, informers and allies he wove throughout the empire. As a reliable officer, he quickly won the favor of the emperor Carus, who seized the imperium from Probus in 282. That led to command of the *Protectores Domestici*, the elite Household Cavalry, and in 283 to a consulship.

In 284, after briefly pacifying the Danube, Augustus Carus gambled on waging war against ever-threatening Persia. So he left his vicious elder son Carinus as caesar in the West, and at great risk to the other frontiers, marched an enormous army southeast, through Mesopotamia. With him was his bookish younger son, the caesar Numerian. Somewhere between the Tigris and Euphrates, Carus trounced the Persians. The great cities of Seleucia and Ctesiphon fell into his hands, and with them most of Persia west of the Iranian plateau.

Then Carus died, struck in his tent, it was said, by a lightning bolt. It was an age of suspicion, often well-founded. So, genuine accident or not, the effect of his death on the army was to arouse it. His son, the gentle Numerian, was

Diocletian's choice for caesar was Galerius, a huge, brutal and ignorant man whose sole loyalty was to his priestess mother, a fanatical pagan with a rabid hatred of Christians.

dutifully proclaimed the next augustus. The young man's life expectancy was brief, as he no doubt knew; and as the legionaries began a sad retreat home, they bore the reportedly ailing new emperor in a litter, under the questionable care of the Praetorian Prefect Aper. When the contingent reached Nicomedia, some soldiers rushed Numerian's litter, found him dead within, and arrested Aper. The army council, carefully cultivated by Diocletian, nominated Diocletian the next emperor, and that was the end of the wild boar.

At that point, Diocletian was effectively emperor only of the army in Asia Minor and nearby provinces. Predictably, the Western caesar, Carinus, declared himself augustus, and denounced Diocletian as an upstart usurper. In May, 285, the Western and Eastern legions met at Margus, south of Belgrade, to settle the issue. At the battle's crisis, Diocletian's ranks were broken, and all seemed lost. But Carinus's troops dropped their arms and declared support for his enemy when they learned their general was dead, stabbed through the throat by a staff officer whose wife he had seduced. Thus Diocletian became undisputed ruler of the Roman world.

Along with his other notable qualities, Diocletian was superstitious. The victory at Margus had been narrow indeed. The gods had given him their favor, but that could be easily lost. Unless he moved quickly to master the fickle army and break the whole bloody cycle of military sedition, he himself would soon fall its victim.

The problem was plain enough. Though it was a powerless anachronism, the Senate clung to the fiction that it alone could choose the *princeps* (First Citizen), the augustus. But the augustus would be most importantly commander in chief of the army, and the army had first say. As Carus's sons had discovered, the army was no respecter of the dynastic principle. Further, the Rhine, Danube and Persian fronts each required the presence of an emperor and an imperial army. If a general were appointed to Gaul with the resources to pacify the Rhine, his success would inevitably encourage him to revolt.

Yet if the right general were given political eminence in advance of his victories, he might maintain his loyalty to the emperor. Everything would depend on the man to whom the authority was given.

Immediately, Diocletian adopted as his heir his fellow Illyrian and longtime comrade Maximian, seven years his junior. He made him caesar and commander in the West. This was a shrewd, well-reasoned choice. Maximian was the son of a Balkan tradesman, a general with an energetic, boorish, tough and domineering character; but he was full of fierce loyalty, not given to subtle intrigue. As the historian Gibbon noted, even his vices were useful: "Insensible to pity and fearless of consequences, he was the ready instrument of every act of cruelty which the prince might at once suggest and disclaim." Maximian needed delicate handling, but he recognized Diocletian's political wisdom, and his own lack of it. He was content to defer on matters of policy, and in return, Diocletian lavished on him all appropriate honors.

Maximian's first test came quickly. The peasantry of northern Gaul revolted, driven to despair by yearly barbarian raids. These Bagaudae had sacked sixty towns. Then came the consequences—grievous depopulation and ad hoc "taxation" by passing legions. There was no glory in putting down such a ragged rabble, but through early 286, Maximian's cavalry harried rebellious peasants along dark forest tracks and soggy valleys. The next summer, a real campaign began, this one against the source of the trouble, the Franks on the other side of the lower Rhine. For his success in subduing the Franks, Maximian became a full augustus, or co-emperor. Diocletian took the divine name of Jupiter, father of the gods, and labeled Maximian as Hercules, the god who labored on Jupiter's behalf.

In general, Diocletian had chosen well in Maximian. Unfortunately, Maximian made a poor choice in one of his own subordinates. To counter Saxon pirates pillaging the English Channel ports, he appointed a competent Gaul, Carausius, as commander of the channel fleet. Backed by the fleet and three legions, Carausius declared for British independence,

In a carving at the base of a porphyry column, the two co-emperors Diocletian and Maximian embrace in a display of affection that was closer to reality than usual among Rome's augusti.

and announced himself as augustus of Britain. Lacking the means to challenge him and facing problems everywhere else, Diocletian for the moment acquiesced.

Franks, Burgundians and Alamanni pushed against the Rhine. The Kabyles raided western North Africa and Spain. The Persians once again took Armenia. Rebellion shook Alexandria and Carthage, threatening the empire's all-important granaries. The restoration of the empire could be delayed no longer. In 293, Diocletian instituted a four-man rule. Each of the two augusti announced a caesar and successor. Maximian at Milan would control Italy, Africa and the Rhine-Danube headwaters. Under him, Constantius at Trier would have Gaul, Britain and the Rhine. In the East, Diocletian himself, based at Nicomedia (see map page 131, E3), would hold Asia and Egypt. His heir, Galerius, would control Illyricum and the Danube.

With this new tetrarchy, the empire's constitutional problem seemed solved. As long as the two augusti "brothers" stayed friendly, they could always rein in a rogue caesar. And when the augusti retired, their successor "sons" would need only concord and prudence to pick competent and loyal new caesars— presumably the children of the newly retired augusti.

The choice of one of these caesars would prove pivotal. Constantius, surnamed Chlorus, was another

The imperial statue of the tetrarchy of Galerius, Diocletian, Maximian, and Constantius is now displayed at St. Mark's Basilica in Venice. In what might have been prophetic intuition by the sculptor, their show of fraternity is juxtaposed with the fact that each has a hand firmly on his sword.

Illyrian, brave and mild-tempered but with a sickly constitution. He strongly heeded the advice of his wife Helena, a former tavern keeper (not an entirely honorable trade), who in the early 270s had borne Constantius a son—by name, Constantine. Helena was friendly to Christianity, and though Constantius would divorce her to make a dynastic marriage, she would retain profound influence over their son, upon whom great events would soon turn.

The other caesar, Galerius, stood in shocking contrast. He had been a plowman in Illyricum, a huge man, brutal and ignorant, who habitually belittled and bullied those around him. If Diocletian thought he had in Galerius another Maximian, he possibly mistook boorishness for simplicity. Galerius's only enduring loyalty was to his mother, Romula, a German born priestess of the mountain gods with a fanatical hatred of Christianity.

In the case of Diocletian and Galerius, the boundaries between the augustus's and the caesars's territories were hardly observed, with the less warlike elder employing his violent subordinate as his field commander. This enabled Galerius, over the next decade, to cultivate a decisive influence over Diocletian, with disastrous consequences to the Christians.

For the next five years, each of the four emperors had a fight going on every frontier, the two augusti supporting their caesars by sending in reserve troops whenever necessary. Constantius defeated incursion after incursion by the ravenous Alamanni, subdued the rebellious Frisians between the Scheldt and Rhine, and settled his prisoners of war in the depopulated tracts of Gaul. When the upstart Carausius was assassinated in Britain, Constantius invaded and brought Britain back into the imperial fold. Maximian crossed the Mediterranean, pacified northwest Africa and restored the imperial presence at Carthage.

For eight months, Diocletian besieged rebellious Alexandria; and when it fell, he punished the city until, as he had vowed, "the blood reached his horse's knees." The brutish Galerius bungled. He tackled the Persians in Mesopotamia and lost most of a legion, jeopardizing Diocletian's confidence in him. But he went back the following year and butchered the great Eastern enemy in a night attack on the Euphrates, restoring Armenia as a Roman buffer state and himself to the augustan approval.

By 300, the tetrarchy had shown what the empire could still do. Its sovereignty was secure and united. The Rhine-Danube tribes, though not quite crushed, had been whipped into submission, and the Persians were reduced to a sulky peace. Popular civic rebellion had been shown to be hopeless and military rebellion suicidal, all in sharp contrast to the preceding fifty years.

Any sustained recovery of the empire would have been impossible, however, without real constitutional reform, reaching down to the hundreds of great and small cities and their all-important agricultural districts. In the previous century, the empire's municipalities had become impotent, and its huge provinces ungovernable. Wealthy provincial aristocrats fled the impoverishing demands of civic government; governors were wholly absorbed in defense. Taxation was accomplished by military pillaging; and in some areas, Roman law and peace was but a memory. Diocletian, quietly ignoring the venerable Senate, methodically replaced the old Roman governance of aristocratic amateurs with the rule of professional bureaucrats.[1]

After fifteen years, Romans awakened to the fact that the imperial government had been transformed. There were now a civil administration (called the *militia*) and a military administration (the *militia arma*). The forty-three old provinces had been subdivided into 120 smaller ones, ruled by presidents and grouped into twelve "dioceses," overseen by vicars general.

All this allowed Rome's cultured nobility to pursue professional careers without pretending to be warriors while energetic, uneducated Illyrians and barbarians could rise in the army without wrecking the civil administration and without gaining unfettered access to state revenues.

In carrying out his reforms, Diocletian had to confront the Roman establishment: the aristocracy and the senate. The first-century Togato Barberini (above) shows one of these Roman nobles carrying busts of his ancestors. The senators gathered in this frieze, from a sarcophagus of the late third century (below), would have been drawn from the same patrician families, but by that time their influence was minimal.

The judicial and tax codes were standardized, and the provincial courts and finances were held strictly accountable (in theory, at least) to their dioceses.

The northern tribes were subdued because they had been stymied. Diocletian abandoned the old forward defense—in which the legions met the barbarian marauders on the frontier and avenged their raids with punitive counter-raids—and instead developed a defense in depth. Frontier legionary camps were replaced with great stone fortresses—the prototypes of medieval castles—to channel any tribal incursions into predetermined routes, hemmed in by a hundred-mile-deep band of fortified towns. Raiders would be harried by cavalry reserves—including the new, heavily armored lancers, ancestors of the medieval knights, until they either surrendered or were broken up into small bands of starving fugitives.

Economic problems proved much tougher to solve. For a century, the imperial coinage had been continually debased, causing runaway inflation. So the emperor closed the local mints and introduced new coins: the gold *aureus* and the copper *folle*. To resolve labor dislocation, Diocletian instituted what amounted to compulsory nepotism, decreeing that select occupations must henceforth be hereditary, that civil servants, soldiers, sailors, bakers, other tradesmen and especially farmers, must bequeath their jobs to their sons, all carefully identified and enumerated in the Great Census of 290. This legally tied tenant farmers and their sons to their land, prefiguring medieval feudalism.

Now in Rome's Museum of Roman Civilization, this tablet appears to be part of a reckoning done for Diocletian's universal census in 290. It mentions citizens of Tarsus and Laodicea along with those of other cities in the eastern Mediterranean region.

For better or worse, these changes endured. One policy that failed for Diocletian (and would fail again under other leaders) was price control. His soldiers had lobbied him unceasingly for relief from continued inflation, so in a stern edict of 301, he set maximum prices on a wide range of commodities, under the threat of death. The result was predictable. In places where market prices were lower than the maximum, they jumped; where they were already higher, commodities vanished from the shelves and reappeared on the black market. Within a few years, the edict was allowed to lapse.

The hostile Christian historian Lactantius would later describe, acidly, the effect of Diocletian's reforms. There were "more tax collectors than taxpayers," he lamented, while "endless exactions from the provinces" financed the tetrarchy's building spree in the new capitals of Trier, Milan, (see map page 131, C3), Sirmium (see map page 131, D3), and especially Nicomedia, where Diocletian "continually tried to match the city of Rome in magnificence."

---

1. By the fall of the Latin West in the fifth century, the Greek-speaking Eastern empire had long retrenched with its capital at Constantinople or Byzantium—a retrenchment that would endure until Constantinople fell to Islam in 1453.

Farmers found conditions increasingly oppressive. Peace had been purchased at the price of prosperity. Diocletian brought stability; but in the following century, the civil service grew to thirty thousand officials, while the army doubled to 635,000. Moreover, ordinary citizens realized something was missing. What was the *purpose* of it all? What was the empire *for*? Those were spiritual questions, and the empire was spiritually bankrupt. To fill this void, the ever-practical Diocletian had himself declared *Dominus*, meaning "Lord." He draped himself in purple, shod himself with jeweled slippers, wore a sacred diadem, and allowed his subjects to approach him only through an interminable hierarchy, and then to prostrate themselves when finally in his presence.

All this failed to accomplish its purpose. The void was still there, and Diocletian, who privately scoffed at all the hollow pomp, knew it. Even so, he took the old gods seriously. During the sack of Alexandria, when his horse slipped on the bloody cobbles and smeared its knees, he ordered an immediate halt to the carnage, as he had sworn to do (the wry Alexandrians later erected a bronze statue to his horse). In Egypt, he ordered books on alchemy and magic burned. He outlawed Manichaeism in 297 as a "Persian" superstition, burning both its books and its leaders. He became a champion of marital fidelity, issued a noble edict on marriage, thundering to his subjects that chaste and pious homes would bring the gods' favor on Rome, while domestic vice, particularly incest, would attract divine vengeance.

The element in the populace best fulfilling this high rectitude was, obviously to many, the Christians. For most of his reign, Diocletian sustained the Roman tolerance of Christianity that had been decreed by Gallienus when he ended the Decian and Valerian persecutions. Indeed, a Christian influence pervaded Diocletian's immediate family. His wife Prisca and daughter Valeria were known to favor the new faith. Peter, a trusted chamberlain in the imperial household, was a Christian, as were senior court financial and administrative officers like Adauctus and Gorgonius; like Lactantius, the future historian and Latin tutor in his court; like Dorotheus—a presbyter and a eunuch—the emperor appointed superintendent of the imperial dye works; and Philoromus, a senior functionary in Alexandria.

The Christians, with some complications involving a "Trinity" that Diocletian did not pretend to understand, worshiped One God. Traditional Roman religion was moving that way, singling out Sol (the sun) as god and reinterpreting Jupiter and other traditional political gods as divine emanations of the One Sol. The centrist Diocletian could see the sense in that; and under that schema, Christians could be regarded as worshiping the One God too, with their Jesus just another emanation like Jupiter.

Then, too, some nineteen years earlier, after his hairbreadth victory at Margus, Diocletian had sensed a divine mission. He must put things right, the gods had told him. Relatively speaking, things were right—on the frontiers and in the provinces anyway. But at home, in the soul of the empire, there was a void.[2] Things were plainly not right with the gods. Somehow, for a reason that has never been clear, Diocletian became convinced that the way to placate the gods was to exterminate the Christians. The result was the Great Persecution, the Age of Martyrs that many would see as the worst Christian ordeal since Good Friday.

It would last for ten years, 303 to 313, and historians ever since have tried to account for it. They discern three general causes. The first they describe as cultural. Diocletian's was an era of orderliness. The old slogans on the imperial coinage—*concordia* and *libertas*—were replaced by a new one: *disciplina*. Into this new era of centrally directed imperial discipline, the Christians never quite fit. Though they made fine soldiers, for instance, they resisted military oaths that carried pagan implications. Obviously, those in

2. The twentieth-century Christian journalist and essayist G. K. Chesterton observed the same tendencies in "tired" civilizations as well as in individuals. He wrote in *The Everlasting Man*: "There comes an hour in the afternoon when the child is tired of pretending, weary of playing a robber. . . It is then that he torments the cat. There comes a time in the routine of an ordered civilization, when the man is tired of playing at mythology and pretending that the tree is a maiden or the moon made love to a man. The effect of this staleness is the same everywhere; it is seen in all drug-taking and dram-drinking, every form of the tendency to increase the dose. Men seek stranger sins or more startling obscenities as stimulants to their jaded senses. They seek after mad oriental religions. . . . They try to stab their nerves to life. . . . They are walking in their sleep and try to wake themselves up with nightmares."

The famed Colosseum at Rome is a popular site for pilgrims, such as this 1955 Austrian group, to gather in memory of the martyrs. The historical record, however, argued even by high-ranking members of the Roman church, seems to indicate that very few Christians met their end in this giant stadium.

charge declared, discipline must be more sternly applied.

The second cause was personal—the violent Galerius, whose pagan priestess mother had bequeathed to him her venomous loathing of the Christians. The third lay within the church itself. Years of comfort had softened it. "As always happens when there is an abundance of liberty, our lives became indolent and careless," wrote the Christian historian Eusebius, who survived imprisonment in the Great Persecution. "We envied one another and did harm to our brethren. . . . Pretense and damned hypocrisy seemed to reach the limit of their evil height. . . . Those who were supposed to be our pastors disdained divine piety and inflamed their hearts in contests with one another."

There had been a noticeable relaxation of the old Christian rules. Christians now attended the brutal games they had once shunned. Many intermarried with pagans. No great Christian leaders of the stature of Origen, Dionysius, or Cyprian had appeared in forty years. Pagan intellectuals like Porphyry and Hierocles wrote highly influential rants against Christianity; and little attention was paid to Christian attempts to reply to them. When Diocletian gave the order to persecute the Christians, it had some eager supporters; and many devout Christians saw behind it the hand of God himself.

St. Maurice is outfitted as a medieval knight in this sandstone sculpture in the St. Maritius Cathedral at Magdeburg, Germany. The thirteenth-century statue shows the martyr, true to the legend, as being black, a member of the famous Theban legion.

The persecution began with a purge of the armed forces. During his campaign in 286, Maximian demanded that his Theban Legion, which had many Christians, swear a pagan oath in preparation for the fight against the Gallic Bagaudae, many of whom were Christian. The legion's Christian commander, Maurice, and some of his officers who were also Christian, refused the oath. The result was a mass martyrdom (see sidebar, page 107). The legion was disbanded, and a purge of the entire army followed.

Diocletian's personal suspicion of a subversive Christian influence in the army had begun with an incident in the East several years before. He was attending a ritual sacrifice of animals from whose entrails his pagan priests were supposed to foretell the future. Some Christian court officials made the sign of the cross on their foreheads,

The Christian invasion of the army

Though Christ was the 'Prince of Peace,' he had a curious appeal to Roman soldiers, and when one whole Legion went over to him, the emperor ordered them slaughtered

Both in the ancient world and the modern, Jesus Christ was known as a man of peace, one who refused to resist his arrest and Crucifixion and who forbade his followers to take up arms on his behalf. Repeatedly, some Christians have included nonresistance among the obligations of their discipleship. Modern-day secular pacifists have also claimed him as one of their own. Yet he never condemned the Roman soldiery, so hated by many of his compatriots, and his first recorded Gentile convert was a centurion, for whom he had only words of praise.[1] Indeed, the Prince of Peace has always had soldiers among his adherents, and never was this clearer than in the Roman Empire of the third and fourth centuries, when a Christian in the legions had as much to fear from his own comrades as from any barbarian warriors.

The Roman army's success over its more numerous barbaric enemies depended in no small measure on a carefully cultivated group cohesiveness, firmly rooted in communal religious rites and loyalty oaths. For the Romans, any refusal to participate endangered the very survival of the military system and was punishable by death.

So found Victor, a grizzled North African member of Emperor Maximian's own Praetorian or palace guard, stationed in the western empire's capital of Milan. When Victor's Christian beliefs became known, the emperor, an old soldier himself promoted from the ranks, gave him six days in prison without food or water to consider how best "you can escape these terrible tortures which will viciously rip you unless you offer sacrifice." On the seventh day, the unrelenting Victor was stretched upon the rack "beyond the third mark," but continued to denounce the Roman deities as demons.

Maximian offered him a promotion, gold and property. Victor responded, "I will not sacrifice to the gods, but I offer myself as a sacrifice of praise to God." After another respite, Victor again defied the emperor, saying, "Do what you will, for I know that he who fights on my behalf is stronger than you."

More tortures followed, but the once-favored bodyguard endured them resolutely.

Tales of the fantastic later accumulated around him. The emperor orders him covered in molten lead. Victor prays for deliverance and the lead cools without harming him. Finally, he is beheaded, and his body left in the forest to be eaten by animals, perhaps lest it become an object of veneration. That plan fails, too. When soldiers return to the site, they find his corpse undamaged and protected by two beasts. Perhaps fearful of consternation among his troops, the emperor permits Victor's body to be buried.

Not only individual soldiers, but an entire legion paid the supreme price under Maximian. This was the Theban Legion, whose story was recounted first by Eucherius, bishop of Lyon, in about 460. Originating, like Victor, in North Africa, the unit had been brought to Europe and stationed in the Swiss Alps. The entire 6,600 complement were Coptic Christians who refused to participate in persecuting their brothers in the faith, according to one account, or in pagan sacrifices, according to another.

Maximian promptly ordered the legion decimated—that is, every tenth man removed from the ranks and beheaded while his comrades looked on. The command was carried out on the unresisting troops by other units. But the Africans did not waver in their conviction. Their commander, Maurice, went among his soldiers, encouraging each one to follow the example set by their fellows—all the way to heaven, if that was God's will.

The legionaries consequently sent the emperor a message that they would never submit to his unlawful commands, effectively anticipating later church doctrine: "We are your soldiers, O emperor, but God's servants. . . . We have always fought for justice, piety, and the welfare of the innocent. There is no way we can follow an emperor in this, a command for us to deny God our Father, especially since our Father is your God and Father, whether you like it or not." Despairing, Maximian had the entire legion slaughtered, even dispatching execution squads to hunt down members temporarily stationed elsewhere.

Eucherius's account of the Theban Legion also relates, with undoubted relish, the fate of this "savage tyrant" Maximian: "When he contrived the death of his son-in-law Constantine, who was then in power, by means of an ambush, his trickery was discovered, he was captured at Marseille, and was strangled not

---

1. Jesus' attitude toward the use of military force is left ambiguous in the New Testament, as it has been regarded ambiguously by Christians ever since. On the one hand, he warns that "all they that take the sword will perish by the sword," and he refuses to summon the angels to his aid when he is arrested (Matthew 26:52–53). On the other hand, he tells his disciples: "Now, he that has no sword, let him sell his garment and buy one" (Luke 22:36).

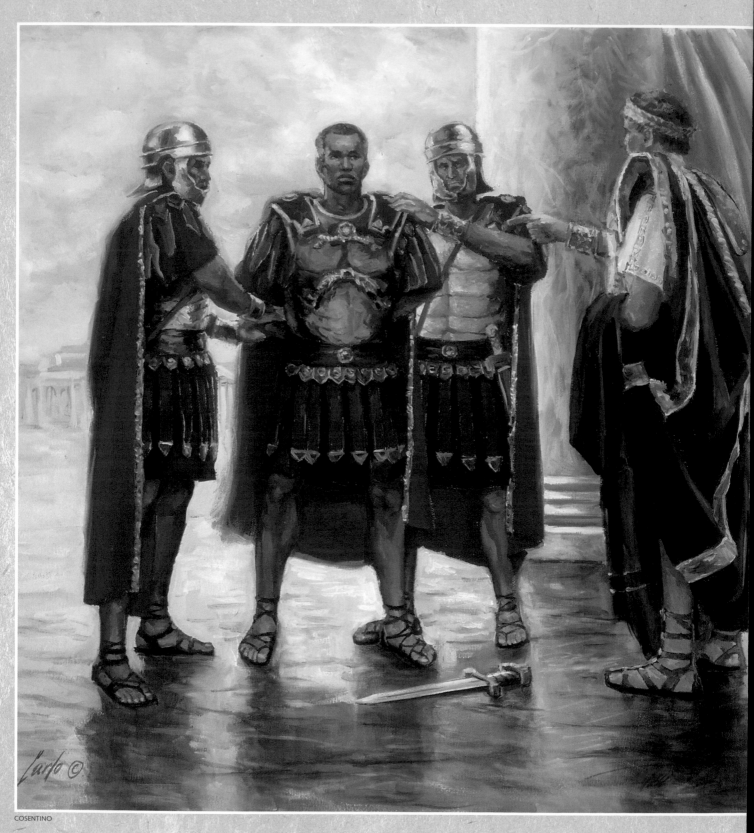

COSENTINO

It must have seemed to the emperor Maximian that the Christians infested each and every corner of his household and empire. Here of his best men, the Praetorian Victor, a loyal and dedicated serva the Empire, spouts unyielding faith in that scoundrel the Christ. N amount of argument, threat or enticement sways the man, and in end Maximian orders Victor's execution.

long afterwards. Punished in this most shameful way, he ended his wicked life with a fitting death."

Another story, that of Marinus, a soldier stationed in Caesarea in Palestine, pinpoints the twin challenges for the Christian soldier of Rome: he faced not only the army religion, but a culture of betrayal that surely undermined the comradeship crucial to fighting units. For Marinus managed to serve loyally and with distinction until singled out for promotion. About to be made a centurion, he was exposed as a Christian by a rival. He refused to recant and was executed.

Informing on one's fellows was apparently a purchased service among civilians. The Romans recognized informers, or *delatores*, as near-professionals, who were paid out of the confiscated estate of those convicted on their word (see earlier volume, *A Pinch of Incense*, chapter 3).

Andrew, a successful general in Syria, also fell afoul of jealousy. After he and a hand-picked cadre of co-believers repelled an invading force of Persians, he and his troops became the darlings of the court of the Syrian governor, Antiochus—until rivals exposed them as Christians. They were tortured but maintained their faith. Because their defiance had drawn too much negative publicity, they were released; Andrew fled, only to be hunted down and slain, after once more refusing to sacrifice to the gods.

On the other hand, Menas, a senior centurion stationed in Egypt, indicted himself. When he first heard the edict from Emperor Diocletian ordering the persecution of Christians, he tore off his badges of office and fled to the wilderness. After a period of meditation, he reappeared in the middle of a stadium during a horse race and professed his faith. Beaten, burned, dragged over a field of iron spikes while his men begged him to recant his faith, he remained steadfast until beheaded.

Likewise another centurion, Marcellus, publicly renounced the symbols of his office upon baptism, declaring that as a Christian, "it is not proper to engage in earthly military service." Another who might better be classified a conscientious objector, but is nonetheless counted among the military martyrs, is the Spaniard Maximian of Tebessa, beheaded in 295. "It is not permitted to me to serve in the army. I am a Christian," he declared, after refusing conscription. It cost him his life.

And then there was Callistratus, a common legionary whose great-grandfather was said to have witnessed Jesus' ministry firsthand and been converted at the first Pentecost. After being discovered at worship, Callistratus endured with such courage several ingenious tortures and a botched execution by drowning, that he converted forty-nine of his comrades. His teachings on Christianity, delivered to them in prison, survive to this day as *The Armenian Apologies*. All fifty were ultimately beheaded.

Sebastian's courage under fire apparently had a similar result. According to old stories that historians now doubt, his efforts to encourage several Christians imprisoned in Rome for their faith led to the conversion of the jailer and sixteen prisoners, as well as the city's governor. Made a captain of the Praetorians, Sebastian persisted in his activities until his discovery. He too was tortured, and after surviving an initial execution attempt at the hands of African archers, he was beaten to death.

How did this many soldiers come to be Christian when the risks were so manifest and the activity seemingly in violation of fundamental Christian teaching? Had not Jesus himself enjoined his followers to love their enemies and turn the other cheek, and ordered Peter to put down his sword? Had not the revered Tertullian at the end of the second century prohibited the faithful from the military life? "The Lord," he had written, "in disarming Peter, disarmed every soldier."

However, Tertullian's opposition to soldiering was based not on pacifism, but on the Roman army's heavy reliance on capital punishment and its pervasive idolatry. Hardly a day passed in the communal life of the legion that did not see a sacrifice of a cow or ox to some member of Rome's tangled pantheon. Moreover, Roman soldiers were required to worship each legion's eagle insignia, climaxing with a religious festival each May.

A few decades after Tertullian, Origen repeated the injunctions against Christians in the military, while contending that the emperor had a duty to take up arms in defense of a righteous cause. Though Origen still wanted Christians exempted from military service, he had planted seeds that would blossom in the late fourth century with the just war doctrine of St. Augustine.

What Augustine articulated, many Christians had already worked out for themselves, joining the legions because they saw the Roman Empire, its peace, its order, and its lawfulness, as an institution worth defending with their lives, despite its unpredictable descents into terrifying persecution and apparently idolatrous ceremonies. For beyond its frontiers, every citizen well knew, lay something far worse: savage hordes, murderous, rapacious, destructive, pagan and anarchic. The legions held them at bay and preserved the Christians' beloved families and church communities no less than their unbelieving neighbors.

Just as Christian values concerning personal rectitude appealed to the better sort of Romans, so too the army's values of loyalty and fortitude in defense of civilization and against violence must have attracted Christians. Surely, many Christians must have reasoned, service with the legions could be honorable. ∎

and the chief priest, who had been unable to foretell anything, blamed his failure on the presence of profane persons. They were displeasing to the gods, he said. An angry Diocletian commanded everyone present to sacrifice immediately under pain of flogging, and ordered that all soldiers in his army should sacrifice or be cashiered. Many chose to be ousted. It seemed, at first, that the matter ended there. "Diocletian offended no further," writes the Christian historian Lactantius.

But it did not end there. That same year, a centurion named Marcellus refused to burn incense in honor of Augustus Maximian's birthday. He flung down the marks of his rank and declared, "I am a soldier of Jesus Christ! If being a soldier means sacrificing to gods and emperors, behold, I cast away my staff and belt and refuse to serve!" He was condemned to die by the sword for his refusal. Witnessing his trial, the court secre-

Books were precious to the Christians and the Romans knew it. So such volumes were targeted for destruction in the early phases of the fourth-century persecutions.

tary, a Christian named Cassian, threw down his pen, declared the sentence unjust, and was himself executed.

Two years later, Galerius undertook to purify the legions under his command. His chief personnel officer, Veturius, ordered all soldiers to sacrifice or to face a reduction in rank or dishonorable discharge; the latter entailed the loss of veteran status and economic ruin. In the West, not wanting to be outdone by the younger Galerius, Maximian imitated the order. Many Christian soldiers resisted and paid with their lives, writes Eusebius—not because they were Christians, however, but for insubordination. What had changed was the enforcement of oaths that had been long relaxed to accommodate Christians who otherwise made excellent troops.

Soon, however, the impatient Galerius found that purification of the army was progressing too slowly. In the West, the moderate Constantius wasn't enforcing it at all. The problem, Galerius well realized, was Diocletian himself, who felt that wholesale bloodshed would interfere with orderly government. Diocletian passed the winter of 302–303 at the palace in his beloved Nicomedia, and Galerius joined him there. They remained closeted for weeks. Galerius badgered unceasingly, and the cautious Diocletian was "unable to break down the obstinacy of that furious man," writes Lactantius. Galerius "wanted all those who refused to sacrifice to be burned," but Diocletian held firm to moderation. There would be a general persecution, but no deaths.

Thus came the First Edict of February 24, 303: Christians refusing to sacrifice

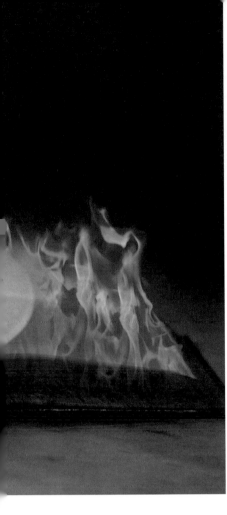

would be stripped of political privileges and tortured. Their churches would be demolished, their meetings forbidden, and their sacred books burned.

The church in Nicomedia was visible from Diocletian's palace, and the day before publication of the First Edict was the feast of the old Roman god Terminus, guardian of the field boundaries. That was a symbolic opportunity too good to be missed, so the emperors turned the household troops loose a day early. Bursting into the church, "they burned all the books of Scriptures they could find and ravaged and looted everything," Lactantius records. "Diocletian and Galerius were watching all this from a high window."

A Christian known as John, finding the posted edict, tore it down and shredded it. For this bravado he was arrested, tortured over a slow fire, and then burned to death. The record of his identity is sketchy, perhaps because Christian leaders at the time generally did not approve of such open defiance. Conscious that most of their flocks were not ready to die martyrs' deaths, they urged them to remain calm, and either hide or flee.

But Galerius was not satisfied. To him, the edict was not forceful enough, the persecution not intensive enough. Christians still openly worshiped. They still seemed everywhere present. *More* needed to be done. Diocletian refused, until what became known as the incident of the fires changed his mind. A few days after the publication of the First Edict, part of Diocletian's palace burned down. Only circumstantial evidence connects the edict with the fire, but Galerius certainly made the connection, accusing the Christians of plotting with palace servants. Terrified, the old augustus ordered an investigation of his household, with the free use of torture and his personal presence at the interrogation. Galerius's servants were excused from questioning.

Then, a few days later, the palace caught fire again. Galerius "had not stopped inflaming the madness of the unthinking old man," Lactantius writes. Galerius thereupon left the palace and Nicomedia. He was fearful, he said, of these Christians; and he took his servants with him.

Diocletian, more terrified still, fell into a paroxysm of rage. His wife Prisca and daughter Valeria, friendly to Christians, were immediately given the choice of sacrificing to the gods or dying. They sacrificed and lived. The trusted chamberlain Peter did not, but died slowly and terribly. The Christian record of his death says that he was whipped until his bones protruded. Still conscious, he felt his torn flesh doused with vinegar and salt. His limbs were roasted over a stove, one small part at a time. "He conquered these dreadful torments,"

The emperor Diocletian looks on with satisfaction as an offense to his eyes and sensibilities is removed at his command. The Christian basilica in Nicomedia stood directly opposite the imperial palace, a galling and strongly symbolic confrontation of the "Kingdom" of the Christians with his empire. Diocletian's first act of persecution was the obliteration of the church.

COSENTINO

records Eusebius, "and gave up his spirit without once being shaken in fortitude." When the servants Dorotheus and Gorgonius protested Peter's treatment, they were ordered to sacrifice. They refused and were immediately beheaded. Lactantius, the court's Latin tutor and future Christian historian, was expelled.

Once the dam broke, there was no holding back the flood. Nicomedia's Bishop Anthimus was beheaded. Priests and ministers were executed with their whole families. People were bound together in groups and cast into huge fires. Slaves were flung into the sea with stones around their necks. The bodies of earlier martyrs were exhumed and dumped into the sea. Altars to the gods and incense burners were set up, not only in the temples but also in the law courts, to sift the population. Those who would sacrifice were spared; those who refused were doomed.

This ferocity did not immediately extend much beyond the emperor's range of view. But Diocletian soon sent formal orders to his fellow augustus, Maximian, and the Western caesar Constantius, to follow his example. Maximian dutifully intensified his efforts; Constantius restricted his to the destruction of a few churches; the sacred Scriptures he is said to have left alone. Still, the junior caesar had to promulgate the order, even without pressing for its execution; so a few of his more zealous governors harvested some isolated martyrs.

The First Edict was directed primarily at the Scriptures, and while the ensuing book-burning was not complete, it was extensive. That's why no complete edition of the Bible today dates earlier than the fourth century, though portions and fragments of the New Testament go back to the early second (see earlier volume, *A Pinch of Incense,* page 34). For generations after, Christians would distinguish the persecution's first phase, "the days of surrender of the books," from the second, "the days of incense burning." Anyone who obeyed the order to surrender the Scriptures, fell into the category of *traditor,* traitor. Many, however, foiled the edict, hiding the rolls or carrying them to distant places. Some women made this their special work.

In the village of Abitina, not far from Carthage, Bishop Fundanus handed over the Scriptures, but a number of Christians, including some Carthaginian visitors, continued to meet in secret for the Eucharist, celebrated by the aged priest Saturninus. One day, the police surprised about fifty of them, including eighteen women and at least one boy, Hilarianus. One by one, they were stretched on a rack and their flesh torn by iron hooks, the blood of each mingling with that of those who had gone before. And when the boy Hilarianus was seized, he cried cheerfully, "Do what you like; I am a Christian." Though one, Felix, is known to have died from flogging, the fate of the rest remains unknown. They are presumed to have succumbed to their wounds immediately or in prison. When the Christians' host was asked why he had allowed Christians in his house, he replied, "They are my brethren and came to celebrate the Lord's Supper, without which we cannot live."

Not surprisingly, however, where the First Edict was strictly applied, many,

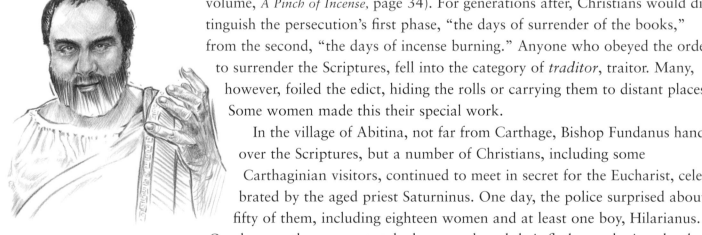

LACTANTIUS ON ROME

While the city of Rome remains, it appears that nothing of this kind [the end of the world] is to be feared. But when the capital of the world falls, who can doubt that the end will have now arrived to the affairs of men and the whole world? It is that city, and only that city, that still sustains all things.

possibly most, Christians either did not resist it or circumvented it. The clever Bishop Mensurius of Carthage replaced all his sacred Scriptures with heretical works and then obligingly ushered the officials into his library to destroy them. Bishop Donatus of Calama slyly handed in a stack of medical treatises. But beginning the persecution with Scripture burning might have been almost diabolically calculated to compromise the flabbier consciences of those tempted to dismiss the order as pertaining not to a test of faith, but rather to a matter of "mere books."

In one well-documented case, the magistrate of Cirta (see map page 130, B4) in North Africa showed up at the door of its Bishop Paul, demanded all his sacred writings, and thus provoked a round of obstruction by the ecclesiastical hierarchy. The bishop said three or four presbyters kept the books. The presbyters said a half-dozen deacons and subdeacons were in charge of them. These in turn referred the magistrate to the four or five lectors who actually held most

Clergy were executed with their whole families, people bound together and cast into huge fires, slaves flung into the sea with stones around their necks.

of the volumes. No one was particularly cooperative, but when the officials were done, they had seized thirty-five volumes—a treasure in the days when books were hand-copied.

In mid-303, there were minor military mutinies in Cappadocia (or western Armenia) and Syria. Diocletian crushed them without discrimination—all the magistrates of Antioch and Seleucia lost their heads, regardless of their religion. But the emperor, still excited by the double arson of his Nicomedian palace, also saw the hand of Christianity in these new troubles, and concluded that the persecution must be intensified. This time, he would attack the church's organization. The Second Edict, issued that year, required that all officials of the Christian church be jailed.

"Everywhere numberless people were imprisoned," said Eusebius, speaking of the Eastern provinces he knew so well. "Jails built for murderers were so full of bishops, priests, deacons, lectors and exorcists that there was no longer any room for common criminals. . . . No one can say how many suffered martyrdom." Shortly thereafter, once all the jails were filled, the palace issued the Third Edict, decreeing that Christian bishops, priests and deacons could be freed only if they sacrificed to the traditional gods, and they should be tortured if they refused.

The aged Bishop Philip of Heraclia in southern Thrace, the southern Balkans, had watched his church sealed in response to the First Edict but had continued to preach to his flock sitting on its steps, encouraging them to prepare for worse to come. Bassus, Thrace's prefect, had a wife who "had served God for some time," but orders were orders, so he had Philip seized

He had been looking forward to a little light entertainment to ease the burdens of his imperial office. But when the emperor Diocletian attends the theater for a performance by the famous satirist Genesius, he is again assaulted by evidence of his biggest headache. After completing a pantomime in which he ridicules Christian baptism, Genesius astonishingly announces to the emperor that he has suddenly accepted the truth of what the Christians were teaching. The actor paid for the declaration with his head.

and tortured together with his loyal priest Severus and deacon Hermes. Wherever the ancient bishop was imprisoned, however, crowds of Christians gathered, once even tunneling into his cell for instruction, while the prefect Bassus looked the other way. After seven months, though, Bassus was replaced by the less lenient Justinus, who transferred the three to Adrianople, where the old bishop was first flogged until his bowels were exposed, and then burned to death with the two others.

Not by any means, however, did all clergy stand so resolutely. "I will not mention those who failed the test of persecution, those who made a shipwreck of their salvation," writes Eusebius. Indeed, a "large number" surrendered. As a longtime resident of Syria and Palestine, Eusebius would have known well the twenty bishops of Palestine; but he does not mention any being martyred. What attitude to take toward "the lapsed" would divide the Christians after the persecution. Should they be readmitted? If so, subject to what conditions? The answers were to prove deeply divisive.

In September 303, Diocletian began his twentieth year of rule, an extraordinary achievement when the average reign of his half-dozen immediate predecessors had been under three years. To mark this anniversary, he agreed to hold his triumphal celebration in Rome, although it was a city he loathed. The procession, November 20, was impressive, marking victories on all the borders of the empire, from Persia and Africa to the Rhine and Britain, complete with trophies, shuffling captives and marching veterans.

But the purple-draped, bejeweled Diocletian was visibly unenthusiastic. The inevitable games in the circus proved to be less garish than expected. The emperor had stinted on them; the crowd knew it, and let him know. A curious incident is recorded of his visit—how reliably, historians dispute. A comedian named Genesius was entertaining a crowd of dignitaries, including Diocletian. In one part of his act, he staged a mock baptism, intended to ridicule the Christians. At this command performance, however, something went wrong. He emerged from the "baptism" act startled and bewildered, then abruptly announced that he had indeed become Christian. The crowd at first chuckled, thinking it part of the act. Rapidly, however, it became evident that Genesius was dead serious. Outraged, Diocletian ordered him tortured and beheaded.[3]

Perhaps this was the incident that threw him into a deeper depression. He dreaded the week-long, midwinter orgiastic feast of the Saturnalia that was just ahead. A week before the feast, without warning and heedless of the weather, he fled Rome for Ravenna in a litter. Some said he had gone mad. By the end of his eight-month journey back to Nicomedia, he had contracted a chronic disease, and reached his palace gravely ill.

Meanwhile, the furious Galerius was wielding the highest authority in the empire. His wish was now Rome's command, and he fervently wished the annihilation of Christianity. The Fourth Edict, issued in the spring of 304, was manifestly Galerius's, and designed to pummel Christianity out of existence. All Christians of any age, sex or rank were obliged to sacrifice to the gods. In the whole empire, there must be no one who could not produce, on demand, a certificate stating that he had made the sacrifice that faithful Christians abhorred. The heavy bureaucratic efficiency built by Diocletian now fell into Galerius's ready hand. Police squads with census rolls cordoned off city blocks, calling out the inhabitants by name and marching them off to the temple to burn a little pinch of incense.

How thoroughly it worked, how many were martyred, how many lapsed, how many somehow escaped the test, how many defiantly continued to preach the gospel—all this is left to be guessed. Nobody was counting. Many bought

Although Diocletian's zeal for persecuting the Christians seemed to flag, the same could not be said for his heir apparent, Galerius, whose particularly brutal purges may well have reflected a thoroughgoing pagan upbringing by his mother, a priestess.

---

3. By tradition, Genesius was buried on the Via Tiburtina. Since historical accounts of the story do not appear until the seventh century, three hundred years after the ostensible event, its authenticity is widely doubted. However, the martyrdom is known to have been venerated as early as the fourth century, and a church was built in his honor at a very early date. The seventeenth-century church historian Sébastien le Nain de Tillemont, in his *Mémoires*, puts forth a case for its validity, and a nineteenth-century oratorio, *Polus von Atella*, by Karl Löwe, and another by Felix Weingartner, dramatize the story.

faked certificates or sent their slaves to sacrifice for them. Flight may have seemed pointless when the Roman Empire covered almost the whole known world, but many fled to the deserts, forests and mountains, often to die there. Others escaped to Armenia or the nominally Roman territory on the upper Tigris, where they were well received. The administration tortured, executed or consigned those they caught to the mines by the hundreds, to a total, over ten years, in the thousands.

The territory of the moderate Constantius—Gaul, Britain and the Rhineland—was another partial refuge. Imperial edicts were still the law there, but the junior emperor showed little enthusiasm for them. Some Christians were undoubtedly martyred, but few enough that there is almost no reliable history, neither from later Christian historians nor from the normally voluminous court transcripts of the times. Ironically, the West was the one area where the empire might have been able to eradicate the church. Christians were few there, one person in five or even one in ten. Because many of these were in the army or civil service, it would have meant officers and judges singling out often well-respected colleagues; most neglected to do it.

In Maximian's Italy, Sicily, and Africa, the persecution bogged down for another reason: bureaucratic procrastination. Christianity was still in part an upper-class phenomenon, so again friends were in no hurry to annihilate friends. Still, some had no friends in high places—like the twelve-year-old Agnes and the gallant soldier Sebastian in Rome, the Sicilian martyrs Agnes and Lucy, and the African girls Maxima, Donatilla and Secunda. All these perished and their names now grace churches all over the world.[4]

In the East, where the church had been spreading much longer, it was much more rooted in the dispossessed and rebellious agricultural population, making it easy to persecute, but impossible to destroy. There was a little town in Phrygia, for instance, where even the magistrates were Christians. After refusing to sacrifice, they fled to their church. Roman officials dispensed justice by burning it down with the agonizing Christians trapped inside. On the other hand, the bustling city of Edessa had only three martyrs because there were so many Christians in its civic government.

Egypt's Christians were particularly hard hit, since that province had recently mutinied and been subdued, and the imperial machinery was still in place to launch a crackdown. "There, thousands and thousands of people, men with their wives and children, despising temporal life according to the teaching of our Savior, suffered all sorts of death," records the eyewitness Eusebius. "After enduring the iron hooks, the racks, the whips and other torments innumerable,

---

4. The bishop of Rome did not escape the persecution. At its beginning, he was Marcellinus, who was said to be "engulfed" by the violence that swept numberless Christians out of this life. He was martyred, probably on October 24, 304. The Donatist rigorists would later claim he was a *lapsus*, a charge affirmed by the *Book of Saints*, published by the Benedictine monks of St. Augustine's Abbey at Ramsgate, Britain, in 1989. Because of the local disruption, the See of Rome remained unoccupied for four years, until Marcellus was elected bishop in mid-308. How many other cities and regions were left without a bishop's care cannot be known.

they were consigned to the flames or drowned in the sea. Others bravely offered their heads to the executioners, or died from torture or hunger; some were crucified like criminals."

Yet throughout the Eastern empire, Christians had been relatives, neighbors, shopkeepers and customers of pagans for two hundred years; and many pagans did their best to protect those they could. Athanasius, destined to become bishop of Alexandria and to play a decisive role in the Christian story, was a child in those days. He later recalled hearing his parents speak of pagans who hid Christians, who saw their own goods confiscated, and went to prison rather than betray them. Except in particular cases of envy or spite, the general population does not seem to have taken much part in the persecutions.

Magistrates had great leeway in how they handled Christians, and many opted to break spirits rather than bodies. They would torture, but in small doses over long periods, sending their victims home in between. Or they would care for the wounds of today that they might be more painful when

Devotion to the martyrs is evident in the earliest examples of Christian art, both in and out of the catacombs. (1) An Egyptian limestone relief of the third century shows two unnamed martyrs—that they are such is evident from the cross each carries, which, along with crowns, was becoming a universal symbol of martyrdom. (2) This arched paving stone (early fourth century) from Jordan is inscribed with a catalog of martyrs. (3) The blood of the martyrs of Pozzuoli, Sicily, including the famed bishop Januarius, is said to have been spattered on the stone wall now protected by this niche.

COSENTINO

reopened tomorrow. One such magistrate boasted that in many years in office, he had not executed a single Christian, but had always succeeded in breaking their constancy.

To enhance their records, some judges would sometimes claim false victories. The accused would proclaim his faith, while his friends shouted him down, and assured the magistrate that he had already sacrificed. Sometimes scuffles would take place between Christians and their friends, and the magistrate would record the loudest shouts as proving the accused's apostasy from Christianity. Sometimes, Christians would deny all recognition of the court by maintaining silence; and a well-meaning neighbor would suddenly recall their having sacrificed—duly recorded and no retractions permitted. Sometimes, the soldiers in the court would strike Christians on their mouths repeatedly until they could not answer, and when they could not deny that they had sacrificed, they were tossed out onto the street.[5]

Not everyone embraced death unresisting. In Gaza, one Valentina had been watching one of her sisters, another vowed virgin, being tortured with iron hooks, and was inspired to tell the judge what she thought of him. When she refused his order to sacrifice, he had her dragged to the altar, only to watch her upend the altar and the tripod holding the fire. She was then ordered burned to death. Similarly, Edesius of Caesarea in Palestine, after watching another group of Christian matrons and virgins being consigned to the brothels, went up to the judge and began kicking and punching him—a satisfaction that quickly earned him excruciating torture and death by drowning.

Meanwhile, after Diocletian's long trip from Rome, he had remained cloistered in his palace. "At times he was actually insane," observes Lactantius. In early 305, he was at last seen at his window, so altered in his appearance by illness that he was recognized only with difficulty. By then, Galerius was fully in charge, the forces at his command larger than the combined forces of Maximian and Constantius in the West. In the expected event of Diocletian's retirement, Galerius warned Maximian in a letter, Maximian would be expected to retire as well.

Finally, in April 305, that day drew near. The blustering Galerius appeared before the man who had made him caesar. He pointed out, for Diocletian's

This response truly horrified Diocletian. After all his work, here was Galerius threatening to return the empire to anarchy. The old man burst into tears.

enlightenment, his patron's advancing years and disabilities, the loss of his physical strength and power of command, and the fact that Maximian would resign rather than risk civil war with him, Galerius. So why not retire now?

Diocletian, shocked but shrewd as ever, objected. If he resigned, there were many who would seek vengeance against him for his past wrongs. However, he proposed, if he made both of the present caesars, Galerius and Constantius, into full augusti, then perhaps he could enjoy a tranquil retirement. Galerius firmly rejected this counteroffer. He was not prepared to spend another fifteen years fighting barbarians in Persia and on the Danube, he insisted angrily, simply to remain the least important of the four emperors.

This response truly horrified Diocletian. After all his work, here was Galerius, actually threatening to return the empire to anarchy. Maximian had already written him, warning him of Galerius's military buildup. And now, here he was. The old man burst into tears and agreed to do whatever Galerius wanted.

What Galerius wanted made Diocletian weep more copiously yet. Galerius asked that he, in Nicomedia, and Constantius, far off in Gaul, would become

---

5. The greatest threat to the survival of individual Christians, especially in the East, was less the work of the imperial police and more the effect of their irrepressible reactions to the sight of the martyrdom of other Christians. In one celebrated case, Pamphilus of Caesarea, a friend of the historian Eusebius, and two of his friends, protested the impending execution of five Egyptian Christians. The protesters themselves were consigned to the flames, as were Pamphilus's slave, another young acquaintance, and then two Christian bystanders, all unable to remain silent while others were being martyred.

Death by drudgery

Christians sent to the mines were lamed, then half-blinded as an identification mark, then worked dawn-to-dusk on a starvation diet, but even there the faith spread

With the full authority of the mighty Roman Empire at his command, the magistrate coldly surveyed the assembled mass of men, women and children, guarded by soldiers. They had been gathered from the surrounding areas, rousted from their homes, sometimes whipped and dragged noisily from their places of worship, chased through woods and fields, discovered in their hiding places. The magistrate looked them over with mixed disgust and pity. These were those loathsome Christians, themselves deceived and deceiving others with absurd ideas attributed to the man Jesus, the crucified Palestinian Jew whom they think actually rose from the dead more than two centuries ago.

It was the magistrate's job to carry out the mandate of the emperor Decius, who was determined to restore to Rome the glories of the past, unifying the empire by reviving worship of the imperial gods, a goal the Christians persistently obstructed. He didn't seek their deaths, but rather their apostasy from their bizarre religion. Their death, though often the only expedient, was nevertheless a defeat. Best of all was one of their leaders publicly renouncing his faith.

However, there was a third option, one of distinct economic benefit to the empire, but still a virtual death sentence. This was service as slave labor in the mines. Few ever came back. Gazing over the prisoners, the magistrate decided that this would be best. *Ad metalla* he declared—"to the mines." (The word in the singular meant metal—gold, silver or iron. In the plural, it meant mines.)

Everyone had heard about the mines and their horrors. A sentence to the mines was deemed capital punishment, because just one in ten had a chance of survival, and unlike decapitation, it was a slow, agonizing journey to martyrdom. So terrible was such a sentence that many decided they would prefer being torn to pieces by animals in the amphitheater.

As the villagers watched, the streams of condemned men, women and children moved past. Usually, the party thus assigned consisted of bedraggled men, common criminals, or political subversives who already had been tortured and imprisoned. These were different, ordinary people, they seemed. "They must be Christians," the crowd would whisper, and then the catcalls began. A few stones were perhaps thrown, though not by all. More and more people secretly admired these Christians, despite their bizarre behavior. They were often generous, kind, helping not only their own members, but others as well.

Throughout the Levant, in Egypt and North Africa, the Romans long had mined gold, silver, salt, and granite. Marble was quarried in Pannonia and Cilicia, copper was mined in Palestine and Cyprus, gold in Spain. Imperial porphyry was found only in the Red Sea mountains of eastern Egypt, where summer temperatures reached 114°F.

Sentencing Christians to the mines and quarries accomplished two quite useful ends: It provided cheap labor to replenish the treasury, and it helped to rid the empire of their obstinate presence. Many mine slaves died from overwork, brutality and starvation, of course, and there were never enough common criminals to replace them. So the Decian persecution relieved the labor shortage.

On arrival, new members of the mine labor force were mutilated for easy handling. One side of their heads was shaved for quick identification in the unlikely event of their escape. The tendon of the left foot was crippled by cauterization, lest they should ever attempt to run. For clearer identification, the right eye was cut out with a knife, or burned through with a hot poker. Boys were castrated.

Then came day after day of hammers and wedges, crushing labor and crushed limbs. Starvation and collapse under loads of rocks were common. Those failing under duress were whipped and beaten until they responded or died. Any who grew too weak to report for work were beheaded.

Prisoners lived in ramshackle villages, Christians and other criminals side by side. The others were occasionally allowed visitors, contact with the outside world, but this was usually forbidden to Christians. Sometimes, a governor inspecting the mines believed life was too soft for the Christians there. If he thought they were living too long, he would resettle them to more miserable conditions, perhaps to the mines in Cyprus, Sardinia, Lebanon or Palestine.

Guards were ever alert to any infiltration of the Christian community by outsiders, particularly by bishops and priests who might wish to minister to these *confessores metallici*—mining-confessors. But many bishops and priests were among the hundreds of Christians who spent their remaining days hauling ore, breathing foul air, wearing bug-infested rags (if anything at all), and dragging iron chains on their feet. If such spiritual leaders were discovered spreading their beliefs among the miners, they were burned alive—that was the fate of the bishops Nilus and Peleus, but not all were discovered.

Despite the vigilance of the guards, however, some communication with Christians occurred. Cyprian, bishop of Carthage, was able to correspond with confessors in some mines, and would write of severe beatings and shackles on the feet of the prisoners. He referred to the miners as "gold and silver vessels." It was astonishing, he said, "that now the nature of the mines has been changed and places which before had been accustomed to give gold and silver have begun to receive them."

He regretted not being with them: "Although it is not granted me to come to you in body and in movement, yet I come to you in love and in spirit . . . considering myself a sharer with you in union of love if not in suffering of body." Three who were martyred managed a letter to Cyprian, hailing him as "greater than all men in discourse, more eloquent in speech, wiser in counsel, simpler in wisdom, more abundant in works, holier in abstinence, humbler in obedience and more innocent in your good deeds."

Even under such terrible conditions, the Christians in the mines often showed the same cheer so puzzlingly demonstrated by Christian martyrs in the arenas. At the Phaeno copper mines, a shanty became a church served by the best shepherds: Silvanus, bishop of Gaza, working tirelessly among the suffering, or the blind lector John, reciting from memory long Scripture passages.

Wondrously, the mines attracted visitors, sometimes from as far as Rome. Christians, at great risk to themselves, sometimes managed, despite the rules, to bring the miners small aids and comforting words. Unfortunately for those at Phaeno, a governor visited one day, found the conditions too easy, and reported directly to the Eastern caesar, Daia. The Christians were scattered to other mines throughout the empire, the four leading clergy were burned to death, and the thirty-nine who were too old or weak to travel— including Silvanus and John—were beheaded.

Throughout their ordeal, the mining-confessors by and large kept hold of their faith and continued their religious practices the best they could. During times of uneasy respite, some rubbed soot from the torches and with their worn and calloused fingers repeatedly wrote the simple word *vita*: life. Centuries later, a graveyard was discovered near an ancient mine, with crosses and headstones attesting to Christians buried there.

After years of darkness, a light finally shone over the mines. The emperor Constantine declared that those imprisoned or shackled in the mines solely for their religious beliefs must be released, protected from danger, and not molested. And so the gates were opened. Villagers who once shouted abuse at those marching off to the mines and quarries were stunned to see lines of folk staggering back in the opposite direction. Despite their lameness, their blindness, their bodies wracked from the effects of starvation, as they passed through the villages, these long columns of men and women sang psalms and hymns, praising God in the highways and city squares. Those who had been punished so cruelly, whose chances of survival had been minuscule, were smiling and laughing, filled with joy.

Bystanders were no doubt astonished. What was it these Christians knew or possessed that they could behave like this after all they had endured? Thus did their light so shine before men, as Jesus had commanded (Matt. 5:16).

Well into the fifth century, mines were used, though not always as brutally, as punishment or exile for Christians engaged in internecine theological, territorial and political disputes. Today, we marvel at the antiquities of the Roman Empire: towering pillars, gigantic temples, aqueducts, roadways, amphitheaters. Unfortunately, the ugly price paid in their construction may be lost in their beauty, a price paid in part by thousands of Christians who suffered, praised God, and laid the foundations of the faith for centuries to come. ■

The mines of the Roman Empire at the turn of the fourth century offered no hope to their inmates. Criminals such as unrepentant Christians could not expect to leave alive. But even here the Christians gathered, quietly, at places of prayer like this one, marked by the sign of the "ship of salvation," one of many symbols used by Christians at the time.

WOOD

the new augusti. However, by the unwritten rule of the tetrachy, Maximian's son Maxentius (married to Galerius's daughter) should have become Constantius's caesar, and Constantius's son Constantine, Galerius's. But Galerius already had his candidates for the two new caesars: his own general Severus, loyal only to himself, to wine and to debauchery, would become Constantius's caesar in Italy; Galerius's great brute of a nephew, Daia, would become Galerius's caesar in Asia.

When Diocletian saw Galerius's choices for his caesars, the decrepit emperor was uncontrollably distraught. The old man had made his mistakes—the biggest being the attempted destruction of the Christians. However, it was with genuine patriotism that he had restored the Roman Empire to stability and unity. Now his own choice for a successor was going to overturn everything he had accomplished. "I've worked long and hard to keep the empire together," he pleaded pathetically. "If things go wrong now, the fault will be all yours."

The changeover took place in May 305. Very much against their wills, Maximian abdicated in Milan, and Diocletian in Nicomedia. The teary-eyed old augustus spoke weakly to his soldiers about age and weariness, passing on the burden, and so forth. Then, much to the surprise of the army—it being fond of young Constantine—Galerius came forward with besotted Severus and brutish Daia as the next caesars, and threw the purple over them. Constantine, a longtime unofficial hostage in Diocletian's court and now in imminent danger, watched impassively from the back of the stage. Then, the old emperor was lifted into his coach and driven off to retirement among his famous cabbages, at his palace at Split.

Since Maximian had always obeyed the senior augustus Diocletian, this new tetrachy marked the first real division of the empire into East and West.

Minted in Carthage on the occasion of Diocletian's abdication, a bronze coin declares him to be "most fortunate"—as indeed he was. Emperors seldom had the option of simply retiring. The reverse side of the coin personifies Foresight and Rest, two qualities associated with the event.

The latter-day citizens of Split, Croatia, have largely usurped Diocletian's memory in the city to which he retired. (1) His lavish palace is now the venue for theatrical and musical events like this 1984 production of the opera Aida. (2) Even his mausoleum has been taken over by the Christians and converted to a cathedral. (3) But the potential for the hometown boy to be a tourist draw is still recognized by the locals, as this striking but inaccurate mural demonstrates.

Under Daia, any pretense that the persecutions were for the common good was abandoned. He simply catered to his own ravenous appetites, particularly as they related to women.

But to Galerius, it was unthinkable that the augustus of the wealthier, more populated and militarily stronger East should obey his nominal superior, Constantius. So from 305, while the persecution of Christians virtually ended in Constantius's West, it became even more ferocious in Galerius's, and especially in Daia's East.

Daia labeled himself *Maximin*, "the Greatest," and helped himself to what he considered the due fruits of office. These began with women. According to the Christian Lactantius, he introduced a "custom" whereby virgins within range of his vision could marry only with his permission, and he then skimmed off the most attractive, presenting them to his slaves when he was done with them. High-born women he requested as gifts, and some pagan officials committed suicide rather than face the humiliation of handing over their wives. And he allowed his officers, most of them barbarians, the same privileges.

Daia was particularly violent against the church in Palestine and Egypt. Apparently, he simply enjoyed inflicting suffering. He issued edicts in 306, 307 and 309, ordering ever-increasing pressures on the church, even to the point of ordering food sold in the markets to be sprinkled with the wine and blood of temple sacrifices, so that all would be forced to taste of them.

Alexandria suffered badly, as the eyewitness Phileas of Thmuis reports:

> Liberty to persecute was given to anybody. Some they beat with clubs, some with straps and cords. . . . Some, with their hands tied behind their backs, were hung from posts, and their limbs pulled in all directions by winches; and while they were hanging, executioners used tools on their bodies, bellies, legs and faces. Others were hung by one hand from a doorway. . . . to stretch their joints and limbs. Others were bound to columns in pairs, face-to-face, in such a way that their feet were off the ground, the cords tightened by the weight of their bodies.

> Some were taken back to prison and lay half-dead for a few days, until they died from their wounds. Others survived in a long imprisonment, and became even braver; when they were again commanded to choose between touching the unclean sacrifice and being freed, or refusing to sacrifice and being killed, they cheerfully went to their deaths.

The historian Eusebius described the horrors visited on the Christians in the area south of the Egyptian city of Thebes: "Women were tied by one leg, hauled into the air and left hanging naked, a cruelly inhuman spectacle. . . . Strong trees were bent together by winches until they met at the top, and a martyr's legs were then tied to each tree, and the trees allowed to spring back. . . . These things were done not for a few days or a short time, but for years. Sometimes, ten were killed at once, sometimes twenty or thirty, sometimes sixty. Once in the space of a day, a good hundred men, women and children were all executed after enduring prolonged tortures." He continues, "We ourselves were witness. . . . One day, the orgy went on so long that the blade became blunt and killed with its weight. The executioners themselves became exhausted and took turns at their work. We also saw the most marvelous inspiration, a force that was truly divine, and the readiness of those who had faith in the Christ of God. Immediately, when sentence had been pronounced on one group, another party came forward from

Galerius was stricken by spreading infection that ate his flesh and laid bare his bowels. In despair he turned to his one perceived hope, the indomitable Christians.

the opposite side, acknowledging themselves Christians. . . . They sang hymns and offered thanksgiving to the God of all until their last breath."

As the exterminations continued month after month, with no sign of success, some administrators may have wondered what was the point of all this slaughter, of citizens who made little resistance. But for the typically ambitious or semibarbarian Roman official, the path of advancement was made perfectly clear by Galerius's ascendance as the first augustus, and Daia as his successor.

What's more, the persecution was now starting to pay for itself. Whether from fatigue or pragmatism, magistrates increasingly began commuting the death sentence for Christians to forced labor: in the mines for the men, in the brothels for the women.

Eusebius records a few cases of saintly virgins like Irene of Thessalonica, who was condemned to sit naked in a brothel but was left undisturbed, because no pagan was shameless enough to disturb her; so she was burned to death. Or the fifteen-year-old Pelagia of Antioch, who was visited by soldiers one day when she was alone in her family house; aware of what being alone with these soldiers would mean, she flung herself from the roof. But for the most part, the later chroniclers pass over the experience in the brothels with a chaste and sympathetic silence.

By now, the Galerian Tetrarchy began dissolving into the usual chaos of competing generals that Diocletian had once repaired and then foreseen. Both Galerius and Daia, scourge of the Christians, met dismal ends. In the ninth year of the persecution, Galerius was stricken by a spreading infection, a hemorrhaging ulcer that began in his sexual organs and then spread throughout his trunk. As the disease ate his flesh and exposed his bowels, it was said the stink of his putrefaction filled the palace and spread to the neighborhood. In vain, he called on the gods. Asclepius, god of good health, failed him. So did Apollo. In his despair, he turned to the only people he thought might help—the indomitable Christians.

Would they pray for him, he pleaded? They doubtless did, and on April 30, 311, Galerius issued an Edict of Toleration. It was a strange document. On the one hand, it blamed the Christians for having abandoned the gods of the fatherland, and explained that punishments inflicted upon them had been designed to bring them back. On the other hand, it deemed them now sufficiently chastised and granted them freedom to worship "in accordance with our normal indulgence," requiring them only to pray to their God for the health of their emperors. For Galerius, however, it was too late. He died a few days later, reeking and in agony.

But for the Christians, "a great light burst out in the midst of the darkest night," wrote Eusebius. Prison doors were opened, and the confessors came out into the light, praising God. The survivors of the mines and brothels

Largely ignoring the new edict, Daia maimed and blinded Christians; then plague struck, his army dissolved before his eyes, and he perished in the birthplace of St. Paul.

limped home, quietly triumphant. Once again, the Christians held public worship; and many of their pagan neighbors, awed by so sudden a change, joined in the celebrations.

Daia lived on, largely ignoring Galerius's edict. Christians may not be killed, he said; but he encouraged their mutilation instead. Nostrils may be slit, hands and feet lopped off, eyes dug out. Meanwhile, he published and distributed what he entitled *The Acts of Pilate*, a collection of coarse slanders against Jesus Christ. Damascus streetwalkers were induced to publish filthy things Christians had done to them. The pagan temples were reorganized with professional priests, bishops and archbishops, all with administrative authority to promote the old gods and obstruct the Christians. Daia even undertook a punitive campaign against the Armenians, for no other reason, apparently, than that they had been harboring Christian fugitives.

Nothing worked. People scoffed at his propaganda. The pagan temples had "bishops," but their priests did not tend the sick, feed the poor or comfort the dying. Then the crop failed, famine spread, and with it, pestilence. Whole villages died, the dogs eating the bodies in the streets. Into this desolate territory wandered Diocletian's wife Prisca and daughter Valeria, Galerius's widow. To shore up his sagging political fortunes, Daia proposed to marry Valeria. She refused. He harried her and her mother unceasingly, killing their servants, menacing their friends, confiscating their goods, and finally exiling them to the Syrian Desert.

By now, the internecine wars for the succession caught up with him. His army fought a rival contender at Adrianople (see map page 131, E3), and crumbled before his eyes. Disguised as a slave, he fled the battlefield, escaped across Asia Minor, and was finally trapped at Tarsus, birthplace of St. Paul. Here he took poison, said the Christian chronicler Lactantius, and died in agony. The year was 313.

Meanwhile, in his splendid retreat at Split in Illyricum, the aging Diocletian was dying too, of a long and painful illness. Some said he was actually starving himself. On his deathbed, he heard not only that Daia was defeated, but that in the aftermath of the battle, Prisca and Valeria had been beheaded. All over the empire, he learned, his successors had thrown down or defaced his statues and monuments. He was buried in a stone sarcophagus he had prepared, bearing on its lid a carving of a boar being speared in the hunt, an ironic memorial to the fate of the luckless Aper.

For the Christians, the night was over, and the sun was in the sky. The great change in their fortunes had begun eight years before in Nicomedia, on that first day of May 305, when old Diocletian had announced his retirement. That launched an era destined to change the empire, change the church, and change the whole course of the Western world. For it was the day when the name Constantine entered the pages of history. ■

LACTANTIUS ON PEACE
If only God were worshiped, there would not be dissensions and wars. For men would know that they are the sons of one God.

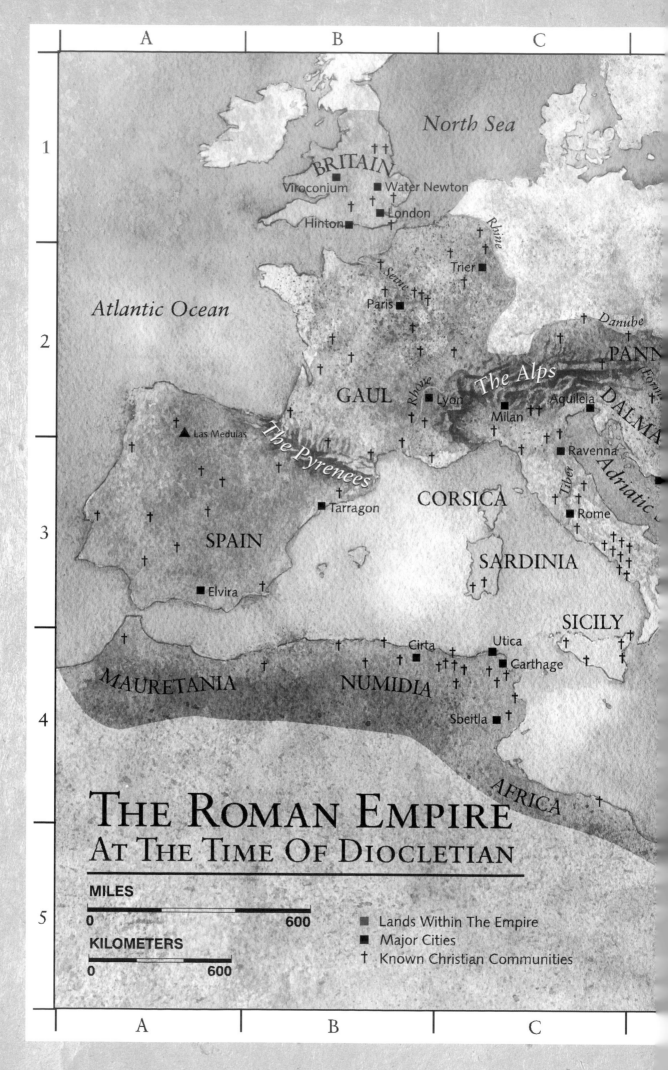

THE ROMAN EMPIRE
AT THE TIME OF DIOCLETIAN

MILES

0 ——————————— 600

KILOMETERS

0 ——————————— 600

■ Lands Within The Empire
■ Major Cities
† Known Christian Communities

North Sea

Atlantic Ocean

BRITAIN

Viroconium ■   ■ Water Newton
†† London
Hinton ■

Rhine

Trier ■

†Seine
Paris ■

GAUL

The Alps

Rhone

Lyon ■

Milan ■

Aquileia ■

Danube

PANN

DALMA

Adriatic

Ravenna ■

Tiber

Rome ■

Las Medulas ▲

The Pyrenees

Tarragon ■

CORSICA

SPAIN

SARDINIA

Elvira ■

SICILY

MAURETANIA

NUMIDIA

Cirta ■   Utica ■
Carthage ■

Sbeitla ■

AFRICA

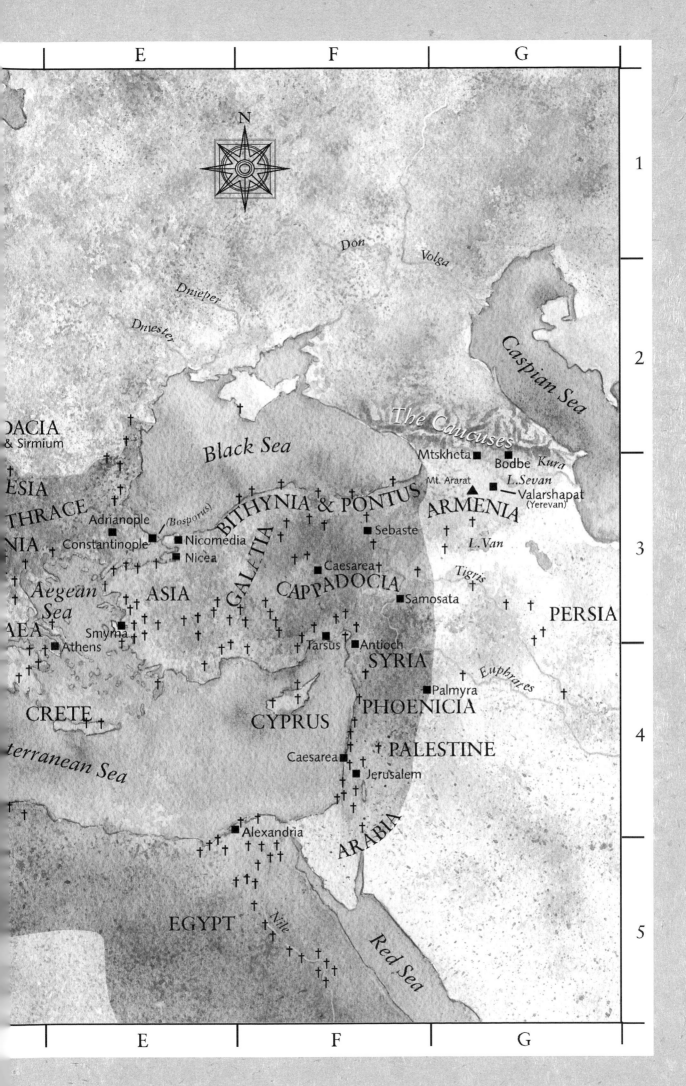

E   F   G

N

1

Don

Volga

Caspian Sea

Dnieber

Dniester

2

ACIA
& Sirmium

Black Sea

The Caucuses

Mtskheta ■   ■ Bodbe   *Kura*

ESIA

Mt. Ararat ▲   *L. Sevan*   ■

THRACE

Adrianople   *(Bosporus)*   BITHYNIA & PONTUS   ARMENIA

Valarshapat
(Yerevan)

NIA   Constantinople   ■ Nicomedia

Sebaste

L. Van

3

■ Nicea

GALETIA

Caesarea

Tigris

*Aegean
Sea*

ASIA

CAPPADOCIA

Samosata

PERSIA

AEA

Smyrna

Athens

Tarsus   ■ Antioch

SYRIA

Euphrates

CRETE

CYPRUS

Palmyra

PHOENICIA

terranean Sea

Caesarea   ■

PALESTINE

4

■ Jerusalem

ARABIA

■ Alexandria

5

EGYPT   *Nile*

Red Sea

What did Constantine see as he marched from Gaul to Rome for what was to be a decisive victory in battle? Was it a cross, or was it some other symbol? The accounts vary. Was the injunction "By this (sign) conquer" given to him in Greek or in Latin? Artist Greg Harlin provides one plausible option. In the end, however, what mattered was that a defining moment in world history had occurred. The future emperor was on his way to becoming a believer—a Christian.

CHAPTER 5

The sign in the sky that changed history

A wild horseback ride across Europe ushered in the era of Constantine, whose march to victory laid the foundations of the Christian empire

The tale is not only romantic, but probably true. The year is 306. A young man arises in the dead of a late spring night in the imperial palace at Nicomedia in Asia Minor. He slips down to the emperor's stables and commandeers the palace horses. He is thirty-two years old, and by all reports quite handsome. He has been a hostage. Now he is making his escape and seeking to delay pursuit.

His name is Constantine, and he is the son of Constantius Chlorus, the Roman emperor in the West. The man from whom he is escaping is Galerius, emperor in the East. As the guest of Galerius, but also his captive, Constantine's life would be forfeited if his father became a little too ambitious and tried to seize the imperial crown of the East, in order to become sole ruler of the empire.

Right now, however, Constantine's captor Galerius is asleep, likely drunk and sated in the imperial bedchamber after a lavish banquet that Constantine had arranged to keep him well-sedated during the getaway. With good reason, Galerius was as suspicious of Constantine as he was of his father, and he had already planned to have the younger man arrested as soon as he got up the next day. If Galerius or anyone close to him had awakened that night and caught wind of what Constantine was doing in the stables, the young man's fate would almost certainly have been instant death.

Kept hostage in Nicomedia by his father's rival Galerius, the young Constantine orchestrated an extraordinary horseback escape. It took him across the breadth of Europe and much of the empire he would one day rule.

Galerius's thick shield of armed bodyguards seemed not to have been on high alert, however, for they neither saw the horses—their well-combed manes glistening under the moon—nor heard their hooves clack along the stones of the palace courtyard as Constantine led them to the gates.

All very improbable of course. It's far more likely that some of the guards had been paid off, or that they simply chose not to sound the alarm. For Constantine, who had already distinguished himself as one of Galerius's top commanders, had a reputation for energy, courage, and initiative, and he was highly popular with the Roman army. Among the imperial guard he undoubtedly had friends and allies who were willing to look the other way.

Thus Constantine and his carefully chosen accomplices were able to unlatch the mighty chains of the palace gates undetected, and to slide back the heavy crossbar—quietly, quietly—and open them—inch by inch—so as not to make a creak. Then they led the horses outside the palace gates and down the narrow cobbled streets until they reached the outskirts of Nicomedia. The open fields, white in the moonlight, lay before them. At last Constantine was free.

He mounted one of the horses, already tacked for that purpose, loosened the reins, squeezed the beast's flanks sharply with his thighs, and no doubt with a few trusted companions, charged off on the high road at full gallop, the rest of the riderless pack thundering after him. The horses were likely the empire's finest: tall, graceful Iberian animals with manes as long as women's hair, the breed from which Bucephalus, the legendary horse of Alexander the Great, was said to have sprung. Like Alexander, the young Constantine wore his hair long, and it must have flown in the night like the horses' manes as they sped westward through the darkened villages, his soldier's cloak billowing behind him.

His escape would become the longest continuous ride on horseback ever recorded in the ancient world—more than sixteen hundred miles from Nicomedia, across the Straits of Bosporus, through the northern Balkans, the Danube frontier lands and the Alpine passes of Austria and Germany, all the way west to Boulogne on the northeast coast of France.

Constantine's dramatic journey with the palace horses, reported by one of his biographers, Lactantius, illustrated his intelligence, ambition and decisiveness. He fully understood that Galerius hated and feared him and was determined to keep him on a short leash indefinitely at the palace. Indeed, Constantine had been living at the court at Nicomedia for at least ten years, serving first under Galerius's predecessor, Diocletian, who also held him as a hostage for his father's good behavior. When Diocletian's retirement in 305 catapulted Galerius to the top position in the East, Constantine's father formally requested that his son be allowed to join him in his campaign against the Picts. According to Lactantius, Galerius outwardly consented, but connived to make it impossible for Constantine to leave.

So Constantine engineered his flight, Lactantius reports, on the very night before he was to have been hauled into Galerius's presence to become a more explicit kind of prisoner. When Galerius awoke at noon the next day and learned from his servants that Constantine was long gone, he burst into tears.

Constantine had taken all the palace horses with him for a reason: so that his pursuers would not have mounts with which to follow him. What's more, none of the individual horses that galloped boldly with Constantine in the moonlight along the high road out of Nicomedia made it even as far as the Bosporus, says Lactantius. That was because at each stable where Constantine stopped to change mounts, he ordered every horse on the premises except his party's own fresh ones to be hamstrung, bloodily crippling the animal. Thus no one from Galerius's court could pursue Constantine without first having to scare up second-rate horses from somewhere. Only when Constantine finally reached the Illyrian border, the dividing line between the Eastern and Western empires, could he relax his frantic pace. In the empire of the West, it was his father's writ that ran, not Galerius's.

At the port of Boulogne (in Latin, Bononia), Constantine met up with his father. Constantius was waiting to cross the English Channel to Roman Britain in order to fight the Picts, the fierce Scottish barbarians who were harrying the empire from the North. Although Constantine probably did not know this, Constantius was already dying when he summoned his son to join him in Boulogne. Just two months later, the old man died in the north of Britain, at York, then called Eboracum. Before he expired, however, his last deed would change the history of Europe and the world. He declared Constantine his heir as augustus of the West. In the coming eighteen years Constantine would eventually become sole Roman emperor, overcoming six powerful rivals one by one, against what must have seemed impossible odds.

When he burst out of Nicomedia in 306, Christianity was still a despised and mercilessly persecuted religious sect, at which most people of his high social standing looked down their noses. Within his lifetime and at his specific direction, Christianity would become the dominant cultural force in the Western world. Indeed, Constantine would inaugurate the process by which would arise "Christendom" (see sidebar page 178). For this, some Christians would go so far as to regard him as a saint. Others would see him as crippling Christianity for centuries by disastrously fusing it to the powers of what Christians call "this world."

Constantine could only assess things as they looked to him in the early fourth century, when the imperial system called for two emperors instead of one. His was not the old Rome of Augustus, which sixteen centuries later would endear itself to Hollywood—with helmeted legions marching on marble avenues toward

When Constantine burst out of Nicomedia, most people looked down their noses at Christianity. Within his lifetime it would become the dominant cultural force in the Western world.

the Capitoline Hill, shouting "Hail, Caesar!" in unison as they passed an emperor splendid in his purple toga, flanked by the vestal virgins in shimmering veils. That Rome was now three hundred years in the past. And even when it lived, the military might, the marble and the poetry of the Augustan Age had masked deep flaws that led to the city's gradual decline as a center of power.

The most glaring flaw was economic. Rome's economy was essentially built on plunder. During the three centuries before Christ, and for a century or so afterwards, the city that had begun as a tiny village, perched on its seven hills above the swamplands of the Tiber, developed military commanders with a genius for organization and strategy, as well as civic leaders who gave it an elaborate system of laws. They built first a republic, then an empire that spread from the Atlantic to the Euphrates, and from Britain to the Sahara, its conquering armies carrying back shiploads of treasure and tens of thousands of slaves to enrich the imperial treasury, serve the gentry and adorn the city.

But Rome created little wealth on its own, and behind its luxurious facade there lurked a deepening squalor. Much of its lower-class populace was unemployed, subsisting in crowded, filthy tenements on free bread handed out by the authorities. The world's real wealth all lay in the bustling, thickly populated, Greek-speaking East, most of it territory long claimed by the ancient empire of Persia. By contrast, western Europe was always poor and thinly settled, harried by barbarian hordes that Rome could check but never control. So, with Persia blocking expansion in the East, and with little to loot in the West, Rome, cut off from its lifeblood of booty, began a long, slow decline.

By Constantine's time, the city of Rome was recognized as an inhospitable place, so noxiously hot and malarial during the summer that few Romans of means and cultivation wanted to stay there any longer than they had to. The administrative center of the western Roman Empire was not Rome, but Milan, strategically located on the main road through the relatively cool, agriculturally fertile plains of northern Italy. The emperor's household, the courts, and the imperial bureaucracy were largely centered in Milan, not Rome.

Then there was the problem of maintaining the huge standing army that the empire needed to protect its thousands of miles of frontiers, an army that could no longer be paid cheaply with conquered land and plunder. It had become a crushing liability, driving taxes to oppressive levels in a stagnant economy. While Constantine was growing to maturity, the whole empire was plagued by rocketing inflation, decreased agricultural production, abandoned farmland, crumbling buildings and monuments, and a seemingly inexorable decline in population. Diocletian's attempts to stabilize the currency and the supply of skilled labor had been heroic, but they did not address the underlying causes of Rome's economic and cultural spiral downward.

Not surprisingly, the empire's center of gravity had slowly shifted eastward. The climate was better and that's where the money was. That was also why Diocletian preferred his palace at Nicomedia, on the sunny Sea of Marmara southwest of the Bosporus—the palace that Galerius was later to occupy and Constantine to flee.

Constantine's father, Constantius, was a career military man, born in Dardania, in what is southern Serbia today. Although Constantius was later said to have sprung from the Dardanian nobility, he was probably as lowborn as Diocletian and the twenty-eight other soldier emperors who preceded him had been. How Constantius acquired the nickname "Chlorus," from the Greek word for "pale green," is not known, but may derive from a sickly complexion. Early in life, he married a woman named Helena (see sidebar, page 247), a barmaid or innkeeper's daughter from the town of Depranum in Bithynia, who in 274 or thereabouts gave birth, in Naissus (modern-day Nish, in Serbia, see map page 131, D3), to Constantine.

Constantius rose quickly—he was made governor of Dalmatia, then probably prefect of the Praetorian Guard, then Diocletian's caesar in the West, then finally augustus in the West. While he was caesar in the West he divorced Helena, at the behest of Diocletian, in order to marry Theodora. She was the daughter of his immediate

By most accounts, Constantius Chlorus (above) was an effective ruler of the western-most parts of the empire. Among exploits that endeared him to Romans, and even to some of those who were made his subjects by military force, was his retaking of Britain after it fell to rebel Roman leaders. The coin shows a grateful Britain kneeling before Constantius as he is crowned by the goddess Victory.

superior Maximian, who was then the western augustus, and all this was part of Diocletian's plan to end, through dynastic marriage and adoption, the mayhem of murder that had claimed the lives of twenty-two of Diocletian's twenty-eight predecessors. Constantius proceeded to have six more children, Constantine's half-siblings, by his new royal wife.

When Diocletian retired in 305, Maximian reluctantly retired as well. Under Diocletian's plan, Galerius and Constantius automatically became the augusti, and were each to name the caesars who would succeed them. But Galerius had a better idea. As the augustus of the much more powerful and prosperous East, he arbitrarily selected both new caesars himself, not only his own but also Constantius's. Severus, an army officer from Pannonia and definitely a Galerian loyalist, was to serve as Constantius's caesar; and the brutal Maximinus Daia, Galerius's nephew, as Galerius's caesar. About this whole arrangement, needless to say, Constantius was not consulted.

The jurisdictions within the new tetrarchy were likewise mapped out by Galerius. Constantius's territory included Gaul, Britain, and Spain; his caesar Severus got Italy, northern Africa and Pannonia. Galerius and Daia split the East between them, with Daia taking eastern Europe and Galerius retaining Asia Minor and points east, including Diocletian's beloved palace at Nicomedia.

There was little love lost between Constantius and Galerius, but the really

The magnitude of the forces opposing Constantine, and his rise to power nevertheless, were astonishing: He faced and overcame six rivals to his imperial claims—three men in each of the empire's two parts.

odd man out was young Constantine. Both he and Maximian's son, Maxentius, who was married to Galerius's daughter, had been passed over for appointment as caesars. Furthermore, Constantine was being held as a veritable prisoner in Nicomedia, and it would be only a matter of time before Galerius—or Severus or Daia—solved the problem of his existence by executing him. Thus Constantine's horseback escape.

And when the dying Constantius named his firstborn son to succeed him instead of Severus, Constantine knew that this act doomed Diocletian's plans for an orderly succession. The Diocletian tetrarchy was smashed and dead before Diocletian himself died. Diocletian was still puttering about in retirement at his estate at Split in his native Dalmatia.

Furthermore, on the very day that Constantius died—July 25, 306—his soldiers proclaimed Constantine the new augustus. As Constantine well knew, this amounted to a declaration of war against the other three tetrarchs—against Severus, the western caesar whom Galerius had foisted on his father; against Daia, the caesar Galerius had appointed in the East and against Galerius himself. Severus, Daia and Galerius were for Constantine three powerful enemies whose domains spanned the Roman Empire.

Constantine realized that he had no place to hide. He was alone and he had to act quickly. He had to seize it all—absolute power over the entire empire, East and West—or be killed ignominiously like the pathetic series of soldier emperors before Diocletian. Constantine was determined not to join them.

But the competition grew even worse. Constantine soon had three other formidable enemies to take into account, each of them with ambitions to rule everything. One of these was Maximian, Diocletian's fellow augustus who had been forced into retirement when Diocletian retired. Now, from his home at Lucania in southern Italy, Maximian had begun reasserting his claim to greater power. Leagued with him was a fifth foe, Maximian's son Maxentius, who lived at Rome and had strong support in the Roman Senate. Finally, from up on the Danube, came a sixth military claimant: Licinius, an old friend of Galerius. Diocletian was persuaded to come briefly out of retirement, affirming by his presence at the ceremony the naming of Licinius as a third augustus.

In other words, the old system of succession by civil war and murder was back. For all seven contenders, it was a case of everything or nothing. To survive at all, Constantine had to overcome the six most powerful men in the Roman world, most of whom commanded armies far more formidable than his.

The immediate enemy was Severus, the man Galerius had named caesar of the West. Had the Diocletian formula been followed, Severus would have automatically become augustus of the West when Constantine's father died, but Constantine now held that title instead. To avoid immediate civil war between Severus and Constantine, Galerius stepped in. He worked out a compromise with Constantine: Severus would remain the augustus and Constantine would be named the new caesar. Constantine saw a benefit for himself in this arrangement. He was already having trouble with his new territories, for although Britain and Gaul had accepted him as the augustus, Spain was balking. He therefore accepted Galerius's offer—for the time being.

Severus, meanwhile, had already made two missteps that would rapidly take him out of the contest. One of his first acts on becoming caesar had been to conduct a tax census, unheard of in the city of Rome, whose residents had lived tax-free for centuries and were infuriated by the idea. Worse yet, he tried to disband the Praetorian Guard. The outraged Guard promptly mutinied, and on October 28, 306, it proclaimed Maxentius, Maximian's son, as the new emperor, although it did not give him the title augustus.

Maximian, the father, bolted north, not only to aid his son's cause but also to reclaim his old title; he was the true augustus of the West, he said. Father and son then united against Severus, first driving him from Rome, and then forcing him to surrender at Ravenna in the spring of 307. That was the end of Severus. Maximian either had him executed or forced him to commit suicide. For Constantine, one rival had been eliminated. But five still remained.

Galerius, furious at old Maximian's effort to return from retirement, marched his powerful army west against the father-and-son challengers at

The homicidal system was back. To survive, Constantine must vanquish the six most powerful men in the world, most commanding far more formidable armies.

Rome. He declared Maximian's comeback illegal, and said his son's occupation of Rome amounted to usurpation. He knew that if he could crush the father and son, he could then turn his army's attention on Constantine.

Old Maximian made his move next. Since Galerius threatened everybody in the West, Maximian made his way to Constantine's camp. If Constantine combined forces with him against Galerius, he said, he would share the title of augustus with him. As evidence of good faith, he offered Constantine the hand of his daughter, Fausta, in marriage.

Constantine, like his father before him, had taken a commoner for his wife when he was offered a more profitable marriage. His first wife's name was Minervina, and she was the mother of his son, Crispus. No matter—following his father's example, he promptly divorced Minervina, and in September of 307, he married Fausta in a dazzling ceremony at Trier, on the Mosel River. After that, at least for a time, he was careful to accord his new father-in-law honor and a show of support, without allowing him to enjoy any real power. After all, Maximian, underneath his surface display of loving kinship, was still one of the five remaining contenders for the rule of the whole empire.

Maximian's son Maxentius proved harder to evict from Rome than Galerius had anticipated. Frustrated, Galerius retreated, and he tried to bestir the aged Diocletian to come out of retirement again and use his muscle to restore the tetrarchy.

Diocletian declined. However, his deft skill at political connivance was far from lost. Still striving to sustain his tetrarchy model, even if he wouldn't personally fight for it, Diocletian persuaded his old colleague Maximian to betray both his son and his new son-in-law, since they were the two who were disrupting the system. The plan called for Maximian to destroy Constantine, then to retire. His son Maxentius, still holding Rome, would be formally declared a public enemy, and a new augustus, Galerius's old friend Licinius, would unseat Maxentius and become augustus of the West, while Galerius would return to the East.

Maximian, the father, waited two years to make an overt move. In 310, while Constantine was on the Rhine frontier battling the barbarians, Maximian seized Constantine's treasury at Arles in southern Gaul and proclaimed himself augustus once more. Constantine retaliated in a flash, sweeping southward through Gaul. Desperate, the old man tried to induce his daughter Fausta to betray the husband he had given her, but she refused. Instead, Constantine's troops caught Maximian at Marseille, where he was forced to commit suicide.

Now there were four rivals. The next year, 311, Galerius, chief persecutor of the Christians, died at Nicomedia after lengthy suffering from an excruciatingly painful disease, as described in the previous chapter.

That left three. All three—Maxentius at Rome, Daia and Licinius in the East—called themselves augustus, and all three had armies to back up their claims. Constantine pondered his options. Licinius and Daia were potentially dangerous, but for now, with Galerius dead, they were locked in murderous rivalry with each other, each claiming the entire empire of the East. Constantine decided to forge a tactical alliance with Licinius, and he arranged in late 311, or early 312, for Licinius to be betrothed to his half-sister Constantia, one of the many children of his father's second wife.

So the remaining immediate problem was Maxentius, his brother-in-law at Rome. Maxentius moved first, ordering that all of Constantine's statues in Italy be knocked down and destroyed. Even though relations between Maxentius and his father had been strained—the old man had lately called his own son a usurper and a public enemy—Maxentius vowed that he must avenge his father's forced suicide at the hands of Constantine. Besides, this same Constantine had now joined up against him with Licinius. To Maxentius, these deeds were unconscionable.

Constantine knew it was time to act. He mounted a preemptive strike against Maxentius, crossing the Alps into Italy in the summer of 312, with a force of at least forty thousand men. Marching south, Constantine stormed, persuaded to surrender, or made allies out of the major cities of northern Italy: Turin, Milan and Verona.

Assaulting Rome itself, however, was a daunting operation. Constantine's forces were outnumbered probably two-to-one by Maxentius's standing troops and cavalry in Rome. Worse, the city was fortified by a twenty-foot-high, twelve-mile-long wall which had been built by the emperor Aurelian in 271 to ward off possible barbarian attacks. Neither Severus nor Galerius had been able to breach that wall, and inside, Maxentius and his huge army waited. It was by now late October.

Maxentius (above), entrenched in Rome, held the symbolic heart of the empire. He openly provoked Constantine by ordering that all statues of Constantine in Italy and Rome be destroyed. For Constantine the next move was obvious: Maxentius had to be toppled.

Constantine so far had only one thing in his favor, but it was considerable: the inhabitants of Rome were completely disenchanted with Maxentius, sick and tired of him. At a series of chariot races organized by Maxentius to celebrate the upcoming anniversary of his accession to power, the crowd taunted him, shouting that Constantine was invincible. Maxentius turned for help to the famous Sibylline Books, with their prophecies on the future of Rome, and there he was told that on his own anniversary date, October 28, the enemy of the Romans would perish. That, thought Maxentius, must surely mean Constantine. He resolved that on that very day he would lead his army out through the city gates and battle his outnumbered rival.

Constantine prepared for battle as well. He was a master strategist whose method was to try to get inside his enemy's mind and anticipate his next move,

Something vital happened to Constantine, something so vital that it would change fundamentally both the course of his own life and the course of the life of the world

and it's likely he guessed that Maxentius would try to leave the city and come at him. So his plans would have allowed for that contingency. But that was not his only insight. There was another that would crown his page in Christian history.

At a point prior to the impending battle, something happened to Constantine, something so vital, so shattering, that it would change fundamentally both the course of his own life, and the course of the life of the world. There are two accounts of this extraordinary event, whatever it was. Eusebius, his biographer who knew Constantine well, tells it this way:

> Constantine called on God with earnest prayer and supplications that he would reveal to him who he was, and stretch forth his right hand to help him in his present difficulties. And while he was thus praying with fervent entreaty, a most marvelous sign appeared to him from heaven. . . . He said that about noon, when the day was already beginning to decline, he saw with his own eyes the trophy of a cross of light in the heavens, above the sun, and bearing the inscription, "Conquer by this." At this sight, he himself was struck with amazement, and his whole army also, which followed him on this expedition, and witnessed the miracle. He said, moreover, that he doubted within himself what the import of this apparition could be. And while he continued to ponder and reason on its meaning, night suddenly came on; then in his sleep the Christ of God appeared to him with the same sign which he had seen in the heavens, and commanded him to make a likeness of that sign which he had seen in the heavens, and to use it as a safeguard in all engagements with his enemies.

Lactantius, another contemporary, tells the story somewhat differently.

> Constantine was directed in a dream to cause the Heavenly Sign to be delineated on the shields of his soldiers, and so to proceed to battle. He did as he had been commanded, and he marked on their shields the letter X, with a perpendicular line drawn through it and turned round . . . at the top, being the cipher of Christ. Having this sign, his troops stood to arms.

Whether Eusebius was right, or Lactantius, or neither—and they could

Though it began as a crude abbreviation painted on shields and carved furtively on coins, houses, and walls, the Chi-Rho became an imperial standard. The large marble version of the monogram (now in the Vatican Museums) is decorated with a laurel wreath, fruit and flowers. To this have been added the first and last letters of the Greek alphabet, alpha and omega (Christ being the First and the Last). However, the smaller medallion from Britain shows the addition was still unfamiliar to some Christians: The omega is upside-down.

both have been right, since there could have been both a dream and a vision—one fact seems conclusive. The man who left Britain to fight for the crown and the man who advanced upon Rome on the morning of October 28, 312, were in certain substantial respects not the same person. From that point on two new terms figure prominently in the thought, language and policies of the emperor. One is God and the other is Jesus Christ.

Perhaps even then he saw, however faintly, that such wars as men fought, wars that up until then he had spent most of his life waging, were but mere shadows of another war, the *real* war, the war between good and evil that rages unseen within the soul of each man. This was the war that the Christians had always understood, and that he would better understand himself in the violent personal struggles that lay ahead of him.

But now the vision was over, and he must attend upon the task at hand. There were, then, on that fateful morning of October 28, tens of thousands of grizzled war veterans working over their shields at dawn, squinting at hastily scribbled drawings of the Chi-Rho that they passed from hand to hand as they tried to reconstruct the symbol with sticks or wire or paint. As they painted Xs on their shields, then put through the Xs vertical lines with rounded tops, they must have scratched their heads in puzzlement. The overwhelming majority of them were pagans who worshiped the bullfighting god Mithras, protector of

Roman soldiers. Christians, after all, still constituted only about ten percent of the Western empire's population at the beginning of the fourth century. And the resemblance to the cross? Even the Christians themselves shirked at using that shameful symbol in their religious art, although their Jesus had died on a cross. The cross was the slave's punishment, grist for gallows humor, not for bearing proudly into battle. But orders were orders.

It seems clear, from everything that followed, that Constantine knew he could defeat Maxentius only with divine help, and that somehow that help was available only from the God of the Christians, not from any pagan deity. Clearly grateful, he did not hesitate later to declare openly his trust in the God of the Christians. So wherever you looked among the ranks of Constantine's army on October 28, 312, you saw among his soldiers the sign of Christ, painted brightly on shields or hoisted high on standards.

As he had planned, Maxentius marched out of Rome with his army, confident the day was to be his. He crossed the Tiber over the Milvian Bridge and continued along the river on the Flaminian Way. About a mile up the narrow defile, he found his path blocked by a phalanx of men with crude, savage-looking markings painted on their shields. To his pagan eyes, the Chi-Rho sign was undoubtedly a

fearful sight: a dancing stick-figure demon. Then he got word that Constantine's forces, advancing to the Tiber on the other fork of the road, had attacked his men back in the lines, at the Milvian Bridge; Constantine seems, with his usual canniness, to have guessed correctly where his enemies would be. Maxentius was trapped. His troops, assaulted at both ends, were forced back in a pincer to the Tiber.

There they were slaughtered like cattle. Panicked, a mob of them, including Maxentius himself, tried to push their way back across the bridge, but failed. Maxentius, along with thousands of others, was shoved over the edge of the bridge and drowned.

So perished Constantine's fourth adversary. Now there were just two.

The next day, October 29, Constantine and his army marched triumphantly through the open gates into Rome. Someone had fished Maxentius's body out of the river, and they carried his head into the city, waving it back and forth atop a spear. The Roman Senate declared Constantine to be augustus, emperor of the West, and senior to Licinius, although Constantine was the younger man. Licinius was certain to resent this demotion, but for now, he and Constantine had an uneasy truce, to be cemented by the planned marriage of Licinius and Constantine's half-sister.

Meanwhile, Daia, Constantine's other remaining enemy, was not doing well in his sorties against Licinius and others. He had lost a battle with the king of Armenia, and his territories were ravaged by plague in the years 312 and 313. He began to fear that the God of the Christians might be behind his misfortunes, and he reluctantly relaxed his anti-Christian policies.

Their battle shields newly adorned with the Chi-Rho that Constantine had received by vision, the emperor's troops rout their opposition. The scene is the Milvian bridge over the Tiber River just north of Rome, which stands only slightly altered today (above). Maxentius, rival to the imperial throne, would die on the bridge, leaving clear for Constantine the road into Rome. With Constantine would go his new battle ensign and standard, proclaiming the words he had been given not long ago: "Conquer by this!"

Clearly, the Battle of the Milvian Bridge—and the perceived intervention of Christ, who had clearly granted Constantine his victory—changed the new emperor's life. The Christian God had deigned to favor him personally; he considered that fact undeniable. So he took the Christians under his wing and became their aggressive protector.

Even before the battle, writes Eusebius, Constantine had ordered a goldsmith to fashion a golden version of the army standard, which he called the *Labarum*, with a crossbar and a jewel-encrusted Chi-Rho. And over the next few years, he launched a massive construction and legislative program to further the Christian cause.

Of far more immediate significance to Christians, however, was a proclamation, drafted by Constantine in 313, that was designed to put an end, once and for all, to official Roman persecution—not only of Christianity, but of all religious practice, and not only in the West but in the East as well. Constantine was able to persuade Licinius, emperor of the East, to sign the document when the two met in Milan in February 313 to celebrate Licinius's wedding to Constantia.

The Edict of Milan, as Constantine's proclamation came to be called, pivotally changed the status of Christians. For the first time since the year 64, when the emperor Nero had declared war on the Christians of Rome and burned them as human torches in his garden, there were grounds for Christian optimism. Perhaps they need no longer fear official reprisals for holding to their faith. For more than two centuries, Christian spokesmen had pleaded for full religious

toleration. Now it might be a reality—no more demands to offer the pinch of incense to the gods, no more tortures with the rack and the red-hot irons, no more burnings and crucifixions, no more lions in the arena, no more mutilations, or deportations to the imperial mines. High hopes had been crushed before, of course, but maybe Christians would finally be free to practice their faith on equal terms with the pagans.

History has preserved the Edict of Milan in the form of a letter by Licinius to the governors of the provinces of the East, where Christians had suffered at Daia's hands.[1] The letter (as quoted by the historian Lactantius) declares: "No one whatsoever should be denied the opportunity to give his heart to the observance of the Christian religion, or that religion which he should think best for himself, so that the Supreme Deity, to whose worship we freely yield our hearts, may show in all things His usual favor and benevolence."

The letter continues: "Now any one of these who wishes to observe the Christian religion may do so freely and openly, without molestation." Of equal importance and more immediate practical consequence, the edict also required the Roman authorities to return to the Christians all property that had been confiscated from them, and all seized Christian churches were to be restored.

The edict did not formally make Christianity the official religion of the empire; it merely offered to place Christianity on a par with the other religions that enjoyed freedom under Rome, in order "that we may not seem to detract from any dignity or any religion." Constantine had to be careful not to alienate the pagans who still formed the vast majority of the empire, especially those in the army, which adored him, but had no sympathy for the Christ he was promoting; and in the Roman aristocracy, on whose support the new emperor depended and who still expected sacrifices to be made to the pagan gods.

Yet it became increasingly clear that Christianity enjoyed Constantine's special favor. Gradually, the old pagan influences began to fade from Constantine's administration. As time passed, he ceased paying the traditional homage to Jupiter on Rome's Capitoline Hill, and ceased striking coins bearing the images of other pagan deities. The Edict of Milan marked the beginning of a new Roman Empire, that before the end of the fourth century would become Christian, not pagan. No wonder Eusebius called the edict the "perfect and thoroughly detailed law on behalf of the Christians."

1. Historians in recent years have concluded that the long-cited Edict of Milan was not an edict at all, but rather an agreement between Licinius and Constantine preserved in the form of Licinius's letter.

That spring of 313, Licinius won a decisive victory against Daia at Adrianople in Thrace (in the southern Balkans), and marched eastward in triumph into Nicomedia. Daia fled and was captured at Tarsus, where he was forced to commit suicide. For Constantine, there was just one rival left, a big one: his new brother-in-law, Licinius, now sole emperor of the East, the empire's larger and richer half.

The showdown started about 314, when Constantine and Licinius began to quarrel over the appointment of new caesars, and Constantine had one of Licinius's nominees executed for treachery. Licinius in turn ordered Constantine's statues knocked down in the town of Emona in Pannonia—the

The edict pivotally changed the status of Christians. For the first time since 64, when Nero had burned them as human torches, there were good grounds for optimism.

equivalent of a declaration of war. Constantine, flushed with a victory in Gaul against the barbarian Franks, promptly marched his army eastward into Licinius's territory. The invasion was hugely successful. At Cibalae, near Sirmium in Pannonia, he won a major battle against Licinius's numerically superior troops, and when it was over he held control of all of Licinius's eastern European holdings, including Pannonia, Dalmatia and Greece—except Thrace.

Temporarily, the pair reconciled. But in 321, Constantine appointed his sons, Crispus by Minervina and Constantine Junior by Fausta, to be consuls, Rome's supreme military and civil magistrates, without seeking Licinius's consent. That heightened the tension, and soon Licinius turned against the Christians within his jurisdiction. Though he did not revoke the Edict of Milan, he began hounding the followers of Christ, forbidding Christians to assemble or worship within the cities. Bishops were arrested and executed, and some churches were demolished.

The most memorable Christian victims of Licinius were a company of Roman soldiers stationed at Sebaste in Lesser Armenia (see map, page 131, F3) who had openly confessed their faith before the Roman prefect. They were ordered stripped naked and left to freeze to death on the surface of a frozen pond. Of the forty, only one yielded and made his way to the warm baths near the lake that the prefect had prepared for any who would apostatize. One of the guards set to watch over them is said to have seen a brilliant light over the dying men. Shedding his garments, he joined them, returning their total number to forty. At daybreak, any of the stiffened bodies that still showed signs of life were burned and the ashes cast into the river. The Christians collected the remains of the other men, and their relics were distributed far and wide to Christian churches. They are known to Christian history as "the Forty Martyrs of Sebaste."

Another victim was a Roman general, exposed as a Christian in Thrace in 319. He was brought before a military tribunal and reprieved as a good soldier

In a last gasp of persecution before his defeat by Constantine, Licinius ordered that all Christians be purged from the ranks of his armies. One of the most famous of the consequent martyrdoms resulted, as forty Christian members of the great "Thundering Legion" were condemned to die on the ice of a pond in the frigid Armenian winter.

who had made a mistake. Set free, he promptly burned down a pagan temple, was rearrested and ordered to recant his Christianity. When he refused, he was flailed, then burned to death. He is known as Theodore the General, sometimes called Theodore the Recruit or Theodore Tyro.

To Constantine, such actions as these justified war, not a mere war of succession, as against Maxentius at the Milvian Bridge, but a full-fledged holy war on behalf of the Christian God. Constantine summoned Christian bishops to aid him, had a tent equipped as his portable chapel, and awarded the gold-covered Labarum with its Chi-Rho the place of honor as the primary standard of his troops. Licinius, for his part, decided to represent the old gods, surrounding himself with pagan priests and soothsayers, and making traditional sacrifices. According to Eusebius, he swore that if he defeated Constantine, he would do his best to exterminate the "atheists," as he called the Christians throughout the empire. The fate of Rome, whether it was to be Christian or pagan, thus lay in the balance.

In 324, the two imperial armies assembled. Constantine was, as usual, outnumbered by Licinius's infantry, cavalry, and vastly superior fleet. On July 3, Constantine, taking the initiative, engaged Licinius at Adrianople, and his seasoned and superbly disciplined veterans, bearing the Labarum in their midst, chased Licinius and his army out of the city. Licinius retreated to the seaside city of Byzantium, at the easternmost end of Thrace, and facing Asia Minor on the Straits of Bosporus, with his navy protecting the Dardanelles. There, Constantine's son, Crispus, who had been placed in charge of his father's fleet, dealt him a decisive blow, sinking nearly half of Licinius's ships.

Licinius and his remaining forces retreated again, crossing the Bosporus to the town of Chrysopolis. But it was already all over for him. On September 18, 324, Constantine's army resoundingly defeated his troops once more. Licinius fled to Nicomedia and sent his wife, Constantia, to her half-brother, to plead for his life. Constantine would have none of this. He did not want another Maximian on his hands, scheming treacherously to get his old title back. Licinius, his final and most formidable rival, was executed.

Constantine was now master of the Roman world. His life had come full circle. The last time he had seen Nicomedia, which lay only about one hundred miles east of Chrysopolis and Byzantium, had been when he galloped out of the city with Galerius's riderless horses behind him, to save his life, some eighteen years earlier. Now all the empire was his. He would settle in Byzantium, renaming it Constantinople, rebuilding and adorning it with treasure as a new Rome, capital of the East. Historians, Christian and non-Christian, would argue

With the last of his foes, Licinius (below), defeated, Constantine assumed the mantle of sole emperor of the Roman Empire. The reverse side of a coin minted at this point in his career shows him dealing brutally with his enemies, while on the coin's other side he lifts his face in prayerful contemplation—to what or whom is unclear. He wears the Greek symbol of royalty, the diadem, not the Roman laurel wreath.

from that time forward over the origins and depth of Constantine's Christianity. Had it all begun with the vision before the Battle of the Milvian Bridge? Was he ever really Christian? Or had he been a believer all his life?

Had he indeed been exposed to Christianity as a child? Some historians believe that he had been, among them the University of Toronto's T. G. Elliott, who holds that both Constantius and Helena were Christians, keeping their faith secret while teaching it to their son. He cites significant evidence. For one thing, Constantius had largely declined to enforce Diocletian's persecution edict in Britain and Gaul. He had knocked down a handful of churches, to be sure, so as

To Constantine, such actions as these justified war, not merely a war of succession, as at the Milvian Bridge, but a full-fledged holy war for the Christian God.

not to call down the displeasure of Diocletian or of Maximian, another enthusiastic persecutor of Christians. But Constantius had refused to arrest, much less punish, any Christians at all. True, Constantine's mother, Helena, was with her son when he married Fausta at Trier, and it was only then, or shortly thereafter that she openly professed the Christian faith. But she might have been a Christian all along.

Constantine himself had given no previous indication that he knew very much about Christianity. It is far more probable that he, like most semi-educated pagans of his time, worshiped a panoply of gods, but regarded them all as manifestations of one supreme God. Along with many of his contemporaries, he would have identified that one God with the unconquered Sun—Sol Invictus— whose feast day was December 25 (a date the Christians later took over as Christmas) and whose shining image appeared on Constantine's coins for many years. From Sol Invictus, it seemed only a short mental step to the God of the Christians and Jews.

In any event, one thing makes the Milvian Bridge incident seem pivotal. After the battle, when he entered Rome in triumph, when the Senate and the whole populace greeted him exuberantly, he ordered a statue of himself placed in the busiest part of the city. He instructed that in his hand be placed a spear in the form of a cross, with an inscription declaring by this sign had the city been delivered. In persistently pagan Rome, this would not have been widely appreciated.

Now the whole Roman Empire belonged to him. But as he saw it, it also belonged to the Christian God. So one of his first acts after his victory over Licinius was to proclaim the empire Christian—in fact, a vast Christian church of which he, Constantine, was protector and leader. "My kingdom is not of this world," Jesus said, but for the moment anyway, it was. ∎

The birth of Christian Britain

Though the traces of the faith are scanty in Rome's most northern province, the convert Alban's martyrdom for trying to save a priest is sound history

No one knows exactly when or how Christianity came to Britain to take its place among many competing religions and pagan cults (including the "elves of hills, brooks, standing lakes and groves," described in Shakespeare's *The Tempest*). In fact, we know less about the introduction and spread of Christianity in Britain than in many other parts of the Roman Empire.

Legends abound. The most romantic of them concerns Joseph of Arimathea, the Sanhedrin member whom Mark's Gospel calls Jesus' "secret disciple" ("a good and just man," Luke adds). According to all four Gospels, Joseph begged Pilate's permission to inter the crucified body of Jesus in his own garden tomb.

Apocryphal sources and some early Christian traditions say that Joseph first cared for Mary, Jesus' mother, and then set out with a small band of followers carrying the Holy Grail (the chalice used at the Last Supper) and came to Britain. Thirty years after the Crucifixion, Joseph is supposed to have built a rudimentary chapel at what later became Glastonbury Abbey (where he is still the patron saint).

Alas, romance must yield here to two intractable facts: one, the legend did not exist prior to the thirteenth century; two, the story derives more from literary than religious sources.

Thriving Christian communities did exist in Britain in the fourth century, however. Sensational confirmation surfaced in 1975, at Water Newton in Huntingdonshire, when a man discovered, in a cultivated field, a treasure trove of Christian artifacts including dated gold coins in a lidded pottery jar. Among other items in what scholars called the Water Newton Treasure was a silver communion chalice, the earliest discovered in the West.

About 340, a portrait of a young, beardless Christ was incised in a stone mosaic later found in a field at Hinton St. Mary, in Dorset (see page 68). Incidentally, the absence of crosses among these early Christian artifacts has led some scholars to speculate that the cross had not yet come into use as a popular Christian symbol.

But on the whole, there is little evidence of Christians in Britain much before the year 300. True, two early church fathers (Tertullian and Origen) boasted that Christianity extended to the furthest reaches of the Roman Empire; in this context, they mention *Brittaniae*, but most scholars treat this not as history but hyperbole.

Nor is there evidence of church buildings in Britain before the fifth century. Worshipers met together outside or in private homes. The first organized dioceses are believed to have been in York and Lincoln. Records show that three impoverished British bishops attended the Council of Arles in 314.

Were Christians subject to martyrdom in Roman Britain? This question, too, is open to scholarly debate. According to a British monk named Gildas (c. 490–570), they were. Gildas wrote of "the nine-year

Discovered in 1975 by a plowman in Water Newton, England, this cup may be a chalice. Vessels and plaques found with it may be the earliest liturgical silver from the Roman Empire yet found.

Although it looks as fresh as if it were far more recent, the mural in the Roman villa at Lullingstone, England, was actually painted in the early fourth century.

Some of England's cities trace their history to Roman settlements and have grown up around early Roman monuments. The city of Bath (above) takes its name from a well-preserved local Roman spa. A man (right) strolls along the Roman wall at Oxford.

persecution by the tyrant Diocletian."

The most comprehensive history of the early church in Britain was written by an eighth-century British monk, the Venerable Bede. His *The History of the English Church and Nation*, which drew upon Gildas, was completed in the year 731.

Bede vividly describes the first British martyr, St. Alban (died c. 304), a pagan living in Verulamium (now St. Albans), who gave sanctuary in his home to a priest fleeing the Roman authorities. After observing how the priest prayed night and day, and put his complete confidence in God, Alban became a convert. In Bede's words, "he forsook the darkness of idolatry and became a wholehearted Christian."

When the Roman authorities received a tip that Alban was sheltering the priest, soldiers were dispatched to Alban's home; but Alban exchanged clothes with the priest so that the soldiers arrested Alban instead. He was brought before a judge who happened, at that moment, to be offering sacrifices to pagan gods. The judge commanded Alban to do likewise. Alban refused and declared himself a Christian; the judge ordered him tortured.

"Though subjected to the most cruel tortures, Alban bore them patiently and even joyfully for the Lord's sake," Bede writes. The judge then ordered Alban executed. He was taken first to the river to be drowned, but as Alban entered the waters, they parted before him, as once they had parted for Moses.

"On seeing this miracle, Alban's executioner threw away his sword, fell to the ground, and "earnestly prayed that he might be judged worthy to be put to death with the martyr." Both men were then taken to a nearby field and beheaded. In a final miraculous twist, Bede records that "the head of the blessed martyr and the executioner's eyes fell to the ground together." Thereafter, Alban became "Saint Alban, illustrious Alban, fruitful Britain's child."

Also believed to have been martyred at about the same time as Alban were St. Julius and St. Aaron, whose feast days are still observed in South Wales. According to Bede, "They were racked by many kinds of torture and their limbs were indescribably mangled, but when their sufferings were over, their souls were carried to the joys of the heavenly city."

After the decade of Diocletian's persecution ended, Bede says Christians emerged from "woods, deserts and secret caverns," where they had been hiding and continued to proclaim the gospel.

Their lives, indeed the lives of all inhabitants of Roman Britain, were (in Thomas Hobbes's pithy phrase) "solitary, poor, nasty, brutish and short." ■

Constructed in 121 to keep out the fierce Caledonians, Hadrian's wall (left) still stretches across the pastures and fields of Northumberland. Farther south, a Roman outpost (top) guards Hardknott Pass in the Lake District. At what is now Wroxeter (above), a garrison town evolved into Viroconium, fourth largest city in Roman Britain.

Like most of Constantine's grand churches, Old St. Peter's in Rome fell victim to redevelopment. A fresco in the present basilica (above) shows a cross-section of the original. The bust of the emperor from his glory days (right) is now in the Louvre in Paris.

CHAPTER 6

It's a whole new era with a whole new peril

An overnight convulsion changes the Christians from outcasts to men of distinction, wealth and power, facing utterly novel problems

For the Christians who lived anywhere in the Roman Empire in the second and third decades of the fourth century—and that included nearly all Christians—the world had suddenly turned right-side-up. Gone was the threat of imminent execution, which had been a lifelong reality for many. No longer did they have to dread public humiliation or slave labor in the salt mines or clothing factories. No longer need they glance back over their shoulders every time they walked down a street. The chill fear of sword, crucifixion, fire and wild beast, which had haunted them on and off for centuries, soon faded from living memory. They were free.

In fact, they were more than free. Their faith, instead of sabotaging their social standing, now elevated them to positions of importance and power. Suddenly the doors to financial prosperity and ownership of the best land swung open wide. Benefits enjoyed by senators, soldiers, veterans and scholars became available to the Christian clergy. Almost overnight, the villains became the builders of the world's greatest empire; the subversives had come out of hiding to run it.

That this astonishing transformation occurred so rapidly was no accident. Constantine pushed for it aggressively. To be sure, he recognized the religious

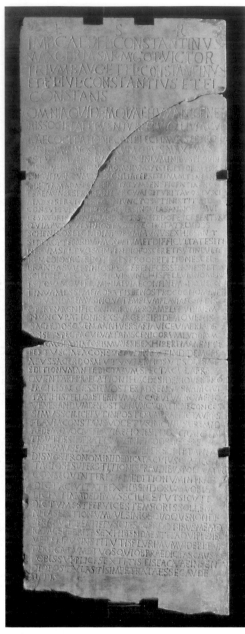

At the beginning of the fourth century, Constantine seemed tolerant of "old religion" of Rome. He granted the city of Spello in northern Italy the privilege of erecting a temple in honor of his family, and the right to celebrate an annual feast in the temple. The tablet inscribed with the edict is proudly preserved by the citizens.

demographic when he took the reins of the empire into his hands: In the West, ninety percent of the population was still pagan, and paganism was woven into the fabric of all of the empire's institutions and customs. But immediately and without unduly upsetting the religious status quo, Constantine began to institute legal and administrative changes, codifying the new freedoms and powers of the Christians that would transform the empire unrecognizably in the years ahead.

However, Constantine was not advancing his Christian agenda in the role of an evangelist. He was preeminently an emperor, and he well knew that only if his realm were unified could it survive. In the days of the old republic, religion had been a powerful force for unity. It must be so again, and the religion he chose to do it with was Christianity.

The Roman government had always been responsible to maintain the *Pax Deorum*, to make sure the gods showered their goodwill on the empire. Thus emperors maintained the cults, especially the imperial cult, and when the gods showed signs of displeasure, the emperors took appropriate steps to placate them. But Constantine no longer believed in pagan religion, let alone that it could unify the empire. He said pagans would not have lost the war against him if their oracles had been true. Worse, he called paganism a devilish deception.

Instead, the newly converted Constantine assumed he had the blessing of the highest divinity. God, he believed, had chosen him and raised him to power to create a Christian empire. It would be a delicate task, but he was convinced the state above all must now support the Christian church and those social and moral principles the church represented. He "enacted many laws for the honor and consolidation of religion," writes the fifth-century church historian Sozomen. To view the reality behind that simple summation, however, is to behold a building and legislative program of staggering dimensions.

Constantine immediately ordered that Christians who had been banished should be permitted to return to their homes. Those who had been sentenced to hard labor in the mines, or weaving and dying works, were released. Christian soldiers who had been stripped of their military ranks for refusing to offer incense to caesar were offered the choice of returning to their previous station, or receiving permanent immunity from public duties.

Next, he showered an array of privileges on the Christian clergy. One of his first acts was to grant them immunity from municipal obligations. This was no mere release from trivial obligation. These civic duties were a great burden under the later empire, entailing heavy personal expenses for those who fulfilled them. Pagan priests and scholars always had been exempted. Now Constantine extended this privilege to the Christian clergy, freeing them to do what Constantine believed they should be doing. Or as he put it, that "without any disturbance, they [may] serve their own law, since the conduct of the greatest worship of the Divinity will, in my opinion, bring immeasurable benefits to the commonwealth."

On a vast floor, symbols of faith

A rediscovered mosaic and its stunning images depict early Christianity's crucial themes for a community of believers who trace their roots back to St. Mark

The port city of Aquileia, established by Rome in 181 B.C. as a stronghold on the river Natissa in northeastern Italy, was evangelized in A.D. 57–58 by St. Mark, according to tradition. By the fourth century its Christian population had grown large enough to merit construction of a basilica, which included a seventy-five hundred-square-foot mosaic floor covered with symbolic images—the conflict between light and darkness, for example, depicted in a rooster-tortoise fight. The basilica was restored several times, and its spectacular pavement, the largest intact early Christian mosaic floor in Western Europe, was rediscovered in the twentieth century.

Bishop Theodore, who directed construction of the original basilica at Aquileia, is remembered in one of the building's splendid floor mosaics (below). The present building (right) is a Romanesque replacement of the first church.

The capitals on the basilica's columns are unique departures from both Greek and Roman styles.

As elsewhere in Christian art of the period, the Good Shepherd is prominently featured in the mosaics at Aquileia.

Whimsical elements such as this lobster are found in mosaics at the Aquileia basilica, along with more traditional religious themes.

Striking in its simple beauty, the basilica in Trier looks much as it did when erected by Constantine in 313. What was originally a civic assembly hall, which was dwarfed by the imperial palace attached to it, is now a Protestant church. The soaring height of the building, nearly 100 feet, is made possible even without buttressing by walls that are eleven feet thick.

But he went further, slowly conferring, not just privilege, but power on the Christian hierarchy. He ordered that court cases begun before an ordinary court could be transferred to the local bishop, even up to the last minute. The bishop's decision would be final, and local civil authorities were to execute the bishop's ruling. Then, to support the high regard for celibacy and continence among Christians, especially among the clergy, he rescinded the clauses of Augustus's centuries-old *Lex Papia Poppaea*, which had penalized those who remain unmarried or childless.

To legal benefits he added financial benefits. He opened both state and private coffers. Setting an example in Rome, he returned property (consisting mainly of cemeteries) to twenty-five churches in the city, then made donations to them from his private funds. He also gave the current bishop, Miltiades, the winter residence of his wife, the Empress Fausta—the palace on the

Lateran Hill that would remain the palace of the bishops of Rome for a thousand years. He ordered provincial governors not only to permit Christians to worship but to subsidize with state funds "the Catholic Church of the Christians." A law of the year 321 allowed Romans to make unrestricted bequests to the church. This, coupled with the rising popularity of all things Christian and the increasing number of wealthy converts, brought a steady stream of gifts and legacies to the church.

Perhaps the most precious gift, and certainly the most symbolic, was an order Constantine made, as his new capital Constantinople, was being built. He told his friend and biographer, Bishop Eusebius of Caesarea, to have fifty great Bibles made in finely bound volumes and distributed to the churches. Many Christians in the last persecution had heard the ugly knock on the door, and the soldier's demand for copies of the Christian Scriptures. Many copies had been handed over, under threat of death. Many had been piled and burned—manuscripts that had taken months to copy, pages filled with the words of life, words that gave instruction and hope to the fledgling movement. Many times had Christians huddled together and wondered whether all their Scriptures were doomed to the ashes. Now the tide had turned. The empire itself was ordering the manufacture of the Bibles, magnificent Bibles at that, and all at state expense. How things had changed.[1]

Nearly all Roman emperors considered themselves builders, each seeking to leave a legacy in wood, brick and stone. But no emperor surpassed Constantine's ambitions or accomplishments, writes University of Toronto classicist T. G. Elliott, who calls him "the greatest builder of all Roman Emperors." Like the others, he built secular buildings—baths, mausoleums, arches, state banquet halls, aqueducts, fortifications and so on. But his greatest architectural bequests to posterity were his churches, the

---

1. Constantine's present of fifty Bibles for the churches was a gift not only to the Christians of that day, but to Western civilization generally. It is possible that the two great biblical manuscripts of the fourth century, the *Codex Vaticanus* (now in the Vatican) and the *Codex Sinaiticus* (now in the British Library), originated in Bishop Eusebius's scriptorium at Caesarea as a result of the emperor's order.

Basilicas built in the early Constantinian era and still functioning as places of Christian worship are rare. The Ekatontapiliani (100 Gates) cathedral on the Greek island of Paros (left), and the church and baptistery in Poitiers, France (right), are two of these exceptional structures.

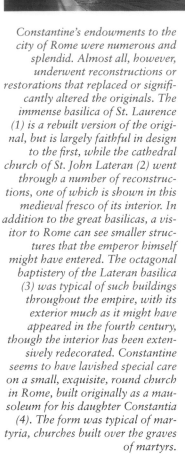

Constantine's endowments to the city of Rome were numerous and splendid. Almost all, however, underwent reconstructions or restorations that replaced or significantly altered the originals. The immense basilica of St. Laurence (1) is a rebuilt version of the original, but is largely faithful in design to the first, while the cathedral church of St. John Lateran (2) went through a number of reconstructions, one of which is shown in this medieval fresco of its interior. In addition to the great basilicas, a visitor to Rome can see smaller structures that the emperor himself might have entered. The octagonal baptistery of the Lateran basilica (3) was typical of such buildings throughout the empire, with its exterior much as it might have appeared in the fourth century, though the interior has been extensively redecorated. Constantine seems to have lavished special care on a small, exquisite, round church in Rome, built originally as a mausoleum for his daughter Constantia (4). The form typical of martyria, churches built over the graves of martyrs.

most visible witness to his Christian program.

The form these usually took was that of the basilica, the large, multi-purpose public hall the Romans usually erected at public squares. Constantine used this form to fulfill a new function. To his architects, the basic basilica design seemed a perfect setting for Christian worship. Thus a typical Constantinian basilica was oblong, usually with side aisles set off from a central nave by arched colonnades. High up in the building, the colonnades supported a brick wall whose windows filtered light to the nave below. The roofs were normally flat and made of wood—the great vaulted ceilings of earlier Roman buildings seeming too pagan, too ostentatious for Christian worship. Besides, they would have distracted attention from the nave, which directed worshipers' eyes toward the semicircular front of the basilica, known as the apse, in which stood the altar.

The effect was astonishing. Typically, light streamed through the nave windows, bathing the congregation in an island of brilliance surrounded by shadows. Increasingly, paintings, mosaics, jeweled robes and precious metal objects (donated to churches by wealthy patrons) magnified the impression. The fourth-century Christian poet Prudentius describes the effect of one basilica whose "ceilings with gilded beams make the whole chamber seem like a sunrise. In the windows glows stained glass, so that they look like fields studded with gorgeous flowers."

The church of St. Clement in Rome allows visitors to travel back through three layers of history. The twelfth-century basilica (above) was built over the fourth-century Constantinian church, which in turn covered ancient buildings including a Mithraic shrine. It is still noteworthy in that the plan, with its distinctive central choir and pulpit, is faithful to the layout of many of the churches of Constantine's time.

Though the city of Rome remained largely pagan in Constantine's day, he did his best to adorn it with Christian churches, including at least six in and around Rome. Most lay outside the city walls, but there were two great exceptions. One was the Lateran Basilica, which he erected next to the palace he had given Bishop Miltiades. Originally dedicated to the Savior and later to John the Baptist and John the Evangelist, it took the endowment of twenty-nine estates to finance it. It had a lofty apse, silver statues of Jesus, and a silver screen with images of the Resurrected Christ between four angels. The apse and sacristy, the adjoining room where the vessels of the Eucharist were kept and where the priests robed, contained seven golden altars, 115 chandeliers and sixty gold and silver candlesticks. It was the first large Christian ecclesiastical building and was proclaimed by the Roman Christians as "the mother and head of all churches."[2]

St. Peter's, the other great church within the city, is considered by many to be the most remarkable. Begun in 332, it was both a basilica and martyrium, built on the site where Peter is believed to have met his death.[3] Like St. John's, it overflowed with precious objects, furnishings, and rich materials of all kinds. Another church built by Constantine, named "Holy Cross in Jerusalem" (though the church, in fact, is in Rome), contained precious relics including, it was said, a part of the True Cross donated by Helena, Constantine's mother, which she had uncovered in the Holy Land (see sidebar page 247).

However, Constantine certainly did not confine his attention to Rome. He wanted to make the entire empire a holy land like Palestine, and he built grand churches in towns small and large nearly everywhere. In Antioch, for example, the lofty Golden Octagon, next to the imperial palace on an island in the River

2. The Lateran Basilica is the oldest of the four great "patriarchal" basilicas of Rome. In ancient times, the site was occupied by the palace of the Laterani, a prominent family. Constantine must have given the Lateran Palace to the Church in the time of Pope Miltiades. A council concerning the Donatists met there in 313. Later, members of the adjoining Benedictine monastery of St. John the Baptist and St. John the Evangelist maintained the services. To this day it is the cathedral of Rome. It was sacked by the Vandals in the fifth century, restored by Leo the Great around 460, and all but destroyed by an earthquake in 896. It burned down in 1360 but was rebuilt. Throughout all of these renovations, it retained much of its ancient form, but restorative work commissioned by Innocent X in the seventeenth century resulted in significant changes to its appearance.

Notwithstanding the splendor of the other great churches he founded in Rome, Constantine's most important endowment was the vast basilica that replaced humbler structures marking the spot of Peter's death and burial. The round structure was the saint's martyrium, the chapel marking the place of his entombment. The obelisk (left) had stood at the Vatican racetrack, the place of the apostle's death, but was moved to be near the tomb.

Orontes, was named the Church of Concord. In Tyre, Eusebius of Caesarea describes the lavish church there—the earliest portrayal we have of a Christian church. But beyond the ornamentation, Eusebius saw something larger, something that was happening inside Christians and inside the church as a result of his emperor's efforts: "A mighty, breathtaking wonder is this [cathedral], especially to those who pay attention only to externals. But far more wonderful are the archetypes or divine patterns of material things: I mean the renewal of the spiritual edifice in our souls."

Constantine's ambitions went with him to the grave unfulfilled—he died before he could see some of his greatest projects completed (like St. Peter's). Even while he lived, his ambition was greater than talent allowed: The empire simply did not have a sufficient number of gifted architects and engineers to properly erect the variety of projects he started, a lack he often complained about in his letters. The result was that within a generation of his death, many

---

3. In the fifteenth century, the Constantinian St. Peter's was demolished because it was falling down. Its reconstruction took more than a century, beginning in 1506, when Pope Julius II laid the first stone of the new church. The new St. Peter's was consecrated in 1626.

CONNOR

of the buildings were already falling into decay. Nonetheless, as classics expert Michael Grant puts it, "Constantine's prolific erection of Christian basilicas and other buildings . . . amounted to an architectural revolution."

However, Constantine did not think his Christian duty began and ended in monuments of stone. He sought also to reshape Roman society so that it would at least begin to reflect Christian principles. Given the numbers of pagans, he still needed them to run much of the state apparatus, but it quickly became clear that he favored Christians in his appointments. Ablabius, for example, whom some called the greatest of his Praetorian prefects, was a Christian of humble origins, and no doubt owed his advancement partly to the faith he shared with the emperor. Not only individuals but whole communities also ben-

Constantine's legislative program reflected a Christian bias. Criminals must not be branded on the face, nor fed to animals, but gladiatorial combat he could not stop.

efited if they were Christian. Thus the villagers of Orcistus in Phrygia, when they petitioned to separate from Nacoleia and be granted their own city charter, reminded Constantine that most of them were Christians. The emperor took favorable notice of this in his reply. The inhabitants of Maiuma, the Christian port of Gaza, and those of Antaradus obtained city status in the same way.

His legislative program vividly reflected the same Christian bias. In 316, he forbade the branding of convicts on the face. Echoing the words of Genesis 1, the face "is formed in the image of heavenly beauty," he said. Within another ten years, he ordered that criminals were no longer to be devoured by beasts or crucified. He also tried to outlaw gladiatorial contests, but their continued overwhelming popularity prevented it. They were to continue in the West for another century.

Several laws show Constantine's concern for the sanctity of marriage and his disapproval of irregular sexual relations. Though his reforms were highly acceptable to fourth-century Christians, those of the twenty-first century would shudder at their severity. He tightened the rules on divorce: Women were no longer allowed to repudiate their husbands, even for drunkenness, gambling or running after other women, but only for murder, poisoning or tomb robbery. Bastards were severely penalized, being denied all rights of inheritance from their fathers. Parents who had sold their daughters or been accessory to their seduction were similarly condemned.[4]

Though Christians as a whole still accepted slavery as a fact of economic life, they did insist on just treatment of slaves. This was reflected in many of Constantine's statutes. For example, he ordered that slave families were not to be

---

4. Constantine's prescribed punishments for criminal acts were notably uninhibited by the Christian virtue of mercy but rather reflected the ferocious penology of his times. For example, parents who prostituted their daughters must have molten lead poured down their throats. If a free woman and a male slave had sexual relations, both were put to death, the slave by being burned alive.

separated when an estate was broken up. The church was empowered to enact manumission when a slave had qualified for it, thereby avoiding bureaucratic processes that could long delay a slave's freedom. This delivered another message. People began to connect freedom with the church. Even so, Constantine's laws on the control of slaves remained much in line with those of the ancient world. A master was not necessarily liable to a charge of homicide if a slave died following a flogging or confinement in chains, but only if the master deliberately killed him or tortured him to death.

In one area, Constantine waged a futile campaign against the greatest curse of the declining empire—the corruption of the civil service. There was nothing that money could not obtain, and without money nothing could be obtained. Litigants could not gain admission to the law courts without greasing the palms of numerous officials, and the wealthy were able to get their cases transferred to friendlier courts if they gave the right people appropriate "gifts." Constantine deplored the system: "Let the rapacious hands of the officials forthwith refrain," he wrote in 331. "Let them refrain, I repeat: for unless after this warning they do refrain, they will be cut off by the sword." It seems, though, that the disgusted emperor found that he could do little more than remain disgusted. Bribery continued as a way of bureaucratic life.

One of Constantine's most lasting secular edicts shows how he balanced his Christian program with pagan realities. In March 321, he decreed that "all judges, city-people and craftsmen shall rest on the venerable day of the Sun," making an exception for farmers, "since it often happened that this is the most suitable day for sowing grain or planting vines, so that the opportunity provided by divine providence may not be lost, for the right season is short." His reasoning isn't specifically Christian, and he makes what seems to be a pagan reference in the process. But his choice of Sunday was no accident, since this was the day of worship for Christians. He also required his troops to say a generically addressed prayer on Sundays, so that, as Eusebius puts it, they "ought not rest their hopes on spears or armor or physical strength, but acknowledge the God over all, the giver of all good and indeed victory itself." Again, there was no specific Christian reference, but assuredly a Christian sentiment.

All these changes could not help but fill Christians with wonder. Eusebius, for example, described how believers felt about the new churches rising before them: "We who had hoped in Christ had inexpressible happiness, and a divine joy blossomed in all our hearts as we saw places that had, a little earlier, been laid waste by the tyrants' malice now reviving as if from a long and deadly injury and cathedrals rising again from their foundations to lofty heights." These changes soon began to fill the churches. Though it is extremely difficult to put specific numbers on it, Christians probably constituted ten percent of the western empire, fifty percent in the East, when Constantine was converted—perhaps 3.5 million believers. By the end of the fourth century over fifty percent of the western empire's inhabitants claimed Christianity as their faith, and the percentages were much higher in the East.

CONSTANTINE ON RELIGION AND STATE

When religion is despised, great dangers are brought upon public affairs; but when legally adopted and observed, it affords the most signal prosperity to the Roman name and remarkable felicity to all the affairs of men.

This became both a blessing and a curse. Many people converted because they were for the first time, able to give the Christian faith a fair hearing. They saw both paganism and Christianity for what they were, and they opted happily for the latter. At the same time, other pagans sensed which way the political winds were blowing. They discerned in Christianity, a sure path to imperial appointment and material reward. It's not surprising that churches soon were brimming with people, many of whom were there from any but spiritual motives.

This created enormous problems for priests and bishops as they strove to introduce thousands of clueless new believers to the intricacies of the Christian faith and practice. Standards simply had to be lowered, both for

> ## Many pagans sensed which way the winds were blowing. They discerned a sure path to imperial appointment and material reward. It's not surprising that churches soon were full.

church membership and for ordination, to keep up with the flood. Many old believers decried the new worldliness that soon became evident within the church. But what is amazing is not that the church lost some of its ardent devotion, but that it retained any at all, in the face of deep tensions produced by popularity, power and wealth.

The churches hardly knew what to do with the new infusion of wealth. It not only introduced greed and materialism into everyday church life, but it also undermined the traditional relationship between the clerics and people. The revenue from which the churches supported their clergy, maintained their buildings and distributed charity to the poor, had always come entirely from voluntary offerings from the faithful. But beginning with Constantine's reign, the old system of voluntary contributions fell into disuse. Clergy now gained their support from the income on church property, which accumulated rapidly, and from state funds. This soon produced a wall between laity and clergy, a wall that only grew higher in coming centuries.

Worse still, the new order of things created a dilemma that would plague the church for centuries: the proper relation of the church and the Christian emperor, or church and state, as later generations would define it. For the first three centuries of its existence, the church had settled its own disputes, hardly ever seeking outside authority because there was no such thing. Now, however, there was such authority. Constantine had ruled for just six months when the Donatists, a rigorist, schismatic sect, having failed in appeals to the bishop of Rome, and before two church councils, now appealed to the emperor (see sidebar page 169). In this instance, Constantine condemned the dissident group, tried persecuting them, quickly gave up when he saw that didn't work, then tolerated them.

For Constantine, it was a sobering lesson with wide implications. He learned, and would learn painfully thereafter, that uniting the empire behind a new religion

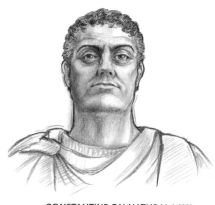

CONSTANTINE ON NATURAL LAW
I reckon that the divine power has been made clear to all, and that those who through fear or want of faith have fallen into sins, and have come to recognize That which really Is, will come to the true and right ordering of life.

was much more difficult than he had imagined. The Donatist affair also provided a foretaste of the awkward new relationship between church and state. Christian groups, it was to be repeatedly discovered, would appeal to the emperor, then protest against state interference if his decision went against them.

For the moment, however, Constantine was not confused in the least: "In matters of faith," he said, "my will is law." He adopted the role of universal bishop, thinking of himself as the final authority in religious as well as secular matters. At first, Christians hardly argued, and it meant that where major controversies divided the church, decisions were often shaped by the intrigues of the imperial court as rival parties tried to manipulate the emperor's support.

Constantine learns a lesson

In his first venture into Christian affairs, he cracks down hard on a dissident sect, meets total failure and leaves them to God

Christianity cannot and should not hide the fact that included among its faithful have been many individuals who mistakenly believed their own preoccupations to be those of the Lord, creating mayhem in the process. Few such characters in early Christianity are more colorful or more significant than the Donatists, who roiled the African church for well over two centuries.

The Donatist schism had its roots in the horrendous Diocletian persecution (303–305). Initially, the demands were that Christians give up their holy books; eventually, Christians were required to sacrifice to Roman gods. Those who succumbed to the pressures faced recrimination from other Christians, especially at the hands of a hard-line party formed in Numidia (southern Algeria), which would become known as the Donatists.

They claimed to have found in Bishop Cyprian of Carthage the only true model of grace under pressure: He had greeted his execution order with a shout of "Praise God!" Like Cyprian, this sect agreed that clergy who handed over Scripture—called *traditores*—must be banned from the church, and that any holy function performed by a traditor was null and void. "Whosoever consorts with the traditores will have no share with us in the Kingdom of Heaven," was their battle cry.

Their wrath soon turned against Mensurius, a successor bishop of Carthage. They especially reviled him for urging, along with his deacon Caecilian, that food parcels be denied a group of Christians who were jailed during the persecution. Mensurius argued that because smuggling food to prisoners was illegal, it would inspire further arrests. His motives were impure, however: He had learned that some of the prisoners were denouncing him, and perhaps the church as well, and he must have thought it would be better to leave them unfed. The storm broke in full after Mensurius died and was replaced, in 311–312, by Caecilian. Among those formally consecrating Caecilian's ascendancy was Felix of Aptunga. Because Felix was regarded as a traditor for handing over Scriptures, his presence at the ceremony made Caecilian's consecration null and void, critics charged.

Caecilian already had other troubles. He had earlier rebuked a woman named Lucilla for her odd habit of kissing a human bone—which, she said, was the relic of a martyr—during the Eucharist. Lucilla departed in a huff. But she was quite rich, and besides possessing an eccentric personality, she was capable of carrying a grudge to extremes. She now had her opportunity to repay the slight. With Lucilla's support, if not her outright financial backing (as some later alleged), Bishop Secundus of Numidia called a council of seventy African bishops in 312. They nullified the election of Caecilian, and they named in his place a man named Majorinus, who was apparently on Lucilla's payroll. The church was now split.

The schismatic (splinter) movement that pressed these events would take its name the next year from Donatus, who was elected as its leader, and who was by all reports an inspiring figure. He strongly believed that the church was not a school for repentant sinners, but was the refuge of the holy alone. "No mercy for sinners" was a Donatist maxim, one they applied especially to candidates

It would take another generation or two before the church as a body could begin exercising independence and exert some pressure on the emperor, though individual bishops and also dissident groups began resisting him from the outset. This reluctance to oppose him formally was partly due to the inchoate organization of the church itself, as well as its frequent internal dissensions. Bishops did not meet regularly, except at provincial synods. General councils could be called only by the emperor, who might summon them merely to endorse a decision he had already made. In the meantime, it was mainly the emperor's informal ecclesiastical advisers—like Eusebius, bishop of Nicomedia

for the priesthood. Right from the start, they made no fetish of mercy.

Constantine, strongly desiring to end this growing internecine dispute in the church, referred it to a council in Rome in 313. The charges were reviewed, and if Donatus had any hopes the assembled bishops would proclaim Donatism the true way, they were quickly shattered. Donatus was criticized for disturbing the discipline of the church and accused of creating outright schism. He and his followers rejected this finding with much vigor. Constantine, who could be very patient, called a synod at Arles the next year to revisit the evidence. This was a massive affair, with six hundred bishops present. Donatus received another sound drubbing (as did, for that matter, the sport of horse racing—banned; and the theatrical professions—excommunicated).

The Donatists responded with what had become their typical disdain. Constantine's patience was growing thin, but in July 315, he told the Donatists that if they could prove anything against Caecilian, he would treat it as if they had won the case. This they could not do, but neither would they be quieted. By 317, his patience had run out. Constantine exiled their leaders, and soldiers confiscated their property. Historian Henri Daniel-Rops calls this "the first time in history the sword was used in the name of Christ."

Donatus, to no one's surprise, raised an army of peasants and thugs from the mountainous regions. These recruits became known as *circumcellions* (circuit riders, rovers and marauders, who lived on those they tried to indoctrinate). They liked to call themselves "Captains of the Saints," and referred to the heavy clubs they wielded as "Israels." Many churches were attacked in Carthage; many clergy and laypeople perished. There was of course retaliation. At one time, imperial troops occupied the three Donatist basilicas at Carthage, and soldiers were accused of taking time from their official duties to rape Donatist women.

All of which had the result of strengthening the Donatist cause. The Donatists argued that they represented the common people and even slaves. Augustine would later comment, "What master was there who was not compelled to live in dread of his own slave, if the slave had put himself under the protection of the Donatists?" By May 321, Constantine—who was waging his military campaign against brother-in-law Licinius—concluded that his attempts to achieve unity were doomed. He granted tolerance, declaring he would leave the Donatists "to the judgment of God."

This was not the end of their story. Persecution renewed in 346–348; during this time, Donatus is believed to have perished. Many martyrs were created, including Maximian and Isaac, whose bodies were supposedly sunk by their jailers, yet somehow swam to shore, according to the Donatist version of events. There is no disputing the resilience of the group. It survived Constantine, and for a time was the predominant religion in North Africa, with three hundred bishops by some estimates, five hundred by others.

The movement began to collapse around 400; in January 412, the emperor Honorius exiled its clergy and confiscated Donatist property. The *circumcellions* responded with a new bloodletting, though all of that was rendered largely moot in 429, when the Vandals conquered North Africa and slaughtered Catholics and Donatists without distinction. Donatism finally died out in the Muslim conquest in the seventh century.

What is to be made of this bloody upheaval? There was a vital theological difference between the Donatists and the Catholics. The Donatists vehemently, sometimes violently, insisted that the validity of clerical functions, such as baptism, depended upon the character of the administrating clergyman, while the Catholics held that the validity of such functions was based on their endorsement by Christ. The same question—how to determine who is a worthy church member or leader and who is not—has been asked elsewhere, without bloodshed. ■

and later of Constantinople—who had the emperor's ear.

If Constantine's impact on the church was convulsive, much more convulsive was his impact on Rome. In effect he rendered the venerable old city obsolete. He did the unthinkable thing. He effectually displaced it as the imperial capital. In the fourth century Rome was still the formal and sentimental seat of the empire. It was the venue of the Senate, the ancient magistrates, the consuls, the praetors and the quaestors. Though all free inhabitants of the empire were "Romans," a citizen of Rome was considered "Roman" in a more esteemed sense.

It had been some time, however, since Rome had been the administrative capital. Emperors lived transient lives, visiting Rome only for brief periods between military and diplomatic campaigns. Each emperor had his favorite residence, where he preferred to conduct state business. Most recently, Diocletian had built himself a palace at Nicomedia, and his successors, Galerius and Licinius, had usually resided there. There was nothing new in an emperor's establishing a semi-official capital in some provincial city nor in an emperor's giving his name to a city. But no capital away from Rome took root as did Constantinople, the city Constantine built on the shores of the Bosporus (see map page 131, E3).

At the time, it was called Byzantium, founded in the second half of the seventh century B.C. by the Greeks. In about 150 B.C., it became a dependency of the Romans and soon after that the eastern terminus of the Via Egnatia, the main road from the Adriatic eastward. Constantine, like Septimius Severus before him, had occasion to lay siege to Byzantium, and his trained military eye

★ Constantinople

A satellite image looks west from the Black Sea to the Sea of Marmara, with Asia on the left and Europe on the right. Dividing the two continents (upper right) is the silver waterway of the Bosporus, the strategic site of the new capital of Constantine's empire. Constantinople became the bridge between East and West. It was approachable by land only on one side, and on this side Constantine and his successors built massive walls that made the capital virtually impregnable.

While his entourage looks on in disbelief (left), Constantine paces out the lengthy perimeter of his new imperial capital, Constantinople, "Constantine's City." Built around the rather unprepossessing city of Byzantium (in the distance), it was dedicated in 330 and a coin with the personification of the city was minted for the celebrations (below). The founder of New Rome was later commemorated in mosaic in the cathedral church of St. Sophia with a model of the city in his hands (above).

must have been impressed. It occupied a key position at the crossroads between central Asia and Europe; it afforded easy access to the Balkan provinces, which played such an important role in the third and fourth centuries; from here, too, the eastern frontier could more readily be reached.

There may also have been personal, religious reasons for the move. Despite his building efforts, Rome remained saturated with pagan buildings and institutions. The senatorial aristocracy clung to their pagan ways; the altar and statue of Victory still stood in the senate house. The people of Rome, for their part, resented an emperor who pointedly omitted the sacrifices customarily made on state occasions. It seemed inevitable then that Rome would never become the

Like the old capital, Constantinople was built on seven hills. There was a senate, but its members ranked below those in Rome. As in Rome, the people received subsidized grain.

Christian capital of Constantine's dreams. Political and strategic considerations dictated the creation of a new capital elsewhere.

So on November 8, 324—a Sunday—Constantine formally laid out the boundaries of his new city, moving them more than two miles further out and roughly quadrupling its territory. According to the fifth-century historian Philostorgius, he traced the line of the future walls on the ground with a spear, in the manner of a Greek founder. The same historian reports that Constantine's companions were amazed at the vast circumference of the new walls. In less than a century, Theodosius II would double the territory of the city once again, and today it is the walls of Theodosius that still stand.

The building and populating of Constantinople were pushed forward with great speed. The emperor offered various incentives to people to settle there, especially if they were skilled in the building trades, and the new walls were completed by 328. In May 330, the new city was formally dedicated with elaborate rites in the Hippodrome. Coins minted that year announced the event to the world. On the obverse of these coins, the figure of Constantinopolis carries a cross scepter over her shoulder, thus emphasizing the Christian character of the city. Like the old capital, Constantinople was built on seven hills and divided into fourteen administrative districts. There was a senate, though its members ranked below the members of the senate in Rome. And like the people of Rome, the people of Constantinople received subsidized grain.

The new capital gave to Constantine an unparalleled opportunity for construction on a grand scale. He enlarged and embellished the existing Baths of Zeuxippos. In the area today occupied by the Mosque of Sultan Ahmed (the Blue Mosque), Constantine built the imperial palace and finished the Hippodrome (begun by Septimius Severus) while enlarging it to a capacity of fifty thousand. The Hippodrome served not only for the entertainment of the people but also for public acts of state, and in the center median the emperor placed the Serpent Column from Delphi (which commemorated the victory the

Constantinople's borrowed glories

His building program for the new capital was meant to create attractions rivaling those of Rome, so Constantine made good use of objects that had been snatched from other historic sites

Constantine had meant his new capital to rival the glories of Rome. But of the monuments and churches he constructed in Constantinople, few of the city's current tourist attractions can be traced to his building program. And even these objects had simply been snatched from existing buildings elsewhere. They frequently ended up in his hippodrome (racetrack), the general layout and location of which is still reflected in the vast open space in the heart of modern Istanbul (1). Among the booty that Constantine arranged along the course of the track was the curious Spiral Column (2) that he had brought from Delphi. In the forum of his new capital, Constantine erected an immense porphyry column, brought from the Apollo temple in Rome and crowned with a statue of the emperor. Originally nearly two hundred feet high, it was severely damaged by fire in the seventeenth century, hence its popular name, the Burnt Column (3). ■

Greeks had won in 479 B.C. at Plataea over the Persians). It was only one of many objects that Constantine appropriated to decorate his new city, a pillaging that caused St. Jerome to remark that "nearly all cities were stripped bare."

In front of the Old Gate of the Severan walls, Constantine built a forum that bore his name. Inside stood the Column of Constantine, nearly eighty feet tall and nearly ten feet wide at the base. The base contained an altar, so the Lord's Supper could be celebrated, and the column was crowned by a statue of Helios, its features adapted so as to represent Constantine—likely a reference to Constantine being Christ's representative on earth.

Constantinople became the heart of what continued to call itself the Roman Empire, though its people spoke Greek. It would stand unconquered for eleven hundred years.

Constantine also began the construction of at least two churches in Constantinople, the Church of the Holy Apostles which he cherished and the church known as *Hagia Eirene* (Holy Peace). Though work on a third church, *Hagia Sophia* (Holy Wisdom), also known as "the Great Church," was probably begun in 326, the dedication did not take place until 360 under Constantius II.[5] These three churches—*Hagia Sophia, Hagia Eirene* and the Holy Apostles—were to dominate the city politically and ecclesiastically for the next eleven centuries.

The founding of Constantinople had vast consequences, secular and religious. For one thing, it hastened the collapse of the Roman Empire in the West. Constantinople controlled all the wealthy provinces of Asia Minor and the East, which contributed the greater part of the imperial revenues. It also had easy access to the Illyrian provinces, which long remained the imperial army's best recruiting ground. Deprived of the East, the West simply didn't have the money or manpower to withstand the barbarian assault that was coming.

But Constantinople survived and became the heart of what continued to call itself the "Roman" Empire, though its capital was nowhere near Rome and its people spoke Greek, not Latin. Late in the fourth century and throughout the fifth and sixth, barbarian peoples would sweep through the West, devastating it and turning much of it into a wilderness. But Constantinople would stand unconquered for more than a millennium.

At the same time, Constantine was so lavish in spending—on the erection of new churches, maintenance of a sumptuous court, corn subsidies, and above all on the building and adornment of his new capital (on which he is said to have spent sixty thousand pounds—by weight—of gold)—he was forced to institute two new taxes. One of these was levied on the poor and proved extremely oppressive; all the authorities, Christian and pagan alike, agree in painting a lurid picture of the terrible distress that was caused when it

CONSTANTINE ON CONFLICT IN THE CHURCH

Often love becomes sweeter when it returns again in reconciliation after hostility is set aside.

---

5. The Church of Holy Wisdom was destroyed twice and finally replaced by Justinian with the building that stands today in Istanbul as the foremost monument of Byzantine architecture. After the conquest of Constantinople by the Muslim Turks in 1453, it became a mosque. In modern Turkey it has been a museum since 1935.

came time to collect these taxes. On the other hand, he also created a stable and abundant gold currency in issuing a gold coin, the solidus. It became the standard coin of the Byzantine Empire, and indeed of the Mediterranean world, for many centuries.

The pagan world in the East watched all these changes with a mixture of chagrin and fatalistic resignation. Though his model metropolis, Constantinople, did contain pagan temples, it was from the start an essentially Christian city, and there, as elsewhere in the East, relatively few pagans openly resisted Constantine's program.

But the Constantine era met with a very different response in the West, especially in Rome. Rome was the perfect urban setting for paganism and its many spectacular cults. Christianity at this stage could not compete with the massive celebrations that marked, for instance, the funeral feast of Attis on March 24. How could Christian worship hold attention against the *taurobolium* (blood-bath), the castration rites, the moaning crowds of flagellating penitents. Romans could watch miracle plays and wild dances, routinely accompanied, said Christian observers, by obscene acts and songs. The pageantry and color appealed to something deep in the Roman people.

At a higher social level, the solemn and ancient state rituals of the pagan Pontifical College, conducted in the superb surroundings of the temples whose history went back in some cases nearly a thousand years, appealed to Roman nostalgia, to patriotism, and to a longing for beauty and order that may never have been but was nevertheless remembered.

It is not surprising, then, that Constantine, in seeking to obliterate paganism, would direct his initial assaults on such externals. Where he had previously tolerated pagan temples, he now tore them down, as at Aphaca (Afqua) on Mount Lebanon, where the cult of Aphrodite had a well-earned reputation for licentiousness. At Aegae in Cilicia, the emperor's soldiers leveled the temple of Asclepius, the center of a popular healing cult. At Antioch the Temple of the Muses was diverted to secular purposes. He built many churches, like the Church of the Holy Sepulchre at Jerusalem and the basilica at Mamre, right on top of pagan shrines, which he destroyed in the process. At Heliopolis (Baalbek) in Phoenicia, he forbade the cult of Venus Heliopolitana, which included ritual prostitution, and ordered the construction of a church. In many provinces, the funds of pagan temples were confiscated and put in the imperial treasury.

A historian of a century later wrote of bands of Christian youths going from town to town, allegedly armed with letters from the emperor, ordering obedience to his decrees and browbeating the populace into abandoning their pagan priests. Statues were destroyed or paraded into the streets, and the people were cajoled and intimidated into ridiculing what their ancestors had venerated.

Nevertheless, such wanton vandalism and callous contempt was not typical

In the passing of a century, Christianity changed from an outlaw sect into the religion of the empire. Reflective of this transformation are these two coins. In the first (top) a Christian has dared to deface an imperial coin by scratching the symbol of Christ on it. In the second, minted at Amiens in France in the mid-fourth century, the Christian symbol is prominently displayed.

of Constantine's rule and was not widely practiced until the era of the Emperor Theodosius I later in the fourth century. While some pagan temples were destroyed by Constantine, many remained open. His law prohibiting the restoration of decayed temples was more typical of his approach. It's also noteworthy that there are no records of pagan martyrs under Constantine.

In fact, Constantine himself retained a few pagan superstitions. Whether they were a vestige of his pagan past or just a diplomatic gesture to seek the support of leading pagans is difficult to say. At any rate, we know he invited the neo-Platonist philosopher Sopater to his court and asked him to consult the

The birth of Christendom

By making Christian morality the basis of the law, Constantine launches a tradition that will endure until the late 20th century

The notion of Christendom—a political world in which Christianity enjoyed a privileged position—was slow to take shape, even after Constantine's Edict of Milan, issued in 313. Although the proclamation required complete religious toleration for Christians in the Roman Empire, it did not mandate any special preferences for them. And Constantine did not make Christianity the exclusive religion of the empire. It was not until after 380, under the emperors Theodosius I in the East and Gratian in the West, that pagan temples were closed, and all subjects of Rome were required to become orthodox Christians.

Nonetheless, from 313 onwards, Constantine gradually added the values of Christianity to the legal structure of the empire. He built Christian churches in Rome and elsewhere, made Sunday an official day of rest in 321, and enacted laws forbidding the use of magic and divination. Furthermore, as emperor, Constantine held the title Pontifex Maximus, or highest priest, with the duty of overseeing the Roman religion. After 313, he in effect promoted Christianity as the official faith of the empire. He assumed the authority, though he was unbaptized, to settle church disputes.

So it can be truly said that under Constantine, although the Christian hierarchy and the secular government remained separate entities, what has come to be known as "Christendom" began to emerge. And many of the reforms instituted by Constantine lasted for centuries, their effects so widespread that they linger within the memories of many people in the twenty-first century. There was until very recently an understanding among most people that Christian values underlie public institutions. Until late in the twentieth century, for example, many predominantly Christian countries and states enforced Sunday "blue laws" that forbade transacting business on the Lord's Day—precisely the same

in principle that Constantine had promulgated in 321.

In Christendom, human laws were believed to derive from God's Law, as revealed in the Ten Commandments.

In the ancient Roman world, abortion was widely practiced. Although Roman law punished abortion on the ground that it deprived a father of his children, only Jews and Christians considered the taking of an innocent unborn human life to be morally wrong in itself. It was only in the Christian Roman Empire, during the reign of the emperor Justinian in the sixth century, that the law began to prosecute abortionists severely.

With Christendom came the growth, as the centuries passed, of a Christian culture. Not only did Christian values receive legal support, but Christian belief permeated great art, literature and music, and engendered such customs of daily life as praying before meals or at bedtime. At the center of every Christian community was a Christian house of worship, whether a soaring cathedral or a simple wood-framed chapel. All this was possible because there was a sense of belonging to a society whose members knew that their rulers not only shared, but would protect Christian beliefs, and that the church was a school for citizenship.

From Constantine's day forward, however, a distinction was gradually made between the secular political world and the church. After all, Jesus himself had said, "Give to the emperor the things that are the emperor's, and to God the things that are God's" (Mark 12:17). Christian judges might preside in the law courts, but these officials were not to try to rule the church itself. Even Constantine's imperial title of Pontifex Maximus was eventually taken by the popes. Only rarely did the church attempt to become a secular authority. Instead, church and state existed side by side

A marble relief reflects the worldview of Christians in the early fourth century, before the ascendancy of Constantine altered it radically. Two lambs symbolize the faithful. They gaze up longingly at an empty throne (upon which a crown is laid) awaiting the return of their Lord.

in a sometimes amicable, sometimes uneasy, and occasionally violent relationship.

In the twentieth century, the pendulum swung to the side of the state, and the Catholic intellectual Richard John Neuhaus was one of hundreds of Christian voices, Protestant, Catholic and Orthodox, complaining about moral impoverishment in the "naked public square," from which religion largely has been banned by court fiat. Many public schools and governmental agencies nowadays hesitate to call the winter holiday Christmas, and schoolchildren who in earlier times might have been told to memorize the Ten Commandments have been reprimanded if they quote the Bible approvingly in their homework.

On the other hand, Christendom often discriminated against other religions, Jews especially, but even minority groups of Christians. At its worst, that discrimination could entail ghettoization, the loss of civil liberties, banishment, and even execution. When daily Bible-reading was common in U.S. public schools, the Bible selected was typically the King James Version used by Protestants, making Catholics, Orthodox Christians, Jews, and others uneasy. For these reasons, many Baptists and other conservative Christian groups that historically suffered persecution from other Christians have vigorously supported a hard-line separation of church and state.

As the third Christian millennium dawned, policy makers in both the church and the government continued to wrestle with their relationship to each other. For while there was much negative to be said about the Christendom that Constantine created, there was much good that would, after seventeen centuries, be lost. ∎

As paganism's fortunes waned, Christian communities simply moved into unused temples and refurbished them for their use. (Above) An image of Peter stands in a niche in the sanctuary of Ramses II, Egypt. Christians had once whitewashed the pharaonic reliefs now visible on the surrounding walls. (Right) The massive Rotunda at Thessaloniki, Greece, built as a mausoleum for the emperor Galerius, was turned into a church dedicated to St. George.

omens for a favorable day for the dedication of his new capital.

Still, by Constantine's day, pagan temples were increasingly viewed as public monuments to the past rather than centers of worship. By the time of his sons, paganism was visibly dying in the cities, though in the countryside it hung on tenaciously for a few centuries.

Another surviving religious phenomenon presented him with a somewhat different problem. Because of their rich tradition and exclusivity, the Jews had been regarded as an irritation by many emperors over the years. From the time of their first conquest of Judea, Romans in general harbored a lingering anti-Semitism. But as long as Jews did not challenge or offend the pagan status quo, the empire was happy to let them run their own affairs. However, now with a Christian emperor ascending the throne, things became more complicated. Constantine cared little about the Jewish attitude toward paganism but deeply about their relation to Christianity, a daughter religion that was also a direct rival in many ways—and often anti-Jewish as well.

Constantine inherited this Roman suspicion and antipathy to the Jews, and his Christianity intensified this feeling. He publicly denounced them for, as he said, "murdering the Lord." He enacted legislation that prevented Jews from owning Christian slaves or circumcising any slaves, and from proselytizing in general. Any effort to prevent a Jew from becoming Christian was forbidden by law. On the other hand, he allowed them greater access to the city of Jerusalem and extended to synagogue leaders immunity from municipal obligations, thus giving them equal status with Christian clergy.

Jewish converts to Christianity seemed especially worthy to him, so when he had the opportunity, Constantine liked to shower favors on the new convert. The historian Epiphanius tells of a certain Joseph, a highly respected member of the Jewish community and a disciple of the patriarch Ellel (whom Epiphanius described as hereditary head of all the Jews of the Roman Empire). Joseph spied Ellel being secretly baptized on his death bed and later discovered copies of the Gospels in Hebrew among Ellel's belongings. Scandalized, Joseph hid the Gospels to protect Ellel's reputation but became fascinated with them and was caught reading them. He was publicly whipped by his fellow Jews, who then attempted to drown him. Joseph escaped and became a Christian convert. Hearing the story, Constantine bestowed honors upon

him and an imperial pension. The grateful Joseph helped Constantine build churches in Galilee at Tiberias, Sepphoris, Nazareth and Capernaum. Prejudice there certainly was, but as with paganism, there is no record of Jewish martyrs under Constantine. Alas, this would not remain so in the future.

As to Constantine's own personal Christian commitment, that has been debated for nearly seventeen hundred years. One thing, however, is beyond debate. He laid the foundations of what came to be known as "Christendom," a society at least nominally based on the assumption that Christianity is *true*. In one form or another Christendom was destined to last for nearly a hundred generations. Constantine's contribution, however preliminary, remains remarkable. ∎

Christians of the fourth century apparently had no qualms about incorporating pagan motifs into their artifacts. The Via Salaria Sarcophagus (left) is an eclectic mix of Christian and pagan figures, perhaps made by a workshop that wanted to hedge its bets. Or it may have been produced for a family in which only some members were Christian. A cross and the head of a mythical griffin decorate a third-century oil lamp (above) found near the Baths of Diocletian in Rome.

When paganism held the Holy Land

Reversing Hadrian's bold effort to secularize Jerusalem, Constantine begins to build: Two splendid churches he constructed still hold their central importance for Christians

Jerusalem and its environs had long been holy to the Jews, and after such monumental events as the Resurrection occurred in the region it became deeply significant to Christians as well.

Recognizing its importance to both religions, and having no affection for either, the emperor Hadrian had attempted to secularize the Holy Land. He renamed Jerusalem as Aelias Capitolina and, among other things, erected a pagan temple directly over a site Christians believed to be Jesus' empty tomb.

When Constantine became emperor, he set out to reverse Hadrian's work, beginning a vigorous building campaign in the Holy Land. First, in 333, he constructed a chapel and basilica where the Virgin Mary reportedly gave birth to the baby Jesus. Additions, repairs and reconstructions over the centuries produced the structure that stands in Bethlehem today, the Basilica of the Nativity, the focus of centuries of turbulence and violence as various factions seized and held it. In mid-2002, a group of Palestinian gunmen occupied the church for more than a month in a standoff with the Israeli army. The Basilica of the Nativity is the oldest church still in use in the Holy Land.

Encouraged by his mother, Helena, Constantine also demolished the pagan temple that Hadrian had built on the site of Jesus' Resurrection, replacing it in 336 with the Church of the Holy Sepulchre and summoning a council to Jerusalem to dedicate the new church—arguably the most important site of the Christian world if it was, indeed, built at the place of Christ's Crucifixion, burial and Resurrection. It was destroyed during a sixth-century revolt, and then rebuilt by Justinian. When the Persians invaded the Holy Land in the seventh century, they spared the church while destroying every other major house of worship. As Muslim and Christian forces occupied and defended the building in ensuing centuries, it became increasingly barricaded and buttressed, taking on its present appearance of a fortress. ∎

At Bethlehem in 333, Constantine constructed the first of his shrines in the Holy Land—an octagonal chapel and basilica over the grotto where Jesus is said to have been born. The present structure of the Basilica of the Nativity (left) is a combination of Constantine's first church, reconstructions from the sixth century, massive fortifications against attack, and crusader repairs. Underneath the marble floors over which countless pilgrims have reverently walked, are mosaics of the old basilica (above), here being cleaned by a Greek Orthodox monk.

Constantine dedicated the Church of the Holy Sepulchre in Jerusalem in 336, on the site of Christ's Crucifixion and entombment. It was comprised of a number of buildings, but centered on the Anastasis (Resurrection). This was a round structure surmounted by a dome with an opening for light, supported by twelve columns embellished with silver (as in the model at the church in Aquileia, left). Candles sparkle in the Resurrection rotunda (below) around the monument of the Tomb, created by carving away most of the hill which originally surrounded it. At Madaba in Jordan (above), a huge mosaic of Palestine once covered the floor of a sixth-century church. On it is a map of Jerusalem as it would have appeared in the fourth century, with Constantine's buildings prominently featured.

How Judaism survived

With the Temple gone and revolt quelled, the great rabbis lay a foundation in the Torah that will long sustain the faith

However devastating the destruction of Jerusalem in A.D. 70 to the religious beliefs of the Jewish people, the failure of Simon Bar Kochba's revolt sixty-five years later was, in one respect, worse.[1]

Until the Bar Kochba defeat, the faithful could console themselves by recalling that the Temple had been destroyed once before, in 586 B.C., that time by the Babylonians. Had not Jerusalem been despoiled then too? Had not Jewish fortunes recovered? Had not the people been restored to their city by the Persians fifty years later? Had not a second Temple, ultimately far more impressive than the first, been erected on the same site?

Surely Yahweh would do the same again, and surely the powerful Bar Kochba, hailed by his followers as the Messiah, was God's instrument to make this happen.

But the "son of a star," as he was nicknamed, suffered a complete defeat, and the Roman emperor Hadrian resolved that there would be no restoration of the Second Temple as there had been of the first. He virtually leveled the city of Jerusalem, filling its ravines with rubble. Even before the revolt, he had renamed it Aelia Capitolina. He erected new Roman buildings on the site and promised to execute any Jew who entered the place.

He also laid waste to Judea, destroying 985 towns and villages, rendering the environs of Jerusalem into a wilderness.

The cost of the revolt in human life was vast. An estimated 580,000 Jews were killed, according to the Roman historian Cassius Dio, and so many were sold into slavery that the slave market collapsed.

To the survivors, one truth gradually sank home. Jewry was no longer a nation-state. The day of the Temple and of the ritual sacrifices was over. If the faith was to survive, it must do so through the local synagogue. It must be learned as well as lived. The day of the rabbi, the teacher, was at hand.

The synagogue, with its local congregation, often a great distance from Jerusalem, was anything but a new phenomenon, of course. It had been a central part of Jewish life since the deportation that followed the first fall of Jerusalem seven centuries before. It was through the synagogue that Paul had founded the first Christian congregations in the Hellenistic world. The means by which the Jewish faith could survive without the Temple was already therefore in place.

Christians, both then and ever since, have raised the question: Why did the Jews not simply recognize that Jesus was the Messiah and accept him? To the Jewish scholar Jacob Neusner, research professor for religion

1. See "Ancient Israel's last president," pages 75-76 in *A Pinch of Incense*, an earlier volume in this series.

and theology at Bard College in New York, this question of whether Jesus was the long-awaited Jewish Messiah was the central point at issue. Christians, particularly converts from Judaism, had to ask themselves what they must do now that Messiah had come, whereas other Jews had to ask what they must do while awaiting Messiah. The two attitudes were fundamentally at variance, he writes.

The feminist theologian Rosemary Radford Ruether agrees. In her history of anti-Semitism in Christian history, *Faith and Fratricide*, she views Jesus' identification of himself as the Messiah as "the most fundamental affirmation of the Christian faith."

But to the journalist and historian Paul Johnson, the core issue is deeper than the issue of the Messiah. Rather, it lies in the question of the Messiah's nature. Johnson, in his *A History of the Jews* writes:

> The notion that Jesus was divine—implicit in his Resurrection and in his foresight of this miracle, and in his subsequent epiphanies—was present from the very beginning of Apostolic Christianity. Moreover, it was accompanied by the equally early belief that he had instituted the ceremony of the Eucharist, in anticipation of his death and Resurrection for the expiation of sin, in which his flesh and blood (the substance of the sacrifice) took the form of bread and wine. The emergence of the Eucharist, the "holy and perfect sacrifice," as the Christian substitute for all Jewish forms of sacrifice, confirmed the doctrine of Jesus' apotheosis. To the question, was Jesus God or man, the Christians therefore answered, both.
>
> This made a complete breach with Judaism inevitable. The Jews could accept the decentralization of the Temple. They could accept a different view of the Law. What they could not accept was the removal of the absolute distinction they had always drawn between God and man, because that was the essence of Jewish theology, the belief that above all others separated them from the pagans. By removing that distinction, the Christians took themselves irrevocably out of the Judaic faith.
>
> The Jews could not concede the divinity of Jesus as God-made-man without repudiating the central tenet of their belief. The Christians could not concede that Jesus was anything less than God without repudiating the essence and purpose of their movement. If Christ was not God, Christianity was nothing. If Christ was God, then Judaism was false. There could be absolutely no compromise on the point. Each faith was a threat to the other.

Whatever the core issue, a mutual antipathy rapidly developed. Matthew's Gospel, usually regarded as the most pro-Jewish of the four, has the Jews saying "His blood be on us and on our children" (Matt. 27:25) seeming to reflect the Jews taking upon themselves the responsibility for the Crucifixion. The term "the Jews" appears seventy-one times in John's Gospel, almost always disparagingly. Sometimes it refers to the Pharisees, sometimes the Sadducees, sometimes the Temple authorities, sometimes all the Jewish people (John was himself a Jew). Although the language, as Johnson's history points out, is that of first-century Jewish polemic used by

The fourth-century synagogue at Capernaum in Israel was built atop an earlier one that Jesus may have frequented. Like many synagogues, it was designed in the style of public buildings of the era. In this case, the influences are Hellenistic and Roman.

A rabbi pores over a book of the Talmud, a compilation of rabbinic commentaries and teachings. Orthodox Jews consider the Talmud to be authoritative in matters of faith.

Jews in heated theological argument among themselves, in the centuries ahead these passages would be cited to validate vicious Christian persecution of the Jewish people.

Insofar as language was concerned, the Jewish response to the Christians was equally violent. "Rouse your fury, pour out your rage, destroy the opponent, annihilate the enemy!" had been a curse against Hellenism invoked in the second century B.C., during the Jewish resistance movement. At the end of the first century A.D. it was redirected against the Christians, and thereafter the denunciation of Christianity makes its appearance in Jewish biblical commentary.

But this reference to the Christians forms little more than an incidental aspect of the new Judaism that emerges from the Jewish disasters of the first and second Christian centuries. What came to replace the Temple was the Torah, meaning the Law and the commentaries on it that had been slowly developing over the Temple's final years. Now the Torah

was the only thing left. The refugee rabbis who, settling at Jamnia west of Jerusalem on the Mediterranean coast, gradually developed it into what Johnson calls "a system of moral theology of extraordinary coherence, logical consistency and social strength." The Jews, he writes, "turned the Torah into a fortress of the mind and spirit."

Yet in so doing, the Jews turned in on themselves. Those who had not been lost in the two wars, nor converted to Christianity, formed their own communities within Roman society. But they were largely closed communities. Where Jews had once constituted one tenth of the Roman Empire; had engaged in its philosophical and cultural activity; and had won tens of thousands of converts to their faith and its practices, they now isolated themselves and poured their boundless intellectual energy into the study and development of the Torah.

It was this fact more than any other, says Johnson, that saved them as a people, and conveyed them from the ancient world through the medieval world and into the modern one. By the twenty-first century, the Romans were long gone and the Hellenistic Greeks, the Gauls and the Celts had vanished into other peoples. However, the Jews were still identifiable, and it was their long isolation, holding fast to the Torah in the midst of a sea of Christianity and Islam, that enabled them to do it.

But it was to be a journey fraught with pain, and it began on September 18 of the year 324, when the Christian Constantine became sole emperor of Rome, and their theological foes, the long-persecuted Christians, were now, or soon would be, running the empire. ∎

CHAPTER 7

History's most durable Christians

In Armenia's tradition, the bishop who refused to die heals the murderous king of his beast-like madness and they establish the longest-lived Christian nation

I n the high mountains beyond the Black Sea's south coast, where the two great rivers of ancient history, the Tigris and Euphrates, find their source, there have lived for something close to three millennia a nation of swarthy, tough and fiercely independent people. These are the Armenians. In the last century and a half, they have migrated all over the world. Armenian surnames—identifiable because they almost always end in "ian," sometimes "yan"—crowd the telephone books of Fresno in California's great Central Valley, and appear in the listings of every major North American city. Less familiar to the world at large, however, is Armenian history. They are the first and longest-lived Christian nation; and from the fourth Christian century onward, they have suffered and died for the faith by the tens of thousands.

Armenia is high country; its mountainous plateau averages forty-five hundred feet above sea level, and on nearly every side, it rises above its neighbors like an island of rock. Many of its peaks are extinct volcanoes, which once filled up its plains with flowing lava. This cooled to become a black and pink stone that is a distinctive mark of Armenian architecture. Armenia's most famous peak, of course, is Mount Ararat, the biblical landing place of Noah's Ark, and a

Reflecting the centuries of suffering her people have endured, an Armenian woman prays in a Yerevan church following the earthquake that devastated her country in 1989.

foothold of faith for Armenia's generations of tenacious Christians.

Spirituality apart, Armenia is otherwise decidedly inhospitable. On the high plains, winter is bitter, with ceaseless wind and temperatures falling to forty degrees below zero; many mountains are snow-covered year round. Ancient nomads dug underground burrows to survive the lethal cold. Nomads they had to be, for the craggy landscape of ravines and canyons is uncongenial to all but herders and wanderers. It has been estimated that two-thirds of the land is not fit for human settlement. Yet it was inhabited from the earliest reaches of human history, and some archaeologists believe that several Stone Age migrations into Europe began in Armenia. The ancient historian and geographer Strabo says that the land got its name from one Armenus, a companion of Jason and the Argonauts, heroes of ancient Greek mythology.

However forbidding, Armenia's lands have been a recurrent battleground, not for their potential productivity but for their location. Because of surrounding seas, mountains and deserts, Armenia is a bottleneck in the well-worn human paths from east to west and from north to south.[1] Only by crossing Armenia's rocky terrain and subjugating its people could would-be conquerors securely reach their objectives beyond. Most of those conquerors, people like the Medes and Hittites, have long since faded into history. The Armenians have survived, and surviving is what they do best.

Armenia's political history emerges from the mists of mythology. In the Iron Age, we're told, Queen Semiramis of Assyria, lovesick for Armenia's Prince Ara the Fair, led an army into the land with hopes of making the young man her paramour by force. Instead, he died in battle, defending his honor to the last. The despondent queen then made her way back southward until she came to the shores of the beautiful Lake Van in the nation's center. There, she built a gracious city, and had a magnificent palace for herself

1. David Marshall Lang, author of *Armenia: Cradle of Civilization*, describes Armenia as the geographic center of the world: "The country is seen to be almost equidistant from the Cape of Good Hope and the Bering Straits, and roughly halfway from the Pacific to the Atlantic Ocean."

carved into the sheer face of the cliff above it.

History confirms only that a certain King Aramu was indeed a contemporary of Queen Semiramis in the ninth century B.C., and that during his time, the city of Van was founded and the land's first nation-state, Urartu (note the similarity to "Ararat"), was established. Three centuries later, the biblical prophet Jeremiah mentions Urartu among the enemies of Babylon, but about then the land was overtaken by the Persians, conquerors destined to return many times.

A subsequent Armenian dynasty arose under Orontes I, which was dealt a bitter blow by the invasion of Alexander the Great in the fourth century B.C. About two hundred years later, a third Armenian dynasty brought the nation to its pinnacle of glory and made it briefly ascendant over much of the Middle East. King Tigranes the Great came to the throne about a hundred years before the birth of Christ and spent the next half-century building, and then losing, the greatest empire Armenia has ever known. He seized Syria to the west, and pressed down through Phoenicia to northern Palestine. Parts of Mesopotamia and Parthian Persia to the south, and Iberia to the north, all fell to his armies.

Two enduring symbols of Armenia are visible at this spot about eighteen miles from the capital of the country, Yerevan. The monastery of Khor Virap was built around the pit in which St. Gregory, the evangelist to the Armenians, was held prisoner for more than a decade. Looming over it, but now across the border in Turkey, is the seventeen-thousand-foot volcanic cone of Mt. Ararat, where Noah's ark is said to have run aground following the great flood.

Ultimately, he ruled over one hundred thousand square miles, of which only a tenth remains to Armenia today.

Tigranes was his own worst enemy. After he executed a messenger for bringing him bad news, no one dared tell him the truth about other crises as they arose. He executed two sons on suspicion of plotting to unseat him; a third son sought to save himself by conspiring with the king of Parthian Persia to bring an army against his father. Meanwhile, the king found himself surrounded by hostility. He had forced citizens of conquered lands to migrate and populate his new city, Tigranokerta. These were now eager to betray him and escape.

It was Rome, however, that smashed Tigranes' empire. In 69 B.C., Tigranokerta readily fell to the general Lucullus; and much of the imported population speedily returned to their native lands. Three years later, the general Pompey marched into Armenia to do battle with the Parthian army mustered by Tigranes' son. Tigranes, now nearly seventy-five, was at the end of his strength. He surrendered and spent his last days as a puppet king, paying docile tribute to Rome.

Antioch's wealthy fled. The poor hoped Shapur would bring benevolent rule. Instead, his men sacked the city, raping, murdering, burning.

The fall of Tigranes ended Armenia's era of worldly glory. Thereafter, and for the next seventeen hundred years, it would play the unenviable role of buffer state between great empires—Persia to the east; Rome, Byzantium and later Turkey to the west; the militant Islamic Arabs to the south; and one day Soviet Russia to the north. But at the dawn of the Christian era, the most dangerous enemy lay to the east, where the Parthian rulers of Persia, who were sometime allies of Armenia, would gradually lose control, to be replaced in the year 226 by far more aggressive successors, the Sassanids. They would set in motion the events that led to Armenia's conversion to Christianity.

It was Persia, not Armenia, which had long been Rome's bane. The two empires, so different in faith and culture, remained locked in a battle of East versus West for more than a century before Christ and six centuries after. To the Romans, Persia was a wall that successive assaults failed to bring down. Thus, the Roman general Crassus met his doom at the Battle of Carrhae in 53 B.C. Plutarch finishes the story. A wedding was being celebrated, he writes, between family members of the king of Parthia, Orodes II, and the king of Armenia, Artavazd II (yet another of Tigranes' sons). The two kings were enjoying a post-nuptial performance of Euripides' "Bacchae," when a soldier strode into the room, bowed to the monarchs, and tossed Crassus's severed head into the crowd. This action elicited much glee, and an actress seized the gory object, using it as a prop while dancing and reciting her lines as a passion-deranged bacchante.

For the first two centuries of the Christian era, Armenia remained a disputed territory, with Parthian Persia and Rome each striving to maintain a favored candidate on Armenia's throne. For much of the time, Armenia was officially a vassal of Rome, while its ruling family was tied by blood to the kings of Persia, the Parthians. However, in 226 the Parthian dynasty fell to the bellicose Sassanids, who had no familial connection with the Armenian royal house. The Armenians now discovered that formerly friendly Persia was an enemy. Henceforth, it must look westward for support.

The Sassanids were to rule Persia for the next four hundred years. They began with a major offensive against Rome, based on an ancient claim. The Romans had seized territory that was properly Persia's, they said. It was territory conquered by the Persian Darius the Great seven hundred years ago, and it included all the Middle East and all of Asia Minor. For the new Sassanid king, Ardashir, and his son Shapur I, the first objective was the subjugation of Armenia. Beyond Armenia lay a far more tempting prize—luxurious Antioch, jewel of Syria, third largest city in the Roman Empire, and launching site of Paul's Christian mission to the Gentiles.

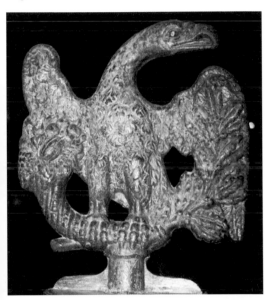

Antioch was also headquarters of the Roman army of the East, but that did not impress Shapur I. In 256 or thereabouts, his army crossed into Mesopotamia, defeated the Roman frontier guard, and drew up before the city. It was a frightening spectacle— the nobility on horseback, peasants trailing after as foot soldiers. Then came mounted knights, known as cataphracts; both they and their immense horses were covered with armor from head to foot, the men peering through narrow eyeholes and carrying long

A competitor to the Roman eagle, (top) a fourth-century Sassanid version of the regal bird, is now on display in Cairo's Coptic Museum. (Bottom) Ardashir I, founder of the Sassanid dynasty, receives his crown from the god Ahura Mazda. This cliff carving is part of a treasure trove of such monuments located at Bishapur in western Iran.

lances. Even the horses wore spiked helmets. Faced with such a galloping horde, gleaming in the sun and pounding the ground towards him, the opponent was expected to panic and run, and in fact often did.

But it turned out that Shapur did not need force to take the city. A highborn citizen named Mariades betrayed it into his hands—if betrayal is the right word. The city's poor were growing increasingly resentful of Rome, and viewed Persia as a deliverer. Mariades himself chafed under the expensive obligation, laid on his family by Rome, of supplying horses for the public entertainments. Some say he had used his position to embezzle, and had been ousted by the Romans in disgrace. Certainly there had been recent unrest in Antioch, so disruptive that the crowds at the chariot races had split into Roman and anti-Roman factions; and the resulting riots had caused cancellation of the events. Perhaps Mariades was in a position to know that the time was ripe for rebellion, and connived with Shapur to surrender to the city.

As Shapur encircled the place, the wealthy classes fled in confusion, taking with them all the valuables they could carry, and leaving the gates unguarded. The poor who remained hoped, no doubt, that Shapur would usher in a benevolent rule. They were to be bitterly disappointed. Shapur's soldiers rampaged through the city, sacking the houses and temples, raping and murdering, and finally burning much of Antioch to the ground. Mariades, too, was killed—perhaps by his own countrymen, perhaps by Shapur, who figured the turncoat to be just as capable of betraying him as he was of betraying the Romans.

Shapur returned to Persia leading a long line of prisoners. Some were destined for the slavery that usually befell captives of war, but Shapur also took care to abduct whomever he could find of the city's remaining intellectual and scientific community. He settled these men in Persia, requiring them to produce wisdom for the good of their new home. One of these prisoners was the Christian bishop, Demetrianus.

The Roman emperor Valerian arrived too late to defend Antioch, found the city nearly deserted, and began to rebuild, though trouble erupting on other borders distracted him, and the work was not completed. In the summer of 260, his troops were sick and low in spirits. Then the unthinkable happened. Under circumstances that have remained obscure, the emperor Valerian himself was taken captive, an unprecedented disaster (see chapter 1 of this volume).

Then Shapur returned to Antioch—so suddenly, it was said, that an actor in a play at an outdoor amphitheater looked up toward Mount Silpius and asked the audience, "Am I dreaming, or have the Persians arrived?" The answer came in the form of a shower of arrows raining down into the audience. Shapur's army immediately swept into the city, and once again looted, burned and took prisoners. Back home, Shapur built himself a city which he triumphantly named "Shapur's Better-than-Antioch."

Meanwhile, Armenia had not been idle. Its king, Khosrov I, as notable for daring as for military strategy, harassed and even invaded the Persian kingdom. Shapur repeatedly counterattacked into Armenia. It was in this decade of high tension and uncertainty that events began to unfold that would result in the

Among the royal Sassanid carvings at Bishapur in Iran is this twenty-three-foot statue of Shapur I, the monarch who halted Rome's imperial advances in the East.

conversion of Armenia to Christianity. The story has one source, Agathangelos's *History of the Armenians*, written in the latter half of the fifth century, a narrative so romantic that the faithful embrace it unexamined almost as readily as skeptics reject it, also unexamined. As far as Armenian Christians are concerned, the events it describes happened.

Agathangelos plunges into the tale with an account of a war council in the Persian court. Dismayed by Khosrov's continued victories, Shapur decided to attempt his assassination. The person who undertook this deed, the king promised, would be raised to second rank in the kingdom, next only to the monarch himself.

A certain Anak accepted the commission. He was a Parthian, a member of the household overthrown by the Sassanids, who still had blood ties to the Armenian monarchy. Together with his brother, they moved their entire families, their sheep and herds, to Armenia, where they claimed to have revolted against the Sassanid rulers. King Khosrov welcomed his relatives, and included them in his deliberations as he planned a new invasion of Persia.

At an opportune time, Anak and his brother asked Khosrov to step aside with them for a private consultation. Their swords, Agathangelos tells us, were already half-drawn. They stabbed Khosrov and fled; but with his last breath, the king ordered that the families of both men be massacred. The dying order was carried out in bloody detail; even the women and children were slaughtered. One son, however, survived. This infant was spirited away by his nurse, and carried to safety in Caesarea of Cappadocia (see map page 131, F3), which was in Roman territory. He would be known as Gregory.

Shapur rejoiced to see Armenia now leaderless and vulnerable. He immediately marched into the country, seizing whatever he could and annihilating the remnants of Khosrov's clan. Khosrov's infant son was rescued, however, and

GREGORY ON HEARING THE WORD

In the same way as laborers first split the tilled ground and break it up, and plough with furrows the black clodded earth and fertilize it; as they cut with sweating toil the worthless growth of grassy weeds, and then sow the productive seed; so with the preaching of the gospel. Unless one first cuts away the debts of the guilt of one's own wild-growing habits of unworthy and voluntary sins—unless you sever from your minds the wild, harmful and destructive roots of sins which are rooted in you and have enveloped with their branches your minds; in the same way, unless you eliminate from yourselves the customs of your upbringing, you cannot receive the seed which will give you profitable fruit.

Gregory replied firmly. He would continue to serve Christ. Death was merely a doorway to his closer presence. Gods like Anahit 'do not really exist.'

delivered to the care of the Romans. While Gregory was being raised in Cappadocia, Tiridates, heir to King Khosrov, was growing up in the home of Licinius, a Roman who would one day become emperor.

There was one significant difference in the education of the two refugee children. Gregory was raised as a Christian. He "became acquainted with the Scriptures of God, and drew near to the fear of the Lord," writes Agathangelos. When he learned, as a grown man, that his father had murdered Tiridates's father, Gregory made a momentous decision. Leaving his two sons, he went to Tiridates, and concealing his parentage, offered himself in humble service to the exiled king.

Tiridates had grown to be a man of immense physical strength. When he accompanied his protector, Licinius, to a battle against the Goths, he performed a feat that astonished his companions. They arrived at the city in the middle of the night, and could find no forage for their horses. Tiridates climbed over a high wall no one else could scale, and threw back armloads of hay until the horses were well supplied, then heaved several useful donkeys over the wall as well.

Licinius had never seen anything like this man. When they came to the place of battle, they found the Roman emperor in dismay; the leader of the Goths had challenged him to single combat, and "because he was weak in bodily strength" Licinius was terrified. He suggested that Tiridates stand in for the emperor. Robed in imperial purple, Tiridates charged the Goth king on horseback and soundly defeated him. He was rewarded with imperial insignia and given command of an army, which he brought to the East, and used it to drive the Persians out of Armenia.

Gregory had accompanied Tiridates obediently all this time. But there was one thing on which he would not compromise—his Christian faith. During Tiridates's first year as king, he brought his court to the city of Erez to worship at the temple of Anahit (a deity corresponding to the goddess known as Venus or Aphrodite in the Greco-Roman pantheon). After Tiridates had made his sacrifices, he adjourned to his tent for feasting and hearty drinking, then ordered Gregory back to make further offerings. Gregory refused.

Tiridates was confused by this first sign of resistance in one who had served him so well, and Gregory's explanations did not please him. "Know that you have made useless the services which you have rendered to me," he declared, threatening his servant with prison and misery for dishonoring Anahit, "the glory of our race and our savior."

Agathangelos recounts Gregory's firm reply. He would continue to serve Christ, and would consider even death merely a doorway to his closer presence. As for Anahit, such gods "do not really exist. . . . Your mind is deranged if you worship them."

Tiridates would not put up with such disrespect directed at himself and his god. He had Gregory subjected to torture, and after each week, brought the prisoner before him to see whether he had repented. Each time, Gregory found opportunity to further expound the faith. Tiridates quickly realized that, for someone dedicated to a God who triumphed over death, threats of execution held no terrors. Instead, he determined to keep Gregory in lingering agony. Gregory was beaten, hung upside down, and his sides ripped open. Tiridates's servants drove nails into the soles of Gregory's feet, then dragged him by the hand, forcing him to run.

Yet after each torture, Gregory resumed his patient teaching. Tiridates was pondering a change of tactics, offering Gregory restoration and honors if he would only submit. He would not. Then a member of the court came to Tiridates with startling news. "All this time he has been living among us and we did not recognize him. He is the son of the treacherous Anak, who killed your father."

A pilgrim honoring St. Gregory of Armenia kneels in the monastery church at Khor Virap, the site of Gregory's imprisonment.

These words sealed Gregory's fate. Tiridates ordered that he be bound hand and foot, and cast down into a cavernous pit below the acropolis in the city of Artashat. There in the blackness Gregory was left to die, utterly forgotten.

Tiridates then busied himself with other exploits, harassing the Persians, and showing himself as a man born to be a warrior. To ensure continued success in battle, he ordered that the gods be duly honored, and that any who behaved toward them with disrespect be turned in for punishment. "He was haughty in dress and endowed with great strength and vigor," Agathangelos writes. "He had solid bones and an enormous body; he was incredibly brave and warlike, tall and broad of stature. He spent his whole life in war and gained triumphs of combat."

Meanwhile, Gregory had not died. For thirteen years, he clung to life. Other prisoners were tossed down beside him and died due to the snakes and fetid stench, but he survived. His endurance was assisted by a widow of the city, who had received the puzzling instruction in a dream to bake a loaf of bread every day and throw it into the pit. That

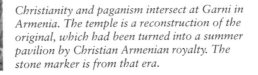

Christianity and paganism intersect at Garni in Armenia. The temple is a reconstruction of the original, which had been turned into a summer pavilion by Christian Armenian royalty. The stone marker is from that era.

meager daily ration kept Gregory on the near side of starvation.

Meanwhile, in Rome, the emperor Diocletian decided to search for a wife of sufficient beauty to equal his status. Portrait painters scoured the empire in search of the fairest faces, and in the course of this quest, broke into a Christian convent where they found women living modest and prayerful lives, who maintained a cycle of worship both day and night. Their abbess was named Gaiane, and the most beautiful of the nuns was named Rhipsime.

Diocletian was delighted with her portrait, and began making wedding arrangements immediately. The nuns, perceiving what was afoot, stole away from the city and made their escape "to a distant land"—Armenia. They settled in the royal city of Valarshapat (see map page 131, G3), and made a shelter in the community winepress. One of the women knew the art of glassmaking, and the community

Rhipsime stretched out her arms and prayed, putting all her trust in God. The nuns crowded around her, but Tiridates's men dragged the young woman away.

was supported by the sale of her glass beads. Diocletian was not about to let them get away so easily, however, and sent an edict to all his territories urging authorities to search for these defiant women and punish them appropriately.

It didn't take long for Tiridates's men to locate the women hiding in the winepress, and within days, gossip about Rhipsime's great beauty had filtered out to the city. Tiridates wanted to see her for himself. He sent a golden litter to pick her up early one morning, and included as well extravagant clothing and jewelry.

As Gaiane looked at these gifts, she recalled Rhipsime's childhood in a wealthy, noble family. "Remember, my child, that you have left and abandoned the honor and splendor of the golden throne of your fathers and the royal purple. . . . So why then will you give your holy chastity as food to dogs in this barbarian land?"

Rhipsime had no such intention. She had "put on faith from the years of her youth like an armored cuirass." She stretched out her arms and prayed "in a loud voice," putting all her trust in God. The other nuns crowded around to her defense, but they were not able to protect her from Tiridates's men, who carried the beautiful young woman to the palace.

Once Tiridates was alone with the girl, he was impressed with her beauty, and decided to sample her charms. He "seized her in order to work up his lustful desires," but Rhipsime was galvanized to feats of strength beyond her natural power, and fought him off vigorously. Tiridates was "worsted by a single girl through the will and power of Christ."

Tiridates decided to try a different tactic. He sent servants to lock a collar around Gaiane's neck and drag her to the palace to talk sense into the girl. Gaiane did agree to speak to her, and while Tiridates and Rhipsime remained alone together in the inner chamber, Gaiane was brought up to whisper through the door. But far from giving the advice they desired, she urged

GREGORY ON THE GOOD SHEPHERD

But why should He, being innocent of death, wish to lay down His life? "I am," He says, "the good shepherd who dies for my sheep." For which sheep then? For the frightened, the fleeing, those about to be eaten by wild beasts.

Rhipsime to remain resolute and to never give in.

"When they realized what advice she was giving, they brought stones and struck her mouth until her teeth were knocked out, and they tried to force her to tell Rhipsime to do the will of the king." Gaiane still refused, and continued to exhort the girl to stand firm in her faith. For this, Gaiane received further beatings that shattered the bones of her face.

Inside the chamber, the battle was going the other way. Rhipsime, still endowed with superhuman strength, battered the king to exhaustion. "She struck him, chased him and overcame him; she wore the king out, weakened him and felled him." She ripped off his elegant clothes and threw away his crown, "leaving him covered with shame." Then, forcing the doors open, she ran out, "cutting through the crowd, and no one was able to hold her." She managed to stop by the winepress to inform her companions of events, then fled to a hilltop outside the city.

It wasn't long before the executioners found her. Rhipsime was stripped and staked to the ground. Torturers then "applied the torches to her for a long time, burning and roasting her flesh." They used stones to disembowel her; and "while she was still alive, they plucked out the blessed one's eyes." Christians from the city hid nearby, hoping to give her body honorable burial; but the torturers caught and killed them as well. They tossed all the remains out as food for dogs and birds.

The next morning, the chief executioner came to the king to learn what he wished done to Gaiane. It seems the events of the day before had unsettled Tiridates's mind; and he asked that a search be made for Rhipsime and that she be persuaded to come back to him. When the executioner remarked that all the king's enemies should perish as Rhipsime had, Tiridates fell to the ground weeping. He ordered the execution of Gaiane and the remaining nuns, who were skinned alive, then decapitated. In all, thirty-seven nuns and Christian townspeople were martyred.

The king continued to grieve for Rhipsime for six days, then arranged a hunting trip to distract him from his sorrows. But as he stood in his chariot preparing to leave the city, according to Agathangelos, "an impure demon struck the king and knocked him down." A scene reminiscent of the madness of the ancient King Nebuchadnezzar was repeated, as Tiridates "began to rave and to eat his own flesh," then to go on all fours, grazing on weeds and behaving like a boar. His servants were not able to restrain him, "partly because of his natural strength, and partly because of the force of the demons who had possessed him." This curse spread beyond the king himself, as other nobles and city

The timeless beauty of this Armenian woman, in David Turnley's striking photograph, echoes that of the nun Rhipsime who so hypnotized her attacker, king Tiridates. Her haunted expression reflects the mixture of defiance and apprehension felt by the nun as she confronted the king.

Tiridates I of Armenia has sentenced Gregory, bishop of the local church, to years of confinement in a refuse pit. The king's sister battles nausea and repulsion as she approaches Gregory on a critical mission. Her reason: Tiridates has a terrifying affliction that reduces his behavior and appearance to that of a wild animal. Unable to bear the outbursts any longer, the princess seeks the prayers of Gregory. By those prayers Tiridates is cured. And, more significantly, he champions the missionary work of his former prisoner.

leaders fell into similar torments, and ruin spread across the country.

Then Tiridates's sister, Khosrovidukht, had a vision in the night: an angel told her that there was a prisoner named Gregory in the city of Artashat who alone could end the torments. "When he comes, he will teach you the remedy for your ills."

The people of the city were skeptical about this vision. Surely Gregory had died within days of being cast into the pit; at this point, it would not even be possible to identify his bones. Khosrovidukht acquiesced. But every night she continued to have the same vision, now accompanied with warnings that if these

Gregory was hauled up, blackened with filth, but alive. They hurriedly dressed him and took him to the king, by this time foraging naked with a herd of pigs.

instructions were not followed, the torments would grow worse. "With great fear and hesitation," Khosrovidukht again brought the message.

This time her words were heeded. A prince named Awtay went to Artashat, where he had a thick rope to be lowered into the depths of the pit. He shouted, "Gregory, if you are somewhere down there, come out. The God whom you worship has commanded that you be brought out." Far below, a hand took hold of the rope and shook it.

Gregory was hauled up, blackened with filth, but alive. They hurriedly dressed him and took him to the royal palace in Valarshapat. King Tiridates, who had been foraging with a herd of pigs, was also brought to the palace. When he saw Gregory, he ran toward him, foaming and tearing his own flesh with his teeth. Gregory prayed, and Tiridates was returned to his senses.

Gregory then asked to be shown the bodies of the martyrs. They were amazed that he knew about this crime. Gregory found the mutilated bodies intact, unharmed by beasts, and wrapped them in their own tattered garments. He then brought them back to the winepress, where he himself spent all night praying "that the Armenians might be converted and find a way to repentance." In the morning, the king returned to his right mind, and came to Gregory with his court. They asked, "Forgive us all the evil crimes that we have committed against you. And beg your God on our behalf that we perish not."

Gregory then began a period of teaching that was to last over two months. "He informed and enlightened them about everything, abbreviating nothing and speaking neither superficially nor hastily," writes Agathangelos. "Like a wise doctor, he tried to find the appropriate remedy that . . . he might heal their souls." Thus, beginning with the royal household, the conversion of Armenia was under way.

About twelve miles west of Yerevan is the cathedral of Echmiadzin, formerly Valarshapat and now the headquarters of the Armenian Apostolic Church. Echmiadzin means "the Only-Begotten One descended," referring to a vision that Gregory had there. Churches have existed on the site since 309.

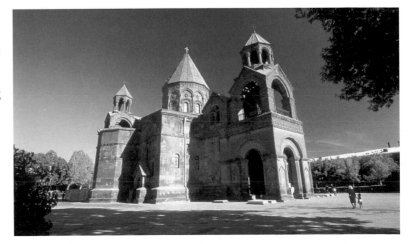

Considered the quintessential example of Armenian church architecture, the Church of the Holy Cross sits on an island in Lake Van, Turkey (1). Built in the early tenth century under the direction of King Gagik I, it recapitulates styles that had been emerging for nearly six hundred years. The high cruciform shape (the seventy-foot height exceeds the measure of both length and width) and conical dome (2) are typical of nearly all Armenian churches, ancient and modern. Its exterior is made even more impressive by engravings and reliefs of biblical scenes and saints (including, again, one of St. George) that richly decorate it (3 and 4).

Armenian church sets a style

Armenia's early architects didn't exactly invent the dome, but they certainly perfected it, and its use in church construction spread as Christianity did, throughout the world

Gregory the Illuminator, national saint and patron of Armenia, gets credit not only for converting the pagan king Tiridates and thereupon the whole kingdom to Christianity, but also for building a church whose influence was profound. A small building constructed of stone in about 301, it was important because of its placement—it marked as sacred the location that today holds a magnificent monastery, one regarded as the religious center of Armenia.

The Monastery of Echmiadzin includes the magnificent cathedral, built in about 480 on the site of Gregory's smaller church. It is the biggest and oldest church still standing in Armenia, and its construction, with a central domed roof atop a square building, set the pattern for numerous churches in Armenia and elsewhere, many of which have survived for centuries. The basic domed-cube style is usually expanded into a cruciform shape, with rounded additions or apses extending from each of the four walls of the interior square building. The dome structure was known elsewhere long before Christianity came to Armenia, but it was nevertheless perfected there, and its widespread use by Armenian church-builders influenced structures from Russia to Western Europe to the New World.

Although the kingdom of Armenia was divided and parceled out long ago, the result of an endless series of brutal conquests, many smaller churches with their Armenian-style domes and plus-sign construction still stand, on land that is mostly Muslim now. ■

The Armenian homeland has been carved up continually over the centuries. Yet evidence of Armenian history is obvious in the myriad small churches scattered across the landscapes of these now predominantly Muslim nations. (1) Armenian peasants gather water near the Ghara Kilissa (Black Church) in the eastern Azerbaijan province of Iran. (2) Artists sketch the ninth-century church of St. Arakelots at Lake Sevan, Armenia. (3) The jewel-like St. Sergius church sanctifies the rugged country of northeast Turkey.

In neighboring Persia, however, Christian fortunes were reversing. Christianity had made some inroads into Persia during the Parthian dynasty, when the national religion, Zoroastrianism, had fallen into neglect.[2] The Sassanids encouraged its revival, developing for it a sacred book, the *Avesta*. Zoroastrianism was a form of religious dualism that envisions two gods, locked in eternal warfare, and requires Zoroastrian followers to obey the good god, Ormuzd, and worship him in the form of fire. Sacred fire was tended in village temples by priests, or "magi," hence the English word "magic."[3]

During their first century, the Sassanids did not directly persecute Christians, perhaps because they were too busy making war, and perhaps

because they presumed that any movement so persecuted by Rome, must be Persia's friend. But during the reign of Shapur II, which stretched through most of the fourth century, the power of the Zoroastrian priesthood began to be felt against anyone who departed from their faith. The brilliant visionary and syncretist Mani, founder of a faith (Manichaeanism) that attempted to blend every known religion of the time, was among its first victims. His body was skinned and stuffed, then hung on a gate in the city of Gundeshabhur. This event was so memorable that the place was called "Mani's Gate" for the next eight hundred years.

Zoroastrianism has existed in various forms for nearly five centuries longer than Christianity. The relief sculpture of its chief deity, Ahura Mazda (left), decorates a wall in the ancient Persian capital, Persepolis. Parsees, modern-day devotees (right), celebrate their New Year around a sacred flame in London, England.

The persecution of Christians wasn't far behind, triggered unintentionally perhaps by the Roman Emperor Constantine the Great. He sent a letter to Shapur II drawing the king's attention to the Christians in his kingdom who had fled there during the years when Constantine's predecessors had persecuted Christianity. He now regarded himself as a "bishop of those outside the [boundaries of the] church," Constantine wrote, and pointed out how many Roman emperors had suffered because they persecuted Christians.

"I heard that the fairest districts of Persia are full of those men on whose behalf I am speaking—the Christians," Constantine wrote. "Imagine my joy. Because your power is great, I ask you to protect them."

Shapur's response was not altogether joyous. He began to harass the Christians, burdened them with exorbitant taxes, seized and demolished their churches, then brought their Bishop Symeon before his court in chains. Despite threats, Symeon refused to worship the sacred fire, and he was forced to watch a

2. Zoroaster was a Persian sage who lived sometime before 1000 B.C., centuries before Confucius or Buddha. Though he left no written records, Iranian tradition recounts him as developing a rational dualistic theology out of the ancient polytheism which he rejected.

3. Some Christian theologians have suggested that the "wise men" mentioned in the second chapter of Matthew's Gospel were Zoroastrian "magi" who studied the stars.

hundred other Christians executed before his own head was struck off.

The following year, just before Easter, Shapur declared that all Christians must die. However, Shapur's beloved eunuch, Azades, was swept up in this annihilation, and the grieving king modified his command. Only those who actually taught Christianity would be executed, he said. Not much of a concession, observes the Christian historian Sozomen, writing in the early fifth century. He estimates sixteen thousand Persian Christians perished under the order.

But in Armenia, Gregory continued his patient, thorough teaching. "He illuminated the hearts and souls of the people by his preaching, seasoning them with

To the horror of the temple priests, St. Gregory of Armenia (right) and King Tiridates send the idol of the goddess Anahit crashing to the floor. Anahit was one of the versions of Aphrodite (deity of love, fertility and beauty) adapted for local worship, and as such represented the benign elements of the pagan pantheon. But for Gregory (known to history as "the Illuminator"), devotion to Anahit was as diabolical and dark as any—something to be eradicated, not tolerated.

The bell tower of the Echmiadzin cathedral, with its typically Armenian cross, is silhouetted against the sun.

divine salt," writes Agathangelos, winning the cognomen by which he would be known to history, "Gregory the Illuminator."

On Gregory's initiative, many pagan temples were destroyed, where for centuries, a confusing array of gods had required bloody sacrifices, including those of human beings. King Tiridates went in person to Artashat to demolish the altar of Anahit, the altar at which Gregory had so persistently, and at the cost of years of imprisonment, refused to make sacrifice.

As well, Gregory told Tiridates that he had had a dream in which the heavens opened and Jesus Christ descended to strike the earth with a golden hammer. A golden pillar emerged, topped by a column of fire and four crosses, which together formed an arch. Above this arch there developed an immense church, with a cupola and a golden cross-topped throne yet above that. On the envisioned site,

Khachkars (stone crosses) have come to symbolize the Christian soul of the Armenians and have been erected by Armenians wherever they have migrated. One khachkar stands outside UN headquarters in New York, commemorating the early twentieth-century genocide which the Armenians suffered at the hands of the Turkish government. The examples on these pages are all in Armenia.

Tiridates helped Gregory raise an elaborate church. The site was the tomb of the thirty-seven nuns and other Christians whom Tiridates had martyred.

The church was a wonder, but no less so was the transformation in Tiridates. To the end of his days, he never stopped confessing his terrible responsibility for the deaths of these martyrs, and thanking God for his unimaginable compassion in granting him forgiveness and salvation nonetheless.

All the while, Gregory had remained a layman, unable to baptize the hundreds who now sought to commit themselves to Christ. Tiridates and his court urged him to accept ordination to the priesthood. He declined what he considered an undeserved honor. Besought by his people and encouraged by an angelic vision, however, he relented and returned with a company of Armenian nobles to the city where he had grown up, Caesarea of Cappadocia. There he was raised to the rank of bishop by Archbishop Leontius.

On his return to Armenia, Gregory tackled his responsibilities with renewed energy. He traveled throughout the land, preaching and baptizing, ordaining clergy and establishing churches. "The whole land was converted, and with all their hearts they were assiduous in fasting and in the service and fear of God," writes Agathangelos, who then recounts what Armenian Christians revere as a sacred moment in their history.

On the banks of the river Euphrates just after dawn, Bishop Gregory meets King Tiridates, his queen Ashken, his sister Khosrovidukht, and the rest of the royal court. One by one, they are baptized in the name of the Father, Son and Holy Spirit. This may be taken as the moment, say the Armenians, when their country became Christian, a position from which, despite fire, sword, misery, hostile governments, seductive propaganda and centuries of persecution, they would never retreat. They were the first nation in the world to officially lay claim to the faith.[4]

In one respect only was Gregory's work hampered. There was no written Armenian language. In the early days, prayers were offered in Greek or Syriac. Translation into written Armenian was difficult, because there are consonants in the spoken language that cannot be represented by letters in the Greek, Latin or Semitic alphabets. The development of an alphabet to represent the Armenian language would not be completed for another hundred years, the work of a traveling preacher named Mesrop-Mashtots, now honored as a saint. He worked out an elaboration of the Greek alphabet, adding letters as needed and altering the shape of others so that all conformed to a single style. Sixteen hundred years later, Mesrop-Mashtots's alphabet is still in use, a tribute to his creative skill.

A young girl recites patriotic poetry for a crowd gathered in front of the statue of Mesrop-Mashtots in Yerevan. While the state was officially atheistic at the time of this photo, it could not ignore the hero status that the Christian inventor of the Armenian alphabet has among his people.

But Armenia's paganism did not die unresisting or quickly. The priests of its cults and surviving temples undertook reprisals against Christians for decades after the conversion of Tiridates. Even a century later, Christians were being martyred in Armenia.

As Gregory aged, Tiridates learned that he had been married long ago, before he came to Armenia, and that he had two grown sons. The king sent an envoy to Caesarea, who returned with Vrt'anes and Aristakes, the latter a monk reluctant to leave his desert retreat. He was persuaded to come, however, when told Christ had more important work for him to do. On their arrival in Armenia, Vrt'anes was ordained a priest, while Aristakes was made a bishop, and took on much of his father's burden of work. For many generations, the rank of bishop would be handed down from father to son among Armenian Christians. It was Aristakes who would represent Armenia at the Council of Nicea in 325.

That is the year, it is said, that Gregory died. He had long before slipped away from active life to spend his time in prayer as a cave-dwelling hermit. No one witnessed his death. Sometime later, shepherds found his body and went

---

4. Armenia is usually recognized as the first Christian state, dating from 301, the year of King Tiridates's baptism. Christianity did not become the "official religion" of the Roman Empire until the reign of Theodosius I (378–395).

back to tell the people of the nearby town, Daranalik, that it was enveloped in a beautiful unearthly fragrance. When they returned to take the body to an appropriate place of burial, however, the cave could not be found. Later still, a monk named Amra was told in a vision where he would find the body. Amra transferred it from the cave, and buried Gregory next to his sons, and a magnificent church was built over the site.

Tiridates died a martyr to his faith. He was poisoned, writes Agathangelos, by pagans in the court circle who were irked by his strict Christian morality.

Gregory the Illuminator departed the scene knowing he had introduced Armenia to Christianity. But the Armenians did not live happily ever after. In the following century, the Persians would pass a law requiring every Armenian to convert to Zoroastrianism. They rose in rebellion, a tiny nation against an enormous empire. ■

GREGORY ON WATER BAPTISM

Just as formerly the Spirit moved over the waters, in the same way He [Jesus] will dwell in the waters and will receive all who are born by it. And at His baptism He vivifies all baptized by having Himself received baptism, and He made baptism honorable by His own descent to baptism.

America's Armenians

As they dispersed throughout the world, many gained distinction in culture, science and sports

Many descendants of Armenian emigrants, dispersed throughout the world during the past two centuries, achieved prominence in science, medicine, business and industry in their new lands, and some have become cultural celebrities. (1) **Aram Khachaturian** (1903–1978), internationally known composer and conductor, said his work is deeply influenced by his native culture: "Being an Armenian, I cannot help writing Armenian music." (2) The author **William Saroyan** (1908–1981) wrote in a spirited style that became known as Saroyanesque, winning the Pulitzer Prize in 1939. (3) Chess champion **Garry Kasparov** (1963–) beat the IBM supercomputer "Deep Blue" in a celebrated 1996 match, though he lost a rematch the following year. (4) **Andre Agassi** (1970–) who burst upon the pro tennis scene at age sixteen with his eye-catching outfits, was the top-ranked player in the world in 1995 and 1999. (5) **Cher**, born Cherylin Sarkissian (1946–), first won fame in the Sonny and Cher TV-recording duo, and later turned to movies, winning the best-actress Oscar in 1987. ■

Triumph of a slave girl

Both fact and fantasy no doubt lie behind the story of how a young woman's faith brought ancient Georgia to Christ

An enchanting account is preserved in both history and legend about the conversion of the people in the ancient land of Iberia, today called Georgia, on the east coast of the Black Sea, south of the Caucasus Mountains.

In the fourth century, during the time of King Mirian III, a young Cappadocian woman known as Nina had been captured and brought to Iberia as a slave, and impressed all who saw her with her prayerful and chaste conduct. She simply told people she worshiped Christ as God.

One day, a mother brought a sick child to Nina, who wrapped the child in her cloak and invoked the name of her Lord, and the child was cured.

When Nana, queen of Iberia, heard of the child's miraculous cure, she went to Nina, hoping that the maiden would cure her illness, and once again, in the name of Christ, the maiden effected a miraculous cure.

The queen told the king, Mirian, about her, but he was unconvinced. However, as the story goes, while on a hunt, Mirian became lost in the mist, and a thick cloud or a solar eclipse darkened the sky. The frightened king's thoughts went to his wife and her new Savior Jesus Christ, and he vowed to believe. Instantly, the mist lifted, the clouds dissipated, the darkness passed. The royal conversion was complete.

The king and queen then took instruction in the faith from Nina.

With a cross made of vine branches in her hand, Nina leads a group of converts into the waters of the Kura River that runs through the ancient kingdom of Georgia. Her preaching and missionary efforts led to the conversion of thousands, followed by the whole nation, earning her the title "Equal to the Apostles."

They proclaimed their conversion throughout the land, and many of the people followed their lead. In the ancient capital of Mtskheta (see map page 131, G2), the king began to build a church, but the builders were stymied by their inability to raise the main pillar, which remained stubbornly at an angle. The scene was set for Nina's next miracle. Throughout the night, she stayed at the construction site and prayed. In the morning, when the king and his people returned to the site, the pillar stood upright above its pedestal, and then settled into its base, perfectly balanced, securing the cathedral of the Living Pillar.

The king then felled a tree sacred to the pagans, where in days past, animals were said to go to heal their wounds, and had the wood fashioned into crosses. He sent an emissary to Constantine, asking that bishops and priests be sent to Iberia. Seeing Iberia embrace Christianity, Nina retreated to a cave on a mountain at Bodbe, where she died and was buried. Her tomb is still located in the local cathedral.

Whatever its veracity, the story of Nina is singularly free of the more hair-raising elements so tragically common in the history of Christianity. It has a luminous, uplifting quality that perhaps helped make its original source, the church history written by Rufinus in about 403, an early best-seller translated into Greek, Syriac, Armenian, Coptic, Arabic and Ethiopic. A durably popular and revered saint, Nina is also claimed by the Armenians, and is often cited as a close relative of St. George, by devout if unverified sources.

The scrupulous historian Cyril Toumanoff, in *Studies in Christian Caucasian History*, works diligently to nail down the dates of the conversion of King Mirian and the people of Iberia.

Much like those of Armenia, the churches of Georgia are a striking and omnipresent reminder of the Christian history of the nation. (Left) The Svetitskhoveli Cathedral in the town of Mtskheta replaces the wooden one built in the fourth century by the newly converted King Mirian. It became the burial site of the nation's kings. A visible reminder of the struggle of Georgian Christians with the pagan milieu of the fourth century, (center) the Uplistsikhe church is built atop caves where the sun was worshiped. (Right) The Metekhi church stands sentinel on the Mtkvari River, just outside Tblisi, the capital.

By comparing (and testing the reliability of) seventh- and eighth-century sources with the date of a solar eclipse which fell on Wednesday, July 17, 334, Toumanoff is able to come close to the historically cited 330 for the conversion of the king, and he further endorses 337 as the year Iberia officially adopted Christianity as the state religion. He establishes Nina's arrival in Iberia in 324, and calculates that she began preaching in 328, and died in 338, fourteen years after her arrival. That would mean that Georgia has been a Christian outpost on the edge of Asia Minor since the time of Constantine.

There is no way of knowing the reliability of Rufinus's own source, an Iberian prince named Bakur; but the cathedral of the Living Pillar, destroyed by Tamerlane in the early fifteenth century and rebuilt, remains a tangible testimony to the power of prayer. And St. Nina's own tomb remains in Bodbe Cathedral, built in 850 on the original site of her church.

The haunting story of the simple slave girl was, however, embellished by the chroniclers of antiquity. Nina acquired many adventures and distinc-

tions over the centuries. In one story, the Blessed Virgin gives her a cross of grapevine wood and sends her to convert the Georgians; in another, Nina becomes one of thirty-eight virgins captured by the lecherous King Tiridates of Armenia (see page 196), and she is, miraculously, the only one to escape. She has also been elevated to the status of Roman princess, and transformed into a niece of the patriarch Juvenal of Jerusalem (who, unfortunately, didn't live until the next century). It is often in her elaborated form that she rests in the hearts and imaginations of contemporary Georgians.

Nina has fortified the Iberians/Georgians throughout their turbulent history. Despite centuries of cruel persecution by Persian, Arab and Turkish invaders, and of course by its own native son, Soviet Russia's Joseph Stalin, Georgia continues to follow the lead of St. Nina. Seventy percent of its population of about five million remains Orthodox Christian today. Thus does the story of the faith of a humble slave girl triumph over the vicissitudes of history. ∎

In a posture reminiscent of the praying figures found in earliest Christian art, a Georgian woman inside the Svetitskhoveli Cathedral lifts her hands in petition.

CHAPTER 8

The Jesus question comes to a head

He was a creature made by God the Father, said
the gaunt, spectral Arius, and the big fight began

Never in his entire life had Alexander, the venerable
bishop of Alexandria, faced an issue that mattered as
much as the one now before him. Never was it so important that he make his
point clear, that he assemble all possible support behind him, that he *win*. Not
only did the fate of his diocese and the success of his ministry depend on it. As he
saw it, the fate of the whole church depended on it, indeed the fate of his own
soul and everybody else's.

The question at hand was as old as Christianity itself: *Who was Jesus Christ*?
To Alexander, there could be but one answer. Jesus was in every sense of the
word the God through whom all things were made, just as he was described in
the opening chapter of John's Gospel. "I and the Father are one," Jesus had said
(John 10:30). Otherwise, Jesus himself must have been *made* by God, a man and
nothing more. And how could the death of one mere man somehow atone for
the sins of another mere man, let alone the sins of *all* other mere men? If Jesus in
the end turned out to be a creature made by God, how could his death have the
power that Christians attributed to it?

Yet here in Alexander's own diocese, a movement had begun that was gaining
alarming momentum, and spreading to other parts of the empire. It was centered

in the church known as the Baukalis, near the port facilities in Alexandria's downtown business district—the largest congregation and oldest church in the city, a church that was said to contain the tomb of St. Mark. The chief spokesman for this new movement was the church's pastor, the priest Arius, recognized as the best preacher in the city. He drew huge crowds. He was revered by hundreds. He was formidable in argument, and he taught his adherents to be the same.

Whatever Christ was, they said, he could not be of the same divine essence as God the Father. Christ had been created by God; he had not in some way sprung out of God. He was *made*, not born of God or "begotten." Such was the almost instantly popular message of Arius. If it took over the whole church, that would be the end of both the church and the gospel.

So, anyway, reasoned Alexander. He had never been known as a controversialist. He did not specialize in argument. This bishop was essentially a pastor, a shepherd of his flock. He loved his people and they loved him. He was certainly not renowned as a persuasive preacher or an eloquent speaker, a sharp logician or theoretician. But now he was being called upon to be all these things and more.

Whatever Alexander's limitations in such a conflict, he saw one thing clearly. Only if Jesus was, as John had described him, "God, the Word"—and only if he was "with God" and also "was God"—could his death change the relationship between Creator and creature. Only then could his death make it possible for each of us to be "born again" as a new being, brought into existence by the same

Arius was a strange, mystical, almost ghostly figure who enchanted hundreds of ascetic virgins while delighting the city's rabble with his lewd songs.

God who made us to begin with, the way Jesus had described it to Nicodemus in John's third chapter. That, reasoned Alexander, was the "good news," the Christian gospel.

As one Christian teacher would observe sixteen centuries after Alexander, if Jesus was a great moral teacher and nothing more, he is of no practical importance at all. "It's quite true," writes the twentieth-century Christian advocate C. S. Lewis in his *Mere Christianity*, "that if we took Christ's advice we should soon be living in a happier world. You need not even go as far as Christ. If we did all that Plato or Aristotle or Confucius told us, we should get on a great deal better than we do. And so what? We never have followed the advice of the great teachers. Why are we likely to begin now? . . . If Christianity only means one more bit of good advice, then Christianity is of no importance. There has been no lack of good advice for the last four thousand years. A bit more makes no difference."

All this seemed obvious enough to Alexander, but not to Arius. He was a strange man, this Arius, a mystical sort of figure, tall, gaunt, emaciated, perpetually

The Gospels record that Jesus was born like all humans and that he grew "in wisdom and stature." While their understanding of the Incarnation proved to be a central stumbling block for Arius and his supporters, the themes of the Incarnation are found early in Christian art. A statue of the adolescent Christ (left) now in the Museo Nazionale delle Terme in Rome shows him as he might have appeared teaching the elders (Luke 2). Depictions of the adoration of the Magi, such as this one (above) from the catacomb of Priscilla, were common in the tombs of Christians.

melancholy, physically frail, almost ghostly. He "seemed altogether half dead as he walked along," writes one ancient historian. It was perhaps understandable that he should hold a powerful influence over the hundreds of ascetic Alexandrian women who had committed their lives to Christ with vows of lifetime virginity. But he also held extraordinary appeal to the rabble of the city, the dockworkers, the sailors. They found hilariously funny the popular songs he wrote to ridicule Bishop Alexander's theology.

This talent for taunt and ridicule reflected the other cast to his character, at least insofar as his contemporary critics would describe it. They portray him as proud, factious, restless, exasperated by opposition, ambitious, insincere and cunning. Twentieth-century historians sometimes seem peculiarly at odds about him. He was a man with "a genius for self-publicity," writes the French historian Henri Daniel-Rops in his *The Church of the Apostles and Martyrs*. "There was nothing insignificant about him, neither his intelligence, character, violence, nor ambition." Notre Dame University's Charles Kannengiesser in his *Arius and Athanasius* views him as "not an adventurous intellectual," but one who "never failed to express his thought in the measured and cautious terms of a man used to silent meditation." Meanwhile, the British theologian R. P. C. Hanson notes dryly in *The Search for the Christian Doctrine of God* that "nobody thought his works were worth preserving" because Arius was "not a particularly serious writer." He just happened to be

ALEXANDER ON BODY AND SOUL

For as when the king is thrown into chains, the city falls to ruin; or as when the general is taken captive, the army is scattered abroad; or as when the helmsman is shaken off, the vessel is submerged; so when the soul is bound in chains, its body goes to pieces. The soul, therefore, governed the man, as long as the body survived; even as the king governs the city, the general the army, the helmsman the ship.

the spark, says Hanson, that set off the inevitable explosion.[1]

It's generally agreed that Arius was born around the year 256 in Roman Libya,[2] which would make him about the same age as his adversary, Bishop Alexander. Early on, he moved to Alexandria, where he appears to have reveled in the city's delicious wealth of theological speculation, so fostered by the great Origen early in the third century. However, as a young man, Arius moved north and became the student of Lucian of Antioch, an experience from which he would never recover.

Neither would many others. Lucian comes down through an assortment of historical records as the preeminent teacher, the man who leaves an indelible stamp on his students. "He inspired a whole generation in Asia Minor and Palestine," writes Columbia historian John Holland Smith in his biography of Constantine, "not only with his own views on Christianity, but also with intense loyalty to himself and to one another."

Besides Arius, Lucian had other notable pupils—like Theognis, the future bishop of Nicea, one of two who would one day stand so resolutely behind his old school colleague Arius that it meant certain exile. And there was Maris, the future bishop of Chalcedon, who would champion Arius's cause through a whole series of church councils that went on for nearly twenty years after Arius's death. Most significant of all Lucian's students was Eusebius, the future bishop of Nicomedia and the confidant of the emperor Constantine. Eusebius would take over the whole leadership of the Arian cause long after Arius himself had become virtually irrelevant to it.

Arianism, as the doctrine came to be known, was in fact a reiteration of the views of Lucian. These, in turn, reflected Antioch's gradually developing answer to the fundamental question posed by Jesus Christ. The question entailed reconciling two assertions, both advanced by Christians as truths: First, there is but

1. Probably the most colorful description of Arius was made in the late nineteenth century by a British scholar, Arthur Penrhyn Stanley, dean of Westminster, which he penned by combining various portrayals found in the ancient historians: "He is sixty years of age, very tall and thin and apparently unable to support his stature; he has an odd way of contracting and twisting himself, which his enemies compared to the twistings of a snake. He would be handsome, but for the emaciation and deadly pallor of his face, and a downcast look, impaired by a weakness of eyesight. At times his veins throb and swell and his limbs tremble, as if suffering from some violent internal complaint—the same, perhaps, that will terminate some day in his sudden and frightful death. There is a wild look about him, which at first sight is startling. His dress and demeanor are those of a rigid ascetic. He wears a long coat with short sleeves and a scarf of only half size, such as was the mark of an austere life; and his hair hangs in a tangled mass over his head. He is usually silent, but at times breaks out into fierce excitement, such as will give the impression of madness. Yet with all this, there is a sweetness in his voice, and a winning, earnest manner, which fascinates those who come across him. Among the religious ladies of Alexandria, he is said to have had from the first a following of not less than seven hundred. This strange, captivating moonstruck giant is the heretic Arius—or, as his adversaries called him, 'the Madman of Ares, or Mars.'"

2. The Libya of Arius's time bore little resemblance to the Libya of today, mostly occupied by the Sahara, which over the centuries has encroached ever more closely upon the Mediterranean. Libya then was Romanized and urbanized and had produced many lawyers, senators and writers. Under the Romans, it was divided into two provinces, Tripolitania in the western part, and Cyrenaica to the east. Cyrenaica consisted of the five cities of the Pentapolis, whose economy was based on the agricultural coastal ridge and which were administered, along with Crete, by a senatorial proconsul. In addition, these cities were an important link in maritime traffic between the cities of proconsular Africa, Tripolitania and Egypt. Similarly, the economy of Tripolitania (western Libya) derived in part from trade and commerce and in part from the olives and wheat grown in the immediate vicinity.

Arius takes the theological debate to the street—or, in this case, to the docks. The songs he composed to ridicule the notion that Jesus is God became highly popular among the Alexandrians. And so did his theological position on the matter.

one God. Second, the Divine Word that was incarnate in the man Jesus is God, while clearly distinct from the Father.

By the end of the second century, two opposing schools of theological thought were being expressed around the Christian world. One of them, now known as Subordinationism, sought to protect the doctrine that God is One by centering the unity of the Divine Being in the Father, and making the Son and Holy Spirit distinctly subordinate to God the Father. The other, which is called Modalism and came in a number of different variations, saw God as appearing first as Father, then subsequently as Son and finally as Holy Spirit. Both theologies were eventually rejected by the Christians, but the process would take the next 250 years. By the end of the third century, Subordinationism tended to center in Antioch, Modalism in Alexandria.

"The approach to Christianity in Antioch," historian Smith explains, "was subtly different from that made by the theologians of Alexandria. At Antioch, emphasis was laid on the uniqueness of God the Father, on the humanity of Christ, and the practical aspects of human life as shaped by the Scriptures. At Alexandria, teachers dwelt on the mystical union between the eternal Christ and the Divine Father, the preexistence of the Word of God and the harmony of heaven. Antiochene theology tended to stress the difference between Father and Son, and to grant the Father precedence; Alexandrian to point to what they had in common, and to insist that they shared it eternally."

Thus Lucian admitted the preexistence of Christ—as a heavenly being created before all visible and invisible creatures. In fact he had created them. But Christ had not existed from all eternity; he was created by the Father out of nothing, and before that he had no existence. It was a doctrine satisfactory to the theological tradition of Antioch, but not at all to that of Alexandria. Arius had learned it well, regarding it not so much as a special doctrine, but as the only rational way of viewing the Trinity. As one historian notes, it led him to the conclusion that the Divine Father was, as it were, the senior partner. Although there is no such thing as "time" in eternity, there was nevertheless "a time when the Son was not."

Antiochene theology reached its extreme in the 260s when Paul of Samosata, the playboy bishop of Antioch, was deposed, not for being a playboy, but for heresy (see sidebar opposite page). He had taught that Jesus was a human being, although united to the Divine Word. Lucian, the teacher of Arius, was ousted from the church along with Paul, though Lucian's teachings little resembled Paul's. The next two bishops of Antioch sustained the condemnation of Lucian; the third readmitted him to the priesthood.

By then, however, the Christians were again under persecution. Lucian was arrested

That the Trinity was an early element of Christian faith is evident from a mosaic (below right) uncovered in 2001 in what archaeologists believe is the oldest church building yet found. Located near the Jordanian town of Rahab and dated to the second century, the inscription begins with an invocation to "Agios Triados," the Holy Trinity. Even the Old Testament seemed to imply the existence of the Trinity, for example, with the visit of the three angels to Abraham in Genesis 18. The Eastern church took up this scene as its inspiration for depicting the Trinity, as in this famous fifteenth-century work by Russian artist Andrei Rublev (below left).

and ordered to appear at Nicomedia before the emperor Maximian. Here, he refused to deny his faith, was jailed and on January 7, 312, was executed. His body was taken to Drepanum on the coast of Bithynia, later named Helenopolis in honor of the emperor Constantine's mother, who took Lucian as her patron saint. A basilica was erected over his tomb.

Arius returned to Alexandria in time to become embroiled in another controversy that had bitterly divided the Christians there. This one, however, was not about doctrine, but discipline, and it broke out not in church or in a church council, but in one of the disease-ridden, rat-infested, filth-filled prisons of

Rise and fall of a desert queen

Zenobia could ride with her cavalrymen and out-drink her generals, and some regard her playboy bishop as Arius's doctrinal ancestor

During a time of great turmoil in the affairs of Rome (between 235 and 284, more than twenty emperors came and went, some within months of each other) a powerful personage moved unexpectedly to center stage. That she was a woman, and a beautiful one at that, makes her story all the more compelling.

It was a period when the *Pax Romana* seemed to be collapsing from within, and although the sack of Rome by Alaric the Visigoth still lay more than a century in the future, Rome was beginning to look more and more vulnerable to its subject nations. The warrior emperors Gallienus, Claudius and Aurelian ultimately defeated the challenges from the barbarians to the north, but another challenge to Roman authority during this period came from Syria in the east, in particular from the fabled queen of the desert oasis of Palmyra.

Perhaps because her death came neither early nor dramatically, or because there is no famous Shakespeare play about her, Zenobia has not achieved the historical staying power of her idol, Cleopatra. But she was certainly no less interesting, physically and politically. She was acclaimed a great beauty, with flashing teeth, penetrating black eyes and rich, dark skin. She could march and ride as well as her cavalrymen, and she could out-drink her generals. In 267, after the death of her husband, the powerful soldier king Odenath, a death in which, according to some reports, she conspired, she became regent of Palmyra, wielding the real power behind the throne of her ten-year-old son Vaballath.

The emperors had become dependent on King Odenath to hold the Persians at bay. After an early attempt to gain favor with the Persian king was arrogantly rebuffed, he had enthusiastically complied. When Odenath died, Rome lost its foremost ally against the Persians and was ready to support his spouse if she proved to be as ready to do the emperor's dirty work.

Zenobia then showed herself to be a great warrior and a great queen, although not the kind Rome was hoping for. Her power grew until, by 270, she controlled Egypt, most of Asia Minor and all of Syria. She drew first-rate thinkers to her desert court; the eminent philosopher Longinus became her foremost adviser. And she sponsored her own interesting heretic, Paul of Samosata, bishop of the great metropolis Antioch in ancient Syria. While there is little direct evidence of the alliance between Paul and Zenobia, he was appointed bishop in 260 over the son of the former bishop, probably because the local clergy knew he would be able to relate more effectively with Zenobia. He remained in place even though he was kicked out of his church and excommunicated after bishops met in Antioch three times to deliberate on his fate.

In Paul, Zenobia had a kindred spirit. When he arrived in Antioch from Samosata (today, Samsat in Turkey), an ancient town on the Euphrates, he was poor and had no apparent skills. But he managed to become the rich and powerful bishop of one of the greatest sees in the East. At the same time, he got himself appointed *procurator ducenarius*, the Roman equivalent of chief financial officer of the city, and it was as procurator, rather than bishop, that he wished to be known. He would stroll through the marketplace, surrounded by his entourage, officiously reading and dictating letters, seemingly oblivious to those around him.

Nevertheless, and much to the disgust of his fellow bishops, he had a flair for religion. His theology is described primarily in the letter of the bishops excommunicating him, so it is difficult to tell exactly what he espoused, but it is clear the bishops believed he taught that Jesus Christ was but a man, a man inspired by the Word, but just a man nevertheless. As Origen had once suggested, he banned hymns to Christ. Unlike Origen,

Alexandria. The year was 303, and the prison was packed with Christian clergy, many of them bishops, rounded up and jailed under Diocletian's Second Edict (described in chapter four).

Up to this point the persecution had been relatively sparing in Alexandria, though there were real horrors to come. However, those who had been imprisoned for life had a lot of time for discussion. One of the topics that could dependably provoke division was the question of what should be done with those countless Christians who had quailed when the edict was proclaimed

he had his congregation sing his own praises instead. Even worse, said his opponents, the hymns were sung by attractive female "deaconesses," a practice upon which the bishops frowned. And while he refused to declare that Jesus came from heaven, Paul allowed some of his own more enthusiastic followers to declare him an angel from above, without correction.

Some historians believe that Paul tailored his theology to suit Zenobia, who may have been Jewish or influenced by Jewish thought. By downgrading the divinity of Christ, he may have been leaving the door open for the declaration of a new messiah, perhaps even one sponsored by a desert queen. It has been argued that his greatest legacy was his influence upon Arius, who seems to have borrowed heavily from his theology, although scholars are careful to point out that there are significant differences in the ideas of the two legendary heretics. To the bishops, however, Paul declared his orthodoxy, and it wasn't until Malchion, a priest skilled in rhetoric, was brought in to interrogate him, that his true beliefs were exposed.

In their audacious, even outrageous behavior, Paul and his queen seemed to neither fear nor heed the authority of a local council of bishops. Despite his excommunication in 268 or 269, Paul continued to run his church as if nothing had happened, counting on Zenobia's sponsorship to keep the bishops from physically ejecting him. Meanwhile, Zenobia finally threw off the thin cloak of fealty to Rome, and declared her son augustus and herself augusta in 271, effectively establishing an independent Eastern empire.

The real emperor, Aurelian, was not amused, and led a powerful force to face and subdue the augusta of the East. Regaining Egypt first, Aurelian routed Zenobia's army outside Antioch. However, Zabdas, her general, still had a trick up his sleeve. He retreated to Antioch and paraded a "captured" look-alike of the Roman emperor before the people, allowing them to think that Zenobia's forces had won the day. That gave Zenobia enough time to retreat across the desert to Palmyra, with Aurelian in hot pursuit.

As her forces were pushed back, and the emperor laid siege to Palmyra, Zenobia took one last wild ride, on a fast she-camel, in a desperate attempt to meet with the Persians and negotiate for their aid. The Romans pursued and captured her when she was on a boat about to cross the Euphrates. At that moment,

Zenobia's dream of empire was over.

Returning to Antioch, Aurelian took time to settle the affair of Paul of Samosata, the historian Eusebius reports. Conscious that Rome was, after all, the capital, he declared that the bishops in Rome and Italy should make such decisions. It is the first recorded case of a Roman emperor endorsing the authority of the bishop of Rome. Perhaps that is Paul's most enduring legacy.

While Paul was executed brutally, with "the utmost indignity," Zenobia fared comparatively well. In 272, she was taken to Rome, where the emperor had her bound in chains of gold and paraded before the enthralled mob. But once her humiliation was complete, she was given an estate in what is now Tivoli, and after marrying a senator, she lived a long and prosperous life, content perhaps to reminisce now and then about the days when her power and fame could be compared to Cleopatra's. ■

Queen Zenobia poses regally with a servant in this marble panel on display at Syria's National Museum in Damascus.

and in various ways repudiated their faith.

The Christian prisoners soon found themselves divided into two camps, much as they had been during the Decian and Valerian persecutions a half century before. The soft-liners were headed by Peter, bishop of Alexandria, a man whose gentle views no doubt masked his fierce insistence on episcopal authority. To Peter, the circumstances of any apostasy should of course be taken into account when a man or woman seeks readmission to the church. There should be adequate evidence of genuine repentance, a form of penance commensurate with the gravity of the applicant's capitulation, and he or she should then be welcomed back into the fold.

The hard-liners were headed by Melitius, bishop of Lycopolis, a small settlement on the upper Nile Valley. To Melitius, what Peter was proposing was simply an abandonment of Christian principle. How could he possibly face the

Melitius inaugurated the 'Church of the Martyrs,' which was to survive another two centuries. He proceeded diligently to ordain deacons, priests and bishops.

widows and orphans of this persecution—one that could very well get much worse before it got better—if he, in effect, had to tell them that the sacrifices made by their kinfolk were regarded by the church as worth no more than a brief fast, or some other almost meaningless act of simulated contrition?

Very rapidly the argument grew bitter. The soft-liners no doubt pointed to the three denials of the apostle Peter, who had been readmitted to the fold by Jesus with nothing more than a thrice-repeated promise of loyalty (John 21:15–18). The hard-liners demanded severe penances, doubtless pointing to the policy of readmission adopted by the Christians in Carthage a half century earlier, in which the lapsed were readmitted only at the point of death after a lifetime of penitence.

It soon became clear from the way the hard-liners were talking, however, that Melitius and his followers were well prepared to go much farther than mere argument. They would quit the church over this issue, they would ordain their own clergy and establish their own church. This directly challenged the authority of Bishop Peter. Not a violent man, but very definite in his view of church authority, he spread a rope across the large room where he and the other Christians were incarcerated. On it he hung a curtain. He did not want to have to look upon Melitius or any of his followers. They should remain on the other side of the curtain, he declared. Historians disagree on how the crowd divided. Some believe most were with Peter, some say they were with Melitius.

In any event, that bizarre curtain in the jailhouse inaugurated the "Church of the Martyrs," as Melitius called it, which was to survive for another two centuries. The clergy were soon released when Galerius called an end to the persecution. Melitius proceeded to ordain deacons, priests and bishops all along the

Nile, including in Alexandria itself. At a synod held between Easter and Pentecost 306, Peter issued an edict setting out the conditions under which the "lapsed" could return to the church. Those who had yielded only after flogging and torture could return after a fast of forty days. Those who gave in after imprisonment must do penance for a year. Those who had capitulated after mere threats, three years. Those who had recanted, but later changed their minds and declared their faith to Roman authorities, immediate pardon. Enraged, Melitius rejected these terms as absurdly lenient and expanded his schismatic activity.

Meanwhile, Arius had been arrested in another roundup of Christians, and turned up in prison with both Melitius and Peter. There, he sided with Melitius. However, when he was released and Peter's edict appeared, he changed his mind and declared for the "catholic" position, as Peter's cause was known. Up until then, Arius had been a layman. Peter ordained him a deacon. Next, seeking to put an end to Melitius's divisive activity, Peter called a synod that excommunicated

Urged by his flock, Peter fled the city. Melitius called it sheer cowardice. Then came another blow. Peter was executed. The 'coward' became a martyr.

Melitius and all of his (as Peter saw it) fraudulent clergy. At this, Arius protested. Peter was going too far, being too high-handed, he said. How could the rift ever be healed that way? With that, Peter ousted Arius as well.

Soon, the Roman Empire's agenda again dictated church events. Daia took over the administration of the part of the empire that included Alexandria and immediately persecuted the Christians far more vigorously than had Diocletian. Urged by his flock, Peter fled the city. That was Melitius's opportunity. He came into Alexandria, began ordaining his own clergy and declared Peter deposed. Sheer cowardice had caused Peter to abandon the see, said Melitius. Then came another blow. It was suddenly announced that Bishop Peter had been executed. The "coward" had turned out to be a martyr. Unabashed, Melitius kept right on ordaining clergy. Then he, too, was arrested and sent as a slave laborer to the mines at Phaeno, in southern Palestine. In the slave camp, he continued building his church and ordaining new priests and deacons.

Peter's successor, chosen by the Alexandrian clergy, was Achillas, a man fated to die within a few months. When he took office, Melitius dismissed him as yet another compromiser of the true faith, but Arius responded very differently. No sooner was Achillas installed as bishop than Arius was on his doorstep, seeking readmission to the church. The new bishop was obviously much taken with him. Not only did he return Arius to full membership, but he ordained him as a priest and appointed him to the Baukalis.

Achillas's precipitous death once again opened the great see of Alexandria to a new candidate, and this time, the man named to the position was Alexander. Ancient historians differ sharply about that episcopal election. Those opposed to

Arianism say that Arius himself sought the appointment, was rejected in favor of Alexander, and conceived a "deep hatred" of Alexander as a result. Most others say that the two enjoyed cordial relations for the first six years of Alexander's episcopate. Then the bomb burst.

The explosion was unforeseen. Arius's popularity in the Baukalis was well established. To the devout, he was the preeminent local "holy man," whose austere life and spectral features pretty much guaranteed that God spoke to him. To the mob, he was the great joker who turned out hilarious songs on religion, all of them jibes at Alexandria's conventional theology—"dinner party songs" is how one ancient opponent acidly described them. He did not, however, enjoy a significant following among the Alexandrian clergy. Sneers the fourth-century anti-Arian historian Epiphanius: "He was the spiritual master of a school that consisted of . . . seven priests, twelve deacons and about seven hundred dedicated virgins."[3]

The initial collision with his bishop occurred when one of Arius's priestly opponents came formally before Alexander and denounced him as a heretic. (The year is debated, but is widely accepted as 318.) The accuser was probably the staunch traditionalist Colluthus, archpriest of Alexandria and Arius's immediate superior.[4] The conciliatory Alexander, loath to have a major theological blowup in his diocese, sought to resolve the problem by holding an exchange of views. He called a hearing at which Arius could explain and defend his position and his opponents could attack it.

To Colluthus and most of the city's clergy, no doubt smarting for years under Arius's torrent of ridicule, this was a cowardly compromise. They wanted a synod called immediately and Arius ousted. Colluthus became so infuriated that he declared Alexander deposed by his inability to act, and named himself as Alexander's successor. So there were now three claimants to the see of Alexandria—Alexander, the legitimate one, as well as a Melitian claimant and Colluthus.

The hearing proceeded, nonetheless, and Alexander opened it by defining his own views on the issue at hand—the relation between the Father and Son in the Trinity. To the bishop's undoubted consternation, Arius arose and condemned him as a heretic. Alexander's explanation was pure Sabellianism, he charged. The hearing appears then to have broken up in disorder, so the bishop adjourned it and called another.

Tempers apparently were more controlled this time. Arius stated his case with characteristic eloquence and reason, so that even Alexander found himself

ALEXANDER ON CHRIST'S PASSION
The new and ineffable mystery! The Judge was judged. He who absolves from sin was bound; He was mocked who once framed the world; He was stretched upon the cross who stretched out the heavens; He was fed with gall who gave the manna to be bread; He died who gives life.

---

3. The reference to seven hundred "dedicated virgins," said to be followers of Arius in Alexandria, is almost certainly an exaggeration for effect. It's noteworthy that Arius was never accused, even by his severest critics, of sexual misconduct.

4. The historian W. H. C. Frend advances the theory that the priest who denounced Arius as a heretic, thereby setting off the controversy that would dangerously divide the church for most of a century, was the same Melitius who had already established himself as a rival bishop of Alexandria over the question of the treatment of the "lapsed." Frend's theory is that, as well as taking a hard line on church discipline, Melitius took an even harder line on church doctrine. The theory is weakened, however, by the fact that the Melitians later joined the Arians in their opposition to the bishop of Alexandria.

admiring the man's talent with words. But he did not agree with him, chiefly because the biblical evidence against him was too strong. Alexander therefore called a synod of the Egyptian churches, where more than one hundred bishops approved a decree condemning Arius's theology. Alexander then called Arius, produced a statement of what he considered the church's position on the issue, and asked Arius to sign it. When Arius refused, Alexander excommunicated him.

Arius—injured, outraged, undoubtedly vengeful—turned immediately to those whom he knew he could count on for support: the other graduates of Lucian's academy, now very highly placed in the new Christian establishment being assembled by the emperor Constantine. Chief among them was Eusebius, bishop of Nicomedia, where the emperor lived, and a close friend of Constantia, the emperor's sister. Moreover, Nicomedia's bishop was a colleague of "the other Eusebius," bishop of Caesarea, the great church historian, now about to write an adulatory biography of Constantine. So Arius was very well connected, and he would now let these illiterate and illogical fools at Alexandria know what that meant.

Describing himself as "the man persecuted unjustly by the patriarch Alexander," he wrote to both Eusebii (an accepted plural of Eusebius). Eusebius of Nicomedia wrote back, declared his support for Arius, and promptly called a synod of his own bishops to take up the case on Arius's behalf. Known as the Synod of Nicomedia, it declared Arius's theology altogether consistent with catholic Christianity, and wrote to the bishop of Alexandria urging that he readmit Arius.

Eusebius of Caesarea wrote back to Arius too, urging him to come immediately

It was one thing to lampoon his bishop, Alexander, in ballads, but when Arius confronts the old man in his cathedral church, even those sympathetic to Arius's cause are shocked. In the midst of delivering his homily, Alexander is shouted down by the priest. It would not be the last episode in the very public dispute between the two men.

to Caesarea. Arius obliged, traveling to Caesarea and possibly on to Nicomedia. Meanwhile, Eusebius assembled a synod of Syrian bishops which likewise approved of his theology, and instructed the Alexandrian church to receive him back.

Alexander's written response to all this advice and direction from those close to the imperial circle reflects a startling change in his congenial disposition—so startling that many historians view the old bishop's letter as having been composed by somebody else. They see it, in fact, as the first appearance in the Arian controversy of the man who in the next half century would take on emperors, bishops, police, judges, church councils and every other manner of opponent, and who would finally prevail over them all. His name was Athanasius, and he left to history the model of the lone figure that fights and defeats established authority. *Athanasius contra mundum*, people would thereafter say, meaning Athanasius versus the world.[5] Because of him—or, as he would be quick to say,

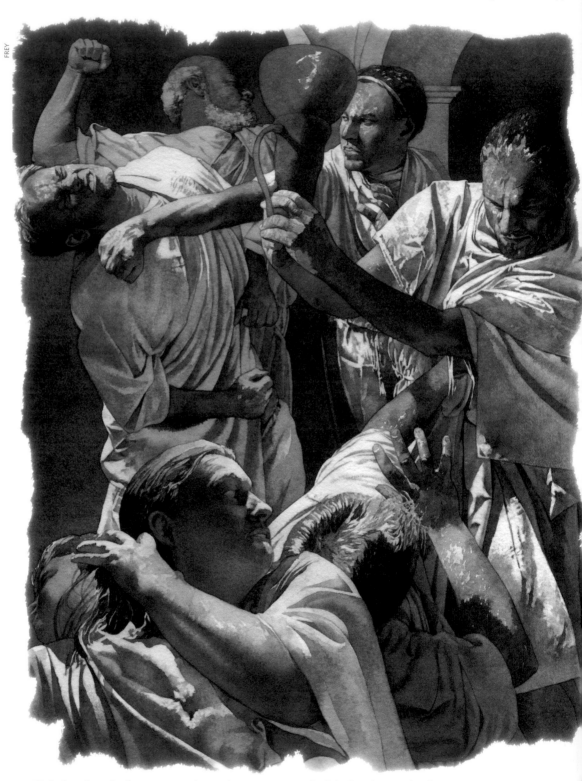

With the edict of toleration issued at Milan, Constantine had declared peace for the Christians. But conflict, sometimes even violence, was to break out within the Church itself. In one of the more physical examples of theological debate, members of one of the many churches in Alexandria come to blows over their differences. Incidents such as this prompted the exasperated emperor to convene a Great Council, where he hoped debate and not fisticuffs would resolve the issues.

because of the grace of God working through him—Arianism would crumble and vanish. But it would be a long, hard struggle for Athanasius, one that would take up the rest of his life, and the struggle may have begun with the writing of Alexander's letter.

The letter, called an "encyclical" or "circular" letter, and probably sent in 319, went to sixty-nine bishops, one of them Sylvester, bishop of Rome. Signed by the bishops around Alexandria in North Africa, it refers to Arius's teachings as "an evil," castigates Eusebius of Nicomedia for "putting himself at the head of these apostates," and charges him with abandoning his former see of Berytus (modern Beirut) in order to acquire the much more prestigious see of Nicomedia, and with trying to "inveigle some of the innocent into this most base heresy which is hostile to Christ."

He was writing, Alexander's letter told the bishops, "that you may know who the apostates are, and also the contemptible character of their heresy, and pay no attention to anything that Eusebius should write you." After setting out a version of Arius's teachings and the case against it, the letter concludes: "We then, the bishops of Egypt and Libya, being assembled together to the number of nearly a hundred, anathematized Arius for his shameless avowal of these heresies, together with all such as have countenanced them."

Meanwhile Arius, wholly endorsed by his highly placed friends in the imperial circle, returned to Alexandria and presented himself to Alexander, apparently assuming that he would now be reinstated as a priest. When Alexander refused, Arius loosed against him a vitriolic propaganda campaign. Pamphlets appeared. The bishop was jeered by rowdies in the streets and rioting broke out. Lawsuits were launched against the bishop. Arius's host of women supporters became particularly active, joining in public protests and holding meetings to vilify the old man.

In 322, Alexander wrote in dismay to a sympathetic bishop in Bithynia that the disturbances threatened to spark another outbreak of persecution. Arius's people, he said, "are both demolishing Christianity publicly and striving to exhibit themselves in the law courts, and to the best of their ability rousing persecution against us where no persecution was. They are daily stirring up divisions and harassment against us, both troubling the law courts by the pleas of disorderly females whom they have duped, and also discrediting Christianity by the way in which the younger women among them immodestly frequent every public street." The uproar, of course, did not take long to attract the delighted attention of the pagan world, as Alexander had feared. The crowds

---

5. Athanasius is assumed to be a native Alexandrian, the son of reasonably prosperous parents who were probably Christian. The church historian Socrates preserves a plausible anecdote of Athanasius's boyhood. He and some other youngsters were "playing church" one day by the sea when Alexander, the bishop, watched them from a nearby seaside apartment where he was meeting with several other clergy. Impressed by the correctness with which the children imitated the church services, he went down to the beach and talked to them, and found they had made Athanasius their "bishop." They also disclosed that they had baptized several of their companions. Alexander went over the baptismal formula they had used, examined the youngsters, found them exceptionally well instructed, and decided that the baptism was valid. He then took personal charge of the education of Athanasius.

razzed the Christians for their internal brawling; new plays in the theaters spoofed the followers of the man who had said, "Blessed are the peacemakers."

Arius fanned the flames by coming up with another song, this one far less ribald, and intended to call attention to his own superior education:

> This is what I have learned
> From those who possess wisdom,
> Well-educated people,
> Instructed of God
> Skilled in all knowledge,
> It is in their footsteps that I walk,
> Even I, that I walk as they do.

It was this education, according to the song, that enabled him to serve God as faithfully as he did:

> I who am so much spoken of,
> I, who have suffered so much,
> For the glory of God,
> I who have received from God
> The wisdom and knowledge that I possess.

The uproar at Alexandria, rapidly spreading throughout the churches of the East, was perceived by the emperor Constantine as a preposterous inconvenience, rooted in the utter irresponsibility of two Christian clergy. He first heard of it as he prepared a state visit to the new provinces in the East that he had acquired with the defeat of Licinius. The news came, no doubt, in a letter from Eusebius of Caesarea, who was then preparing to write the emperor's biography.

Does Arianism really matter?

A materialistic age dismisses such questions as absurd, but for believing Christians the issue is as important now as it was then

Two aspects of the Arian controversy puzzle the twenty-first-century reader. One is the fact that a mere doctrinal dispute could have caused such a rupture in the church. The second, arising out of the first, was the fury and bitterness engendered between committed Christians. It may seem trivial now, with the contest long-ago concluded, the issues so thoroughly hammered out.

But the Arian altercation was crucially important: Since such doctrinal conflicts within the early church led Christians to an understanding of their God and Creator, helping to define what they believe and worship today, they consider the struggle worth it.

"This was a frenzied battle within the Christian soul itself," writes the mid-twentieth-century historian Henri Daniel-Rops. "Men were to hate one another in duels in which no mercy was shown by either side."

That becomes particularly evident in the conduct of Alexander, bishop of Alexandria, who enters the controversy as a man most intent upon resolving conflict, but within a few years is issuing encyclical letters vehemently opposing Arianism.

Arius, on the other hand, was a controversialist from the start, says Daniel-Rops. He was a man who "possessed that inextricable mixture of virtues and defects blended together in the melting pot of pride."

In the course of the next several centuries, as Christians grappled with the doctrinal problems that Christ's words as recorded in the Scriptures had raised, passions and personal animosities would grow worse, often involving physical violence and vicious personal abuse. For example, in 350, Paul, patriarch of Constantinople, was strangled to death as a result of his conflicts with Arius.

All of this would amaze most Christians at the

Constantine immediately wrote to both Arius and Alexander, gave the letter to Bishop Hosius of Cordoba, his trusted adviser on Christian matters, and dispatched him to Alexandria to make peace between, as he saw them, two problem ecclesiastics.

It is a memorable letter. Constantine begins by deploring the "spirit of madness" that has seized the African church, brought on by the "reckless frivolity" that was dividing the Christians into "sects." It has caused "a deep wound, not to my ears only, but my heart" to hear of these conflicts which were, "of a truly insignificant nature, quite unworthy of such bitter contention."

He then addresses his criticism to the two main combatants. "You, Alexander, asked your priests what they thought about certain passages of the law (he meant the Bible) or rather about one insignificant detail of it. And you, Arius, imprudently voiced an opinion which ought never to have been conceived, or, once it was conceived, ought to have been silently buried."

Such things, he continues, ought never to become a public issue. "Disputes of this kind . . . are promoted by argument in unprofitable idleness, even if they take place as some sort of gymnastic exercise. Still it is our duty to shut them up inside the mind and not casually produce them in public synods, nor incautiously commit them to the hearing of the laity. For how great is any individual that he can either correctly discern or adequately explain the meaning of matters so great and so exceedingly difficult? And even suppose someone manages this easily, how many of the people is he likely to convince? Or who could sustain precise statements in such disputes without risk of dangerous mistakes?

ALEXANDER ON THE FATHER
It is necessary to say that the Father is always the Father. He is the Father, since the Son is always with Him, on account of whom He is called the Father.

end of the second millennium, because they could not understand people of faith becoming so intimately involved in matters that, to the twenty-first-century mind anyway, could not be resolved.

"If it seems very remote from our understanding today," asks Daniel-Rops, "is not this perhaps because of weaker faith and blunter emotions?" But such "weaker faith" has an explanation, says the twentieth-century Christian apologist Charles Gore in his *The Reconstruction of Belief*. In Gore's view, a number of influences have combined to destroy religious belief. In particular, he cites the impact of Darwinism, of literary and historical criticism applied to the Bible, and of the reduction of religion to "a branch of abnormal psychology." These have combined to create a widespread disbelief in traditional religious tenets.

Gore's analysis helps identify the reason why the Christian doctrine of the Trinity is perceived by many people as absurd conjecture, and the disputes it provoked as occasioned by sheer pride. That many aspects of Darwinism, criticism, and psychologism have themselves come under scientific attack seems to have had little impact on the general trend

away from religious inquiry.

Protestants, too, may dismiss the questions raised by the Arian dispute as having nothing to do with them, says the Canadian church historian David Priestley (a consultant on this series). But "Baptists and Evangelicals, given our concentration on the Bible, need to be told that we depend on the instruction of the Spirit in and through our catholic ancestors for two key dogmas: the Trinity and the Two Natures of Christ. The very apostolic writings they venerate provide the triadic terminology for God, the exalted descriptions of the Son, and the distinction made between Father, Son and Spirit with their unity. The dogma of the Trinity, and later of the Two Natures, are staples of Baptist and Evangelical conviction."

While many today are unfamiliar with their "classical statement" in human terms, Priestley continues, "we naively extract the tri-unity and 'true God and true man' as self-evident in Scripture and never contested by true believers." But what is "self-evident" now became so only after hard-fought contests between believers centuries ago. ∎

"We must therefore avoid being talkative in such matters. Otherwise, whether because of our natural limitations we cannot explain properly what is propounded, or because with their slower intellect, the audience is incapable of reaching a correct understanding of what is said, one way or the other, the people may be brought inevitably to either blasphemy or schism." And so, he concludes, "please restore my quiet days and untroubled nights to me, so that the joy of undimmed light and delight in a tranquil life may once again be mine."

In other words, observes historian Smith, Constantine "displayed an almost twentieth-century impatience with theology." He was "quite incapable of interesting himself in metaphysical questions," says Monsignor Louis Duchesne in

Thus appeared the man who would take on emperors, bishops, police, councils and every type of adversary and prevail over them all. His name was Athanasius.

The Early History of the Christian Church. His impatience "might perhaps have succeeded with Westerners. But with the Greeks, who were born thinkers, talkers and wranglers, it was quite another matter. The question could not be suppressed; it was necessary to decide it."

So, anyway, Hosius discovered when he arrived at Antioch, called a synod, heard the case of the two disputants, and failed to effect a reconciliation. It was far more than a clash of personalities, he reported to Constantine—it was a major theological issue and it endangered the entire church. Both Arius and Alexander followed Hosius back to Nicomedia, Arius by land to round up his support in Palestine, Syria and other quarters in the East; Alexander direct to Nicomedia by sea. Alexander got there first and to the emperor first, an accomplishment some see as pivotal. Meanwhile, the renowned historian Eusebius of Caesarea ran into trouble at Antioch. An insistent Subordinationist, he spoke his opinions too stridently before an Antiochian synod, and was pronounced a heretic.

Hosius's mission of reconciliation in Alexandria had not been a complete failure, however. He persuaded the inflammatory Colluthus to stop pretending he was a bishop, and to order the men he had ordained to stop pretending to be priests. Colluthus agreed, so there were now only two claimants to the Alexandrian see. Moreover, a major precedent had been set, though no one seemed to notice at the time. The emperor had authoritatively intervened in a purely ecclesiastical and theological dispute. He had asserted a senior role in the affairs of the Christians and they had accepted it unquestioningly.

He now took a far more significant step. In 324, he summoned a council of all the Christian bishops to be held at Ancyra in Galatia, the old province in Asia Minor where Saint Paul had founded the churches to whom he wrote his epistle. This council would resolve the Arian question, Constantine said, as well

ALEXANDER ON CHRIST'S SAVING WORK

Our Lord was made man; He was condemned that He might impart compassion; He was bound that He might set free; He was apprehended that He might liberate; He suffered that He might heal our sufferings; He died to restore life to us; He was buried to raise us up.

as the Melitian question, the question of the date of Easter, and all the other pressing church questions. To Constantine, if Christianity were to serve the empire, its church must be united; and he would take whatever steps were necessary to unite it. Trying to make God a tool of imperial policy was bad theology, however, and dubious political policy as well. Constantine didn't know that, but he was about to find out.[6]

Eusebius, meanwhile, appealed his conviction for heresy to the council at Ancyra. Constantine at the last minute switched the venue to Nicea, where, he explained, the weather was far better and the locale more accessible to bishops from the distant West. Historian Frend suspects another reason. Constantine's friend and biographer Eusebius of Caesarea was far more likely to win an acquittal from a council at Nicea, where the local bishop favored him, than he was at Ancyra where the local bishop did not.

It was now the spring of 325. The palace swarmed with Christians—Hosius, Alexander, both Eusebii, Constantia and possibly the emperor's mother, Helena, whose patron saint was Lucian. All prayed, conferred, schemed, scribbled letters and sought the ear of the emperor as the great day of the council approached. ■

---

6. "Let us be very careful of how we preach that Christianity is necessary for the building of a free and prosperous world," wrote the Christian writer Dorothy L. Sayers in a 1947 essay entitled *The Other Six Deadly Sins*. "The proposition is strictly true, but to put it that way may be misleading, for it sounds as though we proposed to make God an instrument in the service of man. But God is nobody's instrument. . . . To suggest that the service of God is necessary as a means to the service of man is a blasphemous hypocrisy which would end by degrading God to the status of a heathen fetish, bound to the service of the tribe, and liable to be dumped head-downwards in the water-butt if he failed to produce good harvest weather in return for services rendered."

WE BELIEVE IN ONE GOD, THE FATHER
ALMIGHTY, MAKER OF ALL THINGS VISIBLE
AND INVISIBLE; AND IN ONE LORD
JESUS CHRIST, THE SON OF GOD, ONLY-BEGOTTEN
OF THE FATHER, THAT IS, OF THE
SUBSTANCE OF THE FATHER, GOD OF
GOD, LIGHT OF LIGHT, TRUE GOD OF TRUE GOD,
BEGOTTEN NOT MADE,
OF THE SAME SUBSTANCE
WITH THE FATHER,
THROUGH WHOM ALL THINGS WERE
MADE IN HEAVEN AND IN EARTH; WHO FOR
US MEN AND FOR OUR SALVATION
DESCENDED, WAS INCARNATE, WAS MADE
MAN, SUFFERED, ROSE AGAIN THE THIRD
DAY, ASCENDED INTO THE HEAVENS,
AND WILL COME TO JUDGE THE LIVING AND
THE DEAD. AND IN THE HOLY SPIRIT.
THOSE WHO SAY: THERE WAS A TIME
WHEN HE WAS NOT, AND HE WAS NOT BEFORE
HE WAS BEGOTTEN, AND HE WAS MADE
OF NOTHING, OR WHO SAY THAT
HE IS OF ANOTHER HYPOSTASIS, OR ANOTHER
SUBSTANCE, OR THAT THE SON OF GOD
IS CREATED, OR MUTABLE, OR
SUBJECT TO CHANGE, THE CATHOLIC CHURCH
ANATHEMATIZES.

The creed approved at the Council of Nicea in 325 took pains to clarify the relationship of the Father and the Son, and also to denounce the heretical understandings that were anathema, i.e. cursed. It would eventually form the basis of the Nicene Creed used to the present in church liturgies.

CHAPTER 9

Showdown at Nicea: the victory that failed

Constantine's intervention helps carry a vital clause, but Arianism wins over the emperor and prospers; Athanasius becomes the creed's defiant champion

They poured in by boat, caravan and mule cart from across the Roman Empire—from Asia, Syria, Palestine, Egypt, Greece, Thrace—and beyond from as far as Persia and Scythia, 318 bishops by one count, along with their attendants more than one thousand travelers in all, descending upon the bustling commercial city of Nicea in the month of May 325. The emperor, Constantine the Great, had summoned them, and the bishops willingly answered his urgent call. It was he, after all, who had finally put a halt to the torture, enslavement and death that the Roman Empire had, from time to time, visited upon the Christians for the past three centuries, never more severely than in the earlier reign of Diocletian, and its immediate aftermath.

So when Bishop Patamon of Egypt, who had lost an eye in the persecutions, received Constantine's invitation, he responded eagerly. So did Paphnutius, who had one of his eyes bored out, and both of his legs cut off under the reign of Daia; and Paul of Neocaesarea (now Niksar, Turkey), his hands twisted into permanent claws by red-hot irons, under orders of Licinius.

Along with those who carried the scars of persecution in their bodies came delegates who, wrote the historian Eusebius of Caesarea, "were celebrated for their wisdom, others for the austerity of their lives and for their patience, others for their modesty; some were very old, some full of the freshness of youth." All had taken the journey to Nicea to assemble in the Christian church's first-ever general council. They were to consider a growing controversy, one that threatened not only the church, but the hard-won unity of the empire itself.

The voyage to the pleasant lakeshore city of Nicea in Bithynia (now the city of Iznik in Turkey), up from the Mediterranean, along the west coast of the Aegean Sea, and through the Sea of Marmara, was easiest for the Eastern Christians; and of the bishops who attended (the number would vary from day

The Turkish city of Iznik has been renowned over the centuries for its ceramics. When it was known as Nicea, its then great buildings were the site for Constantine's historic council of 325. Cows now graze near the rubble of its ancient walls and towers (left). The church that was the venue for some of the council's debates was later replaced by the Church of St. Sophia (Holy Wisdom), in ruins today (right).

to day and week to week), only about eight came from the West, including those from Spain, Italy, Dalmatia and Gaul. With Pope Sylvester ailing, Rome sent two priests, but no bishop.

From the Eastern metropolises came Alexander of Alexandria, Eustathius of Antioch and Macarius of Jerusalem. From Nicomedia, the Bithynian capital about twenty miles away, came Bishop Eusebius. Also present was the historian, Bishop Eusebius of Caesarea, giving rise to occasional minor uncertainty in the records of the council as to which Eusebius said or did what.[1]

Safe though they were from governmental persecution, a new and even greater concern beset them. For by the year 325, few in the entire church were unaware of the crucial and embittered battle that raged in the East, fiercely dividing its bishops. It centered squarely on the question that had dogged Christians from the beginning. Who was Jesus Christ? There were many items on the agenda for the Council of Nicea, but this one, and this alone, stood paramount.

Indeed, it was chiefly to resolve that question that Constantine had called the council, the first meeting of the whole church since that time in Jerusalem when the apostles had met to resolve another crucial question: Was Jesus Christ for

---

1. The name Eusebius was very common in the early church. According to *The Dictionary of Christian Biography*, at least 137 persons with that name were worth noting in the first eight centuries.

Jews alone, with those few Gentiles prepared to accept circumcision and all the complexities of the ancient Jewish Law? Or was he for all the peoples of the world? That question had been answered. Now there was another. "Who do men say that I, the Son of Man, am?" Jesus had asked his disciples (Matt. 16:13). Three hundred years later, they at last sought to agree on an answer.

Many theories had been advanced over the years, but by 325 they came down to two, one incompatible with the other. The first, though the most easily believed, was essentially negative. It said who he was not. It held that Jesus was

not God, at any rate, not in the way that the Father was God. By this view, the term "God" without modification could be applied only to the Father. The being who became Jesus was actually a creature, something created by God, created before the world was created, but created nevertheless. In other words, there was a time when there was a Father and no Son.

That view was already called Arianism, after the man who had most recently articulated it, the priest Arius, excommunicated by a council called in his home diocese of Alexandria, but later supported by another council called by the two Eusebii.

The advocates of the other view had, for the moment, no name and no firmly agreed upon theology. In general, they believed that God was One all right, but he existed in Three Persons. The First did not create the Second; both had existed eternally, as had the Third, the Holy Spirit. Therefore, there never had been a time when the First existed without the Second and Third. Though all three existed eternally, the Second had lived on Earth as the man Jesus. He had "come down from heaven" at a specific point in created time. Because he was a man, he had suffered and died a human death. Because he was also God, he had saved man from eternal destruction.

But the controversy could not yet be described as the Arian view versus the catholic view. Both claimed to be Catholic, both prepared for a showdown, and both recognized that a key factor in the decision would be the position taken by Constantine. However, the emperor was known to have one purpose only. He wanted the question settled. Period. To him, the theological issue was not central. The unity of the Roman Empire was central, and Christianity was his chosen method to bring that unity about.

This unbecoming brawl over "abstract theology," as he saw it, was most distressing. This "bishop against bishop, district against district," as Bishop Eusebius of Caesarea, the historian, would later describe it, was unacceptable. Who won it, Constantine did not seem to care. The crucial necessity was that *somebody* win it, and the row be over and done with.

Getting the emperor's ear was therefore key. But neither side had any direct experience in lobbying emperors, nor had emperors defined any single way in which to entertain lobbying. Not many years earlier, any Roman emperor who contrived to get so many bishops together under one roof would have done so in order to imprison, torture or kill them. Now the bishops were to be the emperor's favored guests, many arriving in Nicea in carriages he had sent to meet their ships or caravans. He had even raised Nicea's grain quota to make sure everybody had plenty to eat.

In a portrait bust that might have been carved near the end of his reign, Constantine's features have been rendered much softer than the more heroic and stylized versions in this volume. The eyes, however, are unmistakably his.

The priest Arius was among those making the journey to Nicea, of course. So were his top supporters, the two Eusebii. Chief among those arrayed against the "Arian party" was Arius's old foe from Alexandria, Bishop Alexander, and that smart young deacon, Athanasius, who assisted him. Athanasius was a small man, with auburn hair and a beard, who despite his youth, had an inclination to stoop. As a deacon, he couldn't say much to the assembled bishops, but he had a knack for convincingly summarizing the anti-Arian case. Moreover, he wrote voluminously, and seemed incapable of fatigue. Though he was not yet a frontline disputant and would play no visibly prominent role at Nicea, his talents and energy made him extremely dangerous to the Arian cause. Yet he had, as they saw it, a telling weakness. He seemed utterly fearless, more concerned with the assertion of truth than with its political acceptability. Since Constantine's concern was not primarily truth but unity, he might be persuaded to view Athanasius as an obstacle to unity, a chronic troublemaker.

Constantine's entrance during the opening ceremonies, held in the judgment hall of his imperial palace, was accomplished with imperial splendor. As the bishops stood up among their rows of benches, Constantine followed his bodyguards and attendants—conspicuously unarmed—to the front of the room, where he paused before a golden stool, near a table holding the texts of the Gospels. "He wore the purple imperial robes, covered with embroidery, gold and diamonds. With his majestic bearing and dignity, he looked," the enthusiastic Eusebius writes, "like an angel of God come down from heaven."

When the emperor seated himself on the stool, the rest of the assembly sat down too. The Arians, though far fewer in number, then scored a major opening coup. Their most avid and distinguished advocate, Eusebius of Nicomedia, had been chosen as the host bishop to deliver the welcoming address. This would leave the distinct impression that Constantine was on the Arian side, a point that would not be lost on any that may be wavering. Eusebius lavishly praised Constantine and the empire and the leaders of the church.

Next, no doubt to thunderous standing applause, Constantine himself arose. The roar of approval faded, and all fell silent, listening intently, wholly conscious of a momentous occasion. For the first time in history, a Roman emperor yet unbaptized was addressing the Christian church. The man Jesus, crucified by the Romans like a common felon, was now the very center of imperial devotion.

Constantine spoke in Latin, with an interpreter providing a version in Greek, the language of most of those present. He was most grateful that they had come, he said. Divisions and dissent within the church were works of the devil, worse even than civil war. His own military victories, hard-won in an effort to unite the empire, would remain incomplete, if the leaders of the church were torn and distracted by disharmony. He urged those present to speak openly

Amidst thunderous applause, Constantine arose. For the first time, a Roman emperor addressed the Church. Jesus Christ was now at the very center of imperial devotion.

and to make their positions and disagreements clear, but to maintain a spirit of peace and harmony. Such an effort would please not only the emperor, but the God whom they all served.

In a version of Constantine's opening remarks set down by the fifth-century historian Hermias Sozomen, Constantine went further. He told the council: "I deem dissension in the church of God as more dangerous than any other evil. . . . The favor which I seek is that you examine the causes of the strife, and put a consentient and peaceful end thereto, so I may triumph with you over the envious demon who excited this internal revolt, because he was provoked to see our external enemies and tyrants under our feet."

Then in a dramatic act, typically Constantinian, and recorded by another fifth-century historian, Rufinus of Aquileia, he suited the deed to the word. He knew well, he said, that there were disagreements—not only over theological issues, but there was also a buzz of individual spats and power struggles between individual bishops. Even before the meeting began, many bishops had sought him out and leveled charges at one another, he said. Some had drawn up elaborate petitions in which they begged him to rule one way or another in their squabbles.

He quietly sat down. All eyes were fastened upon him as aides, appearing from the wings, swiftly brought forward these written petitions and silently placed them, one by one, in his lap. Then in feigned fury he arose, faced the bishops, raised his hitherto lowered voice to a level of authority and military command, and glared upon them. Their petty quarrels, he declared, were incompatible with their offices as Christ's servants. He had made a point of reading not a single one of their petitions, he said, and with that, tossed them one by one into a brazier, and before their eyes burned them. "Only God," he declared, "can decide your controversies."

It was a stinging rebuke. He had chastised them not only for failing the empire, but also for failing their own Christian ministries, and it doubtless had the effect he sought, pushing local trivialities aside and forcing attention on the

The real Santa Claus

Though Nicholas and Valentine have become festive saints, both suffered for their faith, Valentine paying with his life

Enduring legends often have obscure beginnings, founded on a few basic facts but embellished through the centuries. Such is the case of St. Valentine, who is not known ever to have written a letter of love in the shape of a heart. And St. Nicholas, who lived a holy life of charity and had a deep affection for children, did not deliver presents at Christmas. Yet throughout the Christian realm, both of these two saints, who lived within one hundred years of each other, are commemorated annually, having influenced religious and secular societies alike.

Nicholas was a fourth-century bishop of Myra (on the south coast of the future Turkey), and is honored in both Eastern and Western churches. He shared in the suffering of his era, was thrown into prison during the Diocletian persecution, and was released when Constantine freed Christians who were being punished for their beliefs.

Little else is known of Nicholas, though legend ascribes to him many miracles—he is reported to have leapt out of his mother's womb proclaiming, "God be glorified." It is said that he attended the Council of Nicea, although his name nowhere appears in the historical record. Three hundred years after his death, a church was built in his honor in Constantinople. He became the patron saint of numerous countries; and because of particular miracles, he is also the patron of sailors, children, merchants and pawnbrokers. He is depicted in countless paintings and carvings.

His first biography appeared in the ninth century, collecting the stories that had accumulated around him. The most influential of these stories tells of his rescuing three young women, who were to be forced into prostitution when their father could not provide a dowry. Nicholas is said to have thrown bags of gold through their window so that they could pay a ransom.

By the early tenth century, when this Spanish medallion (left) was crafted, stories of the posthumous miracles of Nicholas had spread throughout the Christian world. At Myra on the coast of Asia Minor (right), the church holding his sarcophagus was a place of pilgrimage until Nicholas's remains were removed to Bari, Italy, in the eleventh century.

main Arian issue, with the implied threat of the imperial wrath if they couldn't reach an agreement.

The details of what happened next are largely lost to history. Though the council's resolutions are well documented, all that remains of the proceedings themselves is a scattering of unrelated facts. Both Eusebius of Caesarea and Athanasius would leave records, but neither provides more than skimpy details on the council's day-to-day workings. If minutes were kept, they are lost. Who presided is not known, though it was probably Bishop Hosius of Cordoba, who as Constantine's chief theological adviser helped convince him of the need for

Residents of the slums of Managua, Nicaragua, trudge past a billboard depicting Santa Claus, patron of the poor, with his beverage of choice.

The deed, celebrated in paintings, gave rise to his fame as patron of children. In Dutch dialectal pronunciation his name, *Sint Nicklaus* became *Sinter Klass*, which in English became *Santa Claus*, and gifts were given children on his feast day of December 6. Dutch and other immigrants to America brought with them the tradition of gift giving; the practice, rescheduled nineteen days later, was eventually made part of the celebration of "Christ's Mass," or Christmas.

Nothing whatever in the life of St. Valentine suggests boxes of chocolates, cupids, pink hearts or the exchange of romantic notions. Several people named Valentine are mentioned in early martyrologies. The one representing what has become St. Valentine's Day was a priest in Rome who assisted martyrs during the third-century persecution of Emperor Claudius II. He eventually was arrested, and having refused to renounce his faith, was beaten and beheaded.

Valentine's feast day, on February 14, has long been linked to celebrations of early spring. The fourteenth-century poet Geoffrey Chaucer, describing the transformation of a long and dreary English winter into the joy of impending spring, followed the tradition that February 14 was the day when birds begin to pair, and wrote the couplet:

> For this was sent on Seynt Valentyne's day
> When every foul cometh ther to choose his mate.

Thus the day became special for devoted couples, and for love-letter writing and the sending of tokens.

Like other Christians who have been declared saints over the centuries, Valentine and Nicholas are revered for the personal holiness they demonstrated during their lives, and Catholic Christians say they certainly went to be with God upon their deaths. They can therefore be addressed even now as eternally living persons:

"I, poor ordinary Christian, have no right to claim God's ear; but you, glorified brother/sister, by your better obedience in this life and present proximity, would you be my intercessor?" the theologian Anselm, who was later proclaimed a saint himself, wrote in the eleventh century.

Lost amid the commercialization of both Valentine's Day and Christmas is the fact that both of the men involved suffered for their faith, one quite probably giving his life for it. ■

For Athanasius, the relationship of the Father to his divine Son could be likened to a waterfall. The Father is the waterfall, the Son the water that is eternally generated and constantly poured out. Or, in his favorite analogy, Athanasius claimed the Father and Son were like light and its brightness. The brightness is not the light source itself, but the two are inseparable.

such a gathering.[2] Even the precise dates of the council are debated; some records say it ran from May 25 to June 19, others that it began earlier and lasted longer, one that it was actually two meetings, spaced two years apart.

This leaves it to historians to reconstruct from the surviving fragments and their own imaginations what probably occurred.

The silver-tongued Arius was doubtless one of the first speakers, and is portrayed as expounding his theology brilliantly. The elegance of his tall, thin frame, his slightly emaciated mien, the carefully unkempt hair and rumpled garments conveyed unmistakably the image of the ascetic that had so enchanted the young Christian women of Alexandria. Could a man so holy, so pious, so self-evidently noble, possibly speak anything but truth?

Eusebius of Caesarea[3] spoke in support of him, followed even more urgently by Eusebius of Nicomedia and others. Was it not easier, more congenial, less problematic, they asked, to think of Jesus Christ as a mere creature like themselves than to see him as the actual creator and preserver of the universe, come to fallen Earth on a mission of salvation? Wasn't a suffering god a contradiction, an oxymoron? How could God suffer while at the same time remaining God?

Alexander and Hosius had contrary observations. If Jesus was not God but merely made by God as men and angels and beasts, how could his sacrifice in any sense redeem fallen humanity? The sacrifices of animals and birds in the pagan religions did not redeem humanity. Were not the sacrifices of creatures in the old Temple of the Jews merely a forerunner of the sacrifice of God himself? Such, surely, had always been the Christian understanding.

However, as the debate unfolded, much to the chagrin of the traditionalists, the Arians would consistently assign their own private meaning to theological terms. "They changed like chameleons," Athanasius would later recall. In this way, they could subscribe to whatever formal statement of Christian belief the council might adopt, avoiding excommunication, while rationalizing the

2. Hosius of Cordoba certainly had a good background. He was a respected church leader, distinguished scholar, knowledgeable in both Christian doctrine and Platonism, and Constantine's personal legate in an abortive mission to Alexandria prior to the council that sought to resolve the Arian controversy.

statement's meaning, and privately maintaining their own beliefs. Or they would frame their own contentions in highly ambiguous language, in order to prevent clarification.

Thus, when the traditionalists rejected Arius's description of the Son as having arisen "out of nothing" and insisted that the Word of God who "became flesh" in the man Jesus, was both "God" and "with God," as the opening verse of John's Gospel describes him, supporters of Arius said they heartily agreed. After all, they declared, everything is "with God" anyway—humans as well as all other creatures.

Or again, when the traditionalists, vainly trying to pin down the point, proposed that "the Word is . . . the eternal image of the Father, perfectly like to the Father, immutable and true God," the Arians would accept that as well. Doesn't the Bible

Was it not easier to think of Jesus as a mere creature? Wasn't a suffering god a contradiction, an oxymoron? How could God suffer and at the same time remain God?

describe man as having been made in God's image and therefore like him? And didn't the apostle Paul's assurance that "Nothing can separate us from the love of Christ" mean that the creature known as man, too, is "immutable" in a sense?

Finally, however, the traditionalists came up with a term the Arians could find no way to compromise. It involved the Greek word *ousia*, which translates into English as "essence" or "substance." Man could not possibly know, of course, what might be the "essence" or "substance" of God, the ultimate quality of the Divine. But whatever that quality is, said the traditionalists, it was shared by both the Father and the Son. They thus developed the expression *homoousios*, "of the same essence" or "of the same substance." The Son, they declared, was of the same "essence" or "substance" of the Father. At this the Arians balked. It was specifically this that they could not accept, they declared.

Throughout all these abstract discussions, Constantine might be expected to have appeared impatient and restless at so much theological hairsplitting. But he did not. He is credited with working steadily throughout the council's meetings to bring accord, always urging moderation and reason. Having sought and won permission to sit with the bishops, he interjected himself directly and forcefully into the discussions. Only occasionally did he urge the participants to stop quibbling

ALEXANDER ON THE DIVINITY OF JESUS

Arius and his followers call in question all pious and apostolic doctrine, denying the Godhead of our Savior, and preaching that He is only the equal of all others. They ignore altogether the passages in which His eternal Godhead and unutterable glory with the Father is set forth.

---

3. Eusebius of Caesarea (c. 263–339), who had trained as a scribe under Pamphilius of Phoenicia, was a prolific writer. Besides his history of the church his works include a number of chronicles, arguments directed against pagans to justify Christianity, and treatises on theology and the Bible. He also composed flattering speeches for Constantine. He was said to be an inexhaustible worker well into his old age, and a scholar of vast range. According to the *Cambridge Ancient History*, he "knew everything, biblical history, pagan history, ancient literature, philosophy, geography, computation, exegesis. . . . He could explain the difficult question of the Passover. . . . It was to him that the emperor Constantine turned when he needed well-written and accurate copies of the Bible; he once asked him for fifty all at once, for the churches of Constantinople." On the other hand, according to the same source, he "did not always avoid the danger of letting his main idea disappear under a mass of documents."

*Eyed with satisfaction by
Constantine and his mother, Helena,
the bishops assembled at Nicea step
forward to sign the resolutions
approved by their council— most
importantly, the creed they have just
hammered out. Among those in the
queue are bishops missing eyes and
limbs, scarred by the tortures of
years of persecution. To the right of
Constantine stands Eusebius of
Nicomedia, who would be instru-
mental in undercutting, by intrigue,
the very decisions being approved on
that spring day in 325.*

over matters that might be understood by God but could only remain mysteries to the minds of men. There was too much asking of frivolous questions, he said, and there were too many unworthy answers. Faith in the Divine Providence, under a united consensus, was the only thing that mattered.

But he no doubt saw, as did they all, that a major doctrine could pivot on the definition of a term. To Hosius, Alexander and Athanasius, and most others present, the point under debate was crucial to the gospel message. God could redeem mankind; man could not redeem man, they said. If Jesus were a creature, like the rest of us, then his death meant no more than the death of any man, and humanity was therefore left unredeemed.

Such was the issue, and it finally came to a head when the Arian Eusebius of Caesarea proposed as the creed of Christianity the one he had learned as a child

> *God could redeem mankind; man could not redeem man. If Jesus was a creature then his death meant nothing: Humanity would therefore be left unredeemed.*

in Palestine. Before what we may assume was a hushed house, he read it to the assembled bishops and the emperor:

> We believe in one God, Father Almighty, Creator of all things visible and invisible; and in the Lord Jesus Christ, the Word of God, God of God, Light of Light, Life of Life, his only Son, the firstborn of all creatures, begotten of the Father before all time, by whom also everything was created, who became flesh for our redemption, who lived and suffered among men, rose again the third day, returned to the Father, and will come again one day in his glory to judge the living and the dead. We believe also in one Holy Spirit. We believe that each of these three is and subsists: the Father truly as Father, the Son truly as Son, the Holy Spirit truly as Holy Spirit; as our Lord said, when he sent his disciples to preach: "Go and teach all nations, and baptize them in the name of the Father, and of the Son, and of the Holy Spirit."

That, Eusebius said, was a statement representing his true beliefs, one that he could wholeheartedly endorse.

The traditionalists listened in dismay. Whatever else it said, the Eusebian creed declared the Son a "creature," so if that creed were adopted, their cause was lost, and the declaration of the redemptive power of Christianity lost along with it. Then came a worse development. The emperor arose. All arose with him. He believed it too, he said. Hearts sank. Frantic prayers ascended. "Lord, have mercy." But then an odd thing happened.

The emperor wasn't finished. However, he continued, he felt that one other phrase ought to be added to this statement of belief, to more fully clarify what was being said. The creed of the Christians must declare, he argued, that the Son is "of the same substance as the Father."

The words no doubt came like a thunderclap, leaving the resulting scene to be imagined. The traditionalists would have grasped one another and wept.

The battle had been won after all. "*Doxa Theou!*" they would cry in Greek, "*Laus Deo!*" in Latin. "Praise God!" Among the Arians, all would have been consternation. That clause, the one they could not explain away, was there, boldly and unmistakably. Someone had obviously "got" to Constantine. Who was it? No one to this day knows, of course, but the best bet was Hosius of Cordoba, the Spaniard, who still had the emperor's ear.

Out of this agreement, the first version of the first Christian statement of faith began to emerge. Known as the Nicene Creed, it would knock the props out from under Arianism. It declared that the Son of God was "begotten, not made," and repeated for anyone who still didn't get it that the Son was "of the same substance [or essence] with the Father."

Going further still, it made clear that anyone pronouncing the Son of God to be of another substance than the Father, or to have been created or to be subject to change was to be declared anathema: formally excommunicated. When the vote was taken, only five bishops refused to sign it, three of whom later relented.[4] The priest Arius himself likewise refused.

With all that and several other issues settled (see sidebar page 244), the council adjourned.[5] Constantine invited the bishops to a sumptuous feast at the imperial palace, celebrating the twentieth anniversary (or *vicennalia*) of his rule. It was a splendid affair. As the bishops entered, they passed through a "hedge" of uniformed soldiers, standing smartly at attention, with swords drawn. Constantine mingled and chatted with the crowd, at one point getting off a quick one-liner.[6]

When the banquet concluded, each of the men received fine presents from the emperor. A few days later, at an official closing session, Constantine asked the bishops to pray for him as they returned home; and with an exhortation that they continue to use their offices to maintain peace, he sent them on their way to report the council's results in their own lands. Constantine also issued letters to all the bishops who had not attended the council, expounding upon the council's decrees, and declaring that they were to be regarded as imperial law. In accord with the council's decision, Arius and the two bishops who had refused to sign

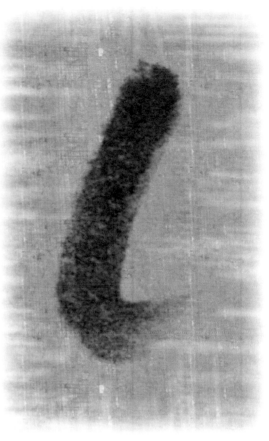

Eventually, a single letter of the Greek alphabet, the iota, separated the Arian and orthodox factions at the Council of Nicea. Were the Son and the Father homoousios or homoiousios? The same or similar substance? The truth hung on this one thin letter.

4. According to the Arian historian Philostorgius, the three bishops who relented and signed the Nicene document did so dishonestly. They wrote the word *homoiousios* instead of *homoousios*. Inserting that one little letter, the Greek iota, into the middle of the word, changed its meaning to "of like substance," or "similar in substance." Thus the Arian controversy was said to have split the church "by one iota."

5. Adjournment brought peace to a contentious meeting that included, in some traditional accounts, a fistfight or two. Lord Runcie, former Archbishop of Canterbury, says that during one heated argument, Nicholas of Myra (see sidebar, page 236) may have "boxed the ears of the leading heretic Arius."

6. Mixing with the bishops at the great banquet which ended the Council of Nicea, Constantine found himself cornered by the Novatian bishop of Constantinople, Acesius, who expounded at great length upon his firm conviction that anyone who commits any sin after being baptized, even if repentant, is unworthy of further consideration by the church. Constantine, likely impatient both with the bishop's long-winded rhetoric and his unforgiving spirit, finally cut him off by interjecting sarcastically, "Very well, then, Acesius, plant a ladder and climb up to heaven alone."

Why Easter falls on Sunday

The Nicene council adopts some twenty canons or decisions that the Paschal feast must occur on 'the Lord's Day'

Apart from the thorny question of Arianism, numerous other issues faced the Council of Nicea, chief among them sorting out the confusion about Easter celebrations.

It was a vexing problem. In the East, many churches observed Easter on the day of the Jewish Passover—after all, they said, Jesus was the perfect Passover sacrifice, the Lamb slain to redeem humankind. But in the West, the Easter holy day was celebrated on the Sunday following Passover, because that was the day when Jesus rose from death and left his tomb empty. To make matters worse, because various calendars were in use and they did not all agree, some Christians calculated Easter to fall on one date, and some on another.

The Council of Nicea must have heard all the arguments on all sides about Easter, but any record of the debates has been lost. After considering the matter, the council unanimously issued the following statement: "We give you good news of the unity which has been established respecting the holy Passover. All the brethren in the East who formerly celebrated Easter with the Jews will henceforth keep it at the same time as the Romans, with us, and with all those who from ancient times have celebrated the feast at the same time with us."

Constantine also issued a letter about the council's decision that he circulated to bishops who were not present during the discussions at Nicea. After asserting that the minds of the Jews had been blinded by error and that their custom for setting the date of the Passover could therefore not be followed, Constantine writes:

"Our Savior has left us only one festal day of our redemption, that is to say, of his holy Passion, and he desired only one catholic church. Think, then, how unseemly it is, that on the same day some should be fasting, while others are seated at a banquet; and that after Easter, some should be rejoicing at feasts, while others are still observing a strict fast. . . .

"To sum up in a few words: by the unanimous judgment of all, it has been decided that the most holy festival of Easter should be everywhere celebrated on one and the same day, and it is not seemly that in so holy a thing there should be any division."

That settled one Easter problem, but a more recent clash of calendars haunts the church today. From the Council of Nicea's decision in 325 until 1582, most of Christianity calculated the date of Easter from the vernal equinox, which occurs on March 21. This unanimity continued even after the Eastern and Western churches split at the end of the first millennium. But in 1582, the Roman Catholic Church switched to the Gregorian reform calendar, while the Orthodox churches retained the old Julian calendar, and used it to set their feast days, as did Protestant Britain, which finally accepted the Gregorian calendar in 1752. Since then, the Orthodox Easter celebration and the Western Christian Easter have usually occurred on different dates.

The council dealt with numerous other issues, foremost among them the division in the church at Alexandria where followers of Bishop Melitius had created their own episcopal hierarchy, because they considered Bishop Peter too soft on those who had lapsed from the faith during the persecutions. The council agreed to allow Melitius to retain his title as bishop, and it pronounced his ordinations valid. However, he and his clergy must remain subordinate to the bishop of Alexandria.

The council adopted at least twenty other canons, as its enactments and decisions were called, covering a variety of church practices. Some of these included very important and long-lasting rules on ordination, on the establishment of patriarchs, and on the movement of clergy between jurisdictions. One canon decreed that a clergyman whose body had been mutilated by physicians or barbarians could remain in office, but if he had mutilated himself, he could not. The "mutilation" referred to was castration, and the discussion was apparently prompted by several cases of young men who, like Origen before them, had made themselves eunuchs.

Another readmitted to the communion was Bishop Eusebius of Caesarea, excommunicated for heresy by a council at Antioch several months before the Nicene council met. Other canons forbade any member of the clergy from dwelling with a woman except his wife, mother, sister or aunt; ordered that those who had supported Licinius during his persecution of Christians should do penance, as should those who had renounced their faith under pressure of the persecutions; that clerics could not lend money at interest and that on Sundays and during Pentecost, prayers should be said standing up. ■

the creed were exiled to Illyricum on the Adriatic. Arius's writings were declared anathema, and all books of his that could be found were gathered up and burned. The Arian dispute had been resolved, the church united. And that, the emperor no doubt told himself, was that.

But that was not that, the Arian crisis was not resolved; the Christians, if anything, were farther from unity than they had been before the council was called. For the Arians left Nicea more determined than ever to take their case directly to the growing Christian intelligentsia, and to convert through them the mass of Christians to the Arian view. One of the first converts they sought to make was Constantine himself. His commitment to the traditional, they knew, was at best tentative. His aim was not the unity of the church so much as the unity of the empire, and hard on the heels of the council came an event that proved the imperial unity as precarious as that of the church.

The trouble centered in the old city of Rome. It remained pagan territory; and pagan hostility focused on this emperor, now openly embracing what had so recently been the despised religion called Christianity. He seemed clearly bent on sweeping away all that the ancient city held dear. Moreover, he fanned the flame of revolt, marking his vicennalia celebration in the city by publicly scorning as meaningless the city's celebration of the victory of the twin pagan gods Castor and Pollux at the battle of Lake Regillus in 496 B.C. where Rome acquired mastery of the Italian peninsula. Open rioting broke out, and a statue of Constantine was hit with a barrage of rocks, knocking off its nose, and badly disfiguring its face. Told of the incident, he smiled grimly, used his fingers to take a careful inventory of his facial features, and said, "I am not able to perceive any wound that has been inflicted upon my face. Both the head and the face appear quite sound." It amounted to a sneer, not calculated to endear him to the Roman populace.

In that climate, and given the well-known Roman penchant for hatching murderous plots against those in authority, Constantine seems to have convinced himself that he was under siege. On October 1, 325, with the Nicene council barely concluded, he issued a public challenge. Anyone with any accusations of any kind that could be leveled against any of Constantine's friends, officials, or intimates was urged to bring such charges forth. The emperor promised to listen and to take any action necessary.

Then came the deed that would permanently blacken his reign, its explanation an enduring historical mystery. Some said it somehow derived from his call for criticism, others from a falsified plot against him, others from a fit of rage. Whatever the cause, the outcome is not in dispute. Beset by gloom and suspicion, he had his first-born son Crispus, offspring of his first wife Minervina, hero of

An enterprising fourth-century collector gathered coins commemorating Constantine and the consulships of his sons Crispus and Constantine II, and had them fashioned into this pendant. However, the owner of the celebratory souvenir had to overlook one dark fact: Constantine had ordered Crispus murdered in 326.

the naval victory that secured the throne for Constantine, and once the apple of his eye, suddenly and without explanation put to death. Hard behind it came the murder of his young nephew, Licinius Licinianus, and others in his immediate household. Soon after, there followed the murder of his second wife, Fausta—locked up in her baths with the heat turned up so high that it killed her. "He departed," records the pagan writer Eutropius, "from his former agreeable mildness of temper. Falling first of all upon his own relatives, he put to death his own son, an excellent man, his sister's son, a youth of amiable disposition; soon afterwards his wife, and later numerous friends."

But why? Speculation abounds. The most plausible theory is that of the Arian writer Philostorgius. Fausta convinced Constantine to put Crispus to death, in an

Although the Nicene council had banished Arius and condemned his beliefs, Arianism gained ground rapidly and very soon became a dominant force among the Eastern bishops.

ambitious attempt to clear the way to power for her own sons, he then discovered Fausta in the act of adultery with one of his grooms, and had her killed. Whatever provoked the killings, writes the historian Lloyd B. Holsapple, in his biography, *Constantine the Great*, "the series of deaths has . . . covered the name of Constantine with shame and degradation."

Meanwhile, although the Nicene council had banished Arius and condemned his beliefs, Arianism gained ground rapidly, and very soon became a dominant belief among the Eastern bishops. They were skeptical about both Nicea and Athanasius, because in their tradition, there must be a strong assertion of the "threeness" in God, and they feared that Nicea did not explain the difference between the Father and Son. Exacerbating their fears was the relentless campaign conducted by Eusebius of Nicomedia, a veritable prototype of the ecclesiastical court politician whose central modus was the vilification of his foes.

To accomplish this, Eusebius must, of course, win the confidence of the emperor. He accomplished this by first winning the favor of the emperor's sister Constantia, then of the emperor himself.

The first victim of Eusebius's machinations was a certain Eustathius, bishop in the powerful see of Antioch, which, as the Arians saw it, belonged in their camp, not that of the traditionalists. Eustathius had loudly opposed the Arians at Nicea, and when he returned to his diocese, refused to ordain any clergy of the Arian school, which meant most of the candidates then presenting themselves.

Historian R. V. Sellers, in his brief biography of Eustathius, describes Eusebius of Nicomedia as traveling through Antioch en route to admire Constantine's new churches in Jerusalem, and stopping at Caesarea to plot with the other Eusebius a campaign against Antioch's bishop. On his return to his see, he recruited a prostitute to name the bishop as the father of her child. Further, Eusebius accused Eustathius of slandering Helena, the emperor's mother, a treasonous offense.

She endeared herself to the world

Through her charities and an amazing journey taken in her late 70s Constantine's mother left an indelible example for Christians

She began as a nobody from nowhere, and raised a son who would become emperor and decisively set the course for the history of the whole Western world. Most historians (though not all) believe she did not come to Christianity until in her sixties. In her late seventies, she embarked upon an unlikely pilgrimage to Jerusalem that gave rise to centuries of legends, traditions and controversies. Through the succeeding centuries, she became a model of humility, charity and faith that would greatly influence Christians for centuries to come.

This was Flavia Julia Helena, born some time between 248 and 250 in Drepanum, a town in Bithynia that served as a Roman military center in the East. Her family was of low social status: Ambrose of Milan reports that Helena was a serving maid, a *stabularia*, in an inn or a hostelry that was probably owned by her parents.

According to a story cherished for centuries in England, Helena was the daughter of the merry old soul King Cole of the nursery rhyme, who was in real life King Coel of Colchester. While there is no credible historical evidence to support the connection, Colchester—Britain's oldest recorded town—makes good use of the story in tourist promotions.

Closer to what was more likely her home, Helena became, around 270, the wife of Constantius Chlorus. Some say she was his concubine, but no moral stigma was attached to the concubine relationship. It simply recognized the disparity in social position between a Roman officer with good career prospects and an innkeeper's daughter. It meant they could not legally marry.

She gave birth to a son, Constantine, in about 274. The obvious affection and regard between mother and son in later life suggest a close and caring upbringing. In addition, descriptions of the elderly Helena's humility, munificence and charity toward others, and of Constantius's intelligence, temperate governance, and tolerance of Christians during the Diocletian persecution, suggest what the family's home life must have been like for some two decades. (The thesis that Helena and her husband were closet Christians who raised Constantine in the faith, is advanced by the University of Toronto's T. G. Elliott. (see chapter 5, this volume.)

In about 293, however, Helena's world came apart. Constantius put her aside to marry Theodora, and thereby secure for himself the rank of caesar; and their son Constantine was sent to live with the augustus Diocletian in Nicomedia, a hostage to guarantee his father's loyalty. Helena, now middle-aged, was left alone, and for more than a dozen years, she disappears from history's notice.

Some time after 306, Constantine, first as caesar and then as emperor, brought Helena to live with him in Trier and Rome, respectively. She was granted the title of Most Honored and Noble Lady, reserved for immediate members of the emperor's family, then the title Augusta around 324. The Sessorian Palace in Rome became her residence, and Constantine granted her access to the imperial treasury. Coins bore her name and likeness; statues were dedicated to her; cities and provinces were renamed in her honor, including her birthplace Drepanum, which upon her death became Helenopolis, in the province of Helenopontus.

Whatever her prior faith commitments, by 312, the sixty-something Helena had become an ardent and active Christian. She "appears to have been more spiritually minded than her son," writes the historian Hans A. Pohlsander. "Her piety was more intense and her conduct more pure. She understood and practiced the Christian virtues of humility and charity. Her life, much more than that of her son, came to be dominated by the Christian faith."

It is not at all clear what motivated this grandmother, something like seventy-eight years old at the time, to travel to Jerusalem on a grueling pilgrimage.

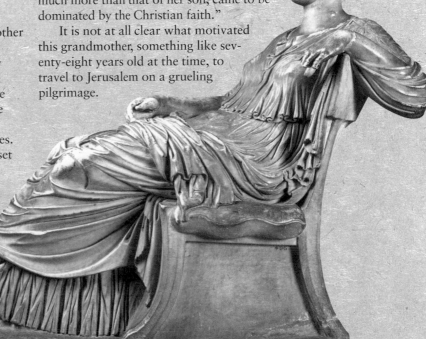

Helena has every reason to look satisfied in this statue in the Museo Capitolino in Rome. Although she had been cast aside when her husband, Constantius Chlorus, sought a more prestigious marriage, she was vindicated by her loving son, Constantine. And by the time she posed for this sculpture in 320, she enjoyed prestige well beyond what she might have expected with Constantius.

While supervising construction of the Church of the Holy Sepulchre, the dowager empress Helena is interrupted. Workers at nearby excavations have uncovered large wooden crosses exactly on the spot believed to be the Place of the Skull (Golgotha), where Christ was crucified. However credible the claim that one of these was the cross upon which Jesus was crucified, Helena's accomplishments in her journey to Palestine helped revere it as "the Holy Land."

Some have suggested that she undertook the journey as penance for Constantine's murder of his wife and son. But whatever prompted Helena's travels, it is recorded that on the road to Palestine and the Eastern provinces of the empire, she lived her faith as devoutly as she had in Rome. She attended services among the people, and used the public treasury to carry out charitable works and to sponsor and therefore accelerate church construction.

Accounts link Helena's name with establishment of the basilica of the Holy Nativity at Bethlehem; the Church of the Mount of Olives in Jerusalem; and the Church of the Holy Sepulchre, built on the site of Hadrian's temple to Venus, over the grotto where Christ was thought to have been entombed. Constantine himself is often credited with directing Bishop Macarius of Jerusalem to replace the pagan temple with the much acclaimed Christian structure. But it is Helena who is credited with having found the site of Christ's tomb.

Helena is also credited with having discovered the true cross at nearby Mount Calvary (Golgotha). It is said that Helena was led to a certain location in Jerusalem by divine direction. Her party managed to dig up three crosses and a title board—"Jesus of Nazareth, King of the Jews." But the joy of discovery was short lived. Which of the three crosses went with the title? Jerusalem's Bishop Macarius suggested that a gravely ill noblewoman be placed upon each of the crosses in turn. When she was healed after resting on the third one, everyone concluded it was the true cross. Helena sent a piece of it to Constantine, who immediately ordered Macarius to build on the site "a basilica more beautiful than any on earth."

While deep Christian devotion, tradition, literature and art over the ensuing centuries became attached to her discovery of the True Cross, its historical credentials date back only to the late fourth or fifth centuries. Credible historians of that time— Gelasius of Caesarea, Rufinus, Socrates, Sozomen and Theodoret—acknowledge the discovery and credit her with the principal role, as do Ambrose, Paulinus of Nola and Sulpicius Severus. But details vary greatly, and neither the highly regarded Eusebius, nor St. John Chrysostom, nor Athanasius mentions Helena in reference to the cross.

With or without that, however, Helena's pilgrimage through the Holy Land is well documented. It profoundly impressed Christians throughout the empire, and prompted a constant stream of future pilgrimages. Because of her efforts, Constantine built impressive structures on many holy sites—his construction in the region, some say, actually turned Palestine into the "Holy Land."

When her work in Jerusalem was done, Helena ended her days in Nicomedia or Constantinople. Sometime between 328 and 330, at about eighty years of age, she died with her son at her side. Her body was taken to Rome for burial in the Via Labicana mausoleum.

Without any doubt, her reported discovery of the True Cross and her establishment of many churches left a profound material legacy. But her manner of living—selfless among the helpless poor and the powerful rich, commoners and rulers, learned theologians and novices—was equally celebrated.

Medieval hymns praised Helena's deeds; Byzantine empresses sought to emulate her humility and charity. As the devotion to Helena took root, churches and monasteries throughout Europe were dedicated to her. European colonization carried her name to South Africa, North America, and to the island in the South Atlantic where Napoleon would be exiled. Invoking her name in France and Germany was said to be helpful in catching a thief or recovering stolen goods. Sowing flax on her Eastern feast day, May 21, would produce a good harvest in Russia and Ukraine. In the West, Helena's feast day is celebrated on August 18. And miners in the Swiss and Austrian Alps claimed her as their patron saint.

Born in obscurity, Flavia Julia Helena crossed the stage of history in a magnificent role as empress and saint, leaving a remarkable heritage in her wake. In the words of British novelist Evelyn Waugh, "What we can learn from Helena is something about the workings of God; that he wants a different thing from each of us, laborious or easy, conspicuous or quite private, but something which only we can do and for which we were created." ∎

Military themes that decorate Helena's sarcophagus seem to contradict the deeply pious and charitable nature of the empress. The massive sarcophagus is now displayed in the Vatican Museums.

Though they were blatantly trumped up, writes Sellers, the charges were enough to persuade Eusebius's handpicked council of Arians to send Eustathius into exile. There he died some thirty years later, having continued to pen letters pouring scorn on the "demented chorus-dancers on the Arian stage," who were "horrible sycophants and accusers" that "concoct their earthborn deceits." He was of course replaced by an Arian bishop; the traditionalists elected a rival bishop, and for the next eighty years, there were two claimants for the see. So much for "unity."

In the meantime, the Arians faced a challenge at Alexandria, which they had fully expected. In January 328, Bishop Alexander died and was succeeded by Athanasius, the young deacon who had assisted him at Nicea. Eusebius of Nicomedia promptly opened another smear campaign against him, but Athanasius was to prove a far tougher target than Eustathius. Almost as soon as he reluctantly took up what was a powerful position in a city second only to Rome, it became clear that the battle against Arianism would fall to him.

In their first move against Athanasius, the Arians made an alliance with the Melitians, who had been received back into the church by the Nicene council, on

The Arians said that Athanasius had murdered another bishop and had cut off the dead man's hand to use it in a diabolical rite. The hand, they claimed, was now in their possession.

the condition they recognize the authority of the bishop of Alexandria. This they now refused to do, and went back into schism under their own bishop, John Arcaph, who with Arian support declared himself the "real" bishop of Alexandria, the Arians contending Athanasius had been elected illegally. They also accused Athanasius of treason. He had sent, they said, a purse of gold to a rebel. Athanasius forcefully rejected the charge, and Constantine circulated a letter saying that the accusation against Athanasius was false.

Undaunted, Eusebius next charged Athanasius with sacrilege. A village church, said the accusers, had been desecrated during a communion service by the priest Macarius, who was acting under orders from Athanasius. Macarius had smashed the church altar, shattered the chalice and burned the holy books. Athanasius quickly assembled evidence proving himself innocent. There was no church in the village, for one thing, he said, and there would have been no celebration of the Holy Communion on that particular day anyway.

None of this seemed to be sticking, so Eusebius arranged a far more bizarre accusation, this one advanced by the Melitian claimant John Arcaph. John's fellow Melitian bishop, a man named Arsenius, had disappeared, he said. He was known to have been murdered, and the killer was obviously Athanasius. Worse still (and here the horror doubtless made the deed too revolting to be easily told), Athanasius had actually cut off the dead man's hand and was using it in a diabolical rite. However, said Arcaph, his own people had actually procured the hand, and he now had it in his possession—in a

Honored eventually as a true champion of the faith, Athanasius became the subject of many religious images soon after he died in 373. This brilliant mosaic, in St. Mark's Basilica, Venice, dates from the thirteenth century.

wooden box. Then, as indisputable evidence, he publicly produced the box and the hand.

All this, said Eusebius of Nicomedia, was too much to be ignored. While some of these charges may seem a little embellished, where there was smoke, there must be fire. He assembled a council in the diocese of his colleague Eusebius of Caesarea, and summoned Athanasius to appear before it. The council assembled in 333, but Athanasius simply refused to attend.

Meanwhile, Eusebius of Nicomedia had scored another victory, the reacceptance into the church of Arius himself. Arius had by no means given up his fight, despite being excommunicated and exiled. He saw in the Nicene council's action, and in the emperor's unprecedented participation in church affairs, a way of rehabilitation. If the church allowed the emperor to involve himself in its policy decisions, then an appeal to Constantine himself would enable him to bypass the church altogether.

Through the influence of Constantia, Eusebius arranged for Arius to be allowed to return from Illyricum, and to begin to reestablish himself. Once in the capital, Arius convinced Constantine that his faith was not really incompatible with that expressed at Nicea, and that he had merely been misunderstood. Seeing once again an opportunity to finally resolve the conflict, the emperor accepted Arius's case, and wrote Athanasius, instructing him to readmit Arius to communion. Athanasius, reasoning that the emperor did not run the church, flatly refused.

Now the fat was really in the fire. Constantine, understanding that Athanasius had set himself defiantly against church authority, ordered him to answer the charges at a church council that was about to meet at Tyre, on the east coast of the Mediterranean. Here, finally, would be the opportunity to make the investigation that could not be made at Caesarea, because Athanasius had not shown up. What about the missing bishop Arsenius? What about the hand?

This time, Athanasius and forty-seven of his bishops from Egypt answered the call, and went to Tyre. Arrayed against them were sixty Eastern bishops, most of them holders of Arian views, including his two arch-foes, Eusebius of Nicomedia and Eusebius of Caesarea. But it soon became obvious that the Council of Tyre was not a church council at all. It was a military commission of inquiry under an army officer named Flavius Dionysius, all the members of the commission being Arians. The accusers made their case, presenting to the commission the wooden box and its macabre contents.

Athanasius acted in his own defense. He had, he said, made certain inquiries when the affair of the hand had first been made known. He had sent a deacon into the back country to look for the missing Arsenius. The deacon had learned that the dead man had been seen very much alive and hiding out in a monastery. Now he was gone. But the deacon had followed his trail, and eventually tracked him down to an inn in this very city of Tyre.

"Does anyone in this council know this Arsenius?" asked Athanasius. Nodding, many said they did. He then brought into the chamber a man wearing a heavy cloak that covered him completely, except for his head and face.

"Is this not Arsenius?" Athanasius asked.

Those who knew the man agreed that yes, that was Arsenius all right.

With considerable drama, Athanasius flung back the cloak to reveal Arsenius's hands and arms, intact and connected undeniably to his body.

"I presume that no one thinks God has given to any man more than two hands," Athanasius observed dryly.

It was all "more magic," shouted the Arians. Athanasius was plainly a sorcerer.

Bishop Arcaph wrote a letter to Constantine repenting for his misdeed, and Arsenius, too, confessed and sought forgiveness. Constantine wrote a public letter, warning that if Athanasius's enemies continued to carry out such false schemes, he would haul them before the magistrates and judge them under the law.

However, the commission would not give up at that. What about the matter of the shattered chalice and the church desecration? That too must be investigated. Having listened to a variety of witnesses—including unbelievers, Jews and catechumens (none of whom would have been present at a Communion service)—the commission maintained that the accusations against Athanasius were true. Athanasius was therefore removed as bishop of Alexandria and ordered exiled.

STIRNWEIS

A church council in Tyre, stacked in favor of the Arian faction, dealt what was supposed to be the final blow to Athanasius. It condemned this fighter for orthodoxy and called for his exile. But Athanasius proved to be a wily and tenacious adversary and slipped away. Just a few weeks later he accosts a surprised Constantine on the highway, begging for an audience in order to yet again plead his case.

But Athanasius did not wait for the decision. He knew full well that he had no chance of exculpation before that commission. He would flee, he resolved, but then found all roads leading out of Tyre were guarded to stop him. That night, therefore, the figure of a very slight man could have been seen boarding a raft on the Mediterranean beach. It vanished into the darkness, and shortly the bishop of Alexandria was aboard a waiting ship and headed for Constantinople. He could hope for justice, he knew, from one man only. That man was Constantine.

But Constantine was in no mood to grant an audience to Athanasius. A few weeks later, however, as the emperor returned to Constantinople from a country palace, he saw a man standing in the middle of the road. Drawing to a halt, Constantine did not at first recognize the man. It turned out to be Athanasius, greatly changed by his tribulations. "Either convene a legitimate assembly or allow me to meet my accusers in your presence," he urged. Doubtless with a sigh, Constantine agreed.

He summoned a meeting in Constantinople where Athanasius's accusers now appeared with a brand new charge: that he had arranged to prevent a number of wheat-bearing ships from sailing out of Alexandria to Constantinople. Preposterous, Athanasius replied. After all, he was just a private citizen and certainly not a wealthy one. He could do nothing of the sort. But Eusebius of Nicomedia assured the gathering that Athanasius was a powerful and influential bishop, and could get away with anything.

Constantine, no doubt concerned about the security of the vital wheat shipments, and no doubt also exasperated with the antics of both Athanasius and his enemies, ordered Athanasius banished to the ancient and magnificent city of Trier in northwestern Germany. Athanasius would spend more than two years there, during which two of the men who had figured prominently not only in his own life but in that of the entire Christian church, would die, one under sordid circumstances, the other nobly.

In 336, Arius was invited to appear before the emperor, who wished to put any lingering dissent to rest. Did he really hold to the teachings of the church as defined at Nicea? he asked. When Arius responded that he certainly did, Constantine ordered that he be received into communion on the following day at Constantinople.

What happened to Arius that day was recorded only by Athanasius, exiled among the Alamanni at the time; and the account is therefore regarded by some historians as suspect, given the lengthy and bitter relationship between the two men. In any event, Athanasius writes that when Alexander, bishop of Constantinople, learned of the emperor's decree, he spent the entire night in prayer, asking God not to allow this to happen. On the next day, when the triumphant Arius was on his way to the church to be readmitted at last, he was suddenly stricken with severe stomach pain. He lurched into a public latrine, where his bowels burst. His companions found him sitting on the toilet, half-clothed, covered with gore and excrement, dead. Christians would recall that, according to the Acts of the Apostles (1:18), someone else had died with his bowels bursting. His name was Judas Iscariot.

During the centuries since his death in 336, Arius has remained a highly controversial figure. Most Christian writers, whatever their denomination, unequivocally condemn him as the quintessential heretic. John Calvin, for example, wrote in the sixteenth century that, "when Arius arose, the Council of Nicea was convened, and by its authority, both crushed the wicked attempts of this impious man, and restored peace to the churches, which he had vexed and asserted the eternal divinity of Christ in opposition to his sacrilegious dogma."

Not everyone takes such a harsh view of the man, however. "I do not think that Arius was a heretic," the twentieth-century historian T. G. Elliott writes in his book, *The Christianity of Constantine the Great*, "and I do not wish to present

ALEXANDER ON COUNCIL DECISIONS

Whatever is determined in the holy assemblies of the bishops is to be regarded as indicative of the Divine will.

him as more wedded to his Arian ideas than he was. He invented what turned out to be a heresy; and he was for some years before 325 fairly busy with it, resisting his bishop and seeking support from other bishops. However, when his ideas were declared heretical by the Council of Nicea in 325, he did not continue, so far as I can see, to develop them. He got back into the church. I take it that Arius did not have the will to be a heretic, and that, in the absence of such a will, he could not have been one."

However, he adds, Arianism is an easy pitfall into which the individual can stray. "Arianism can arise at any moment when a Christian confronts the problem of the relationship between the Father and the Son. It results from a natural way (not the best way) of thinking about this problem, and is always widespread. Arians are everywhere, and when a fourth-century bishop says that they are everywhere, we should not be surprised." Indeed, the Jehovah's Witnesses translate John 1:1 not as "the Word was God," but rather as "the Word was a god."

Constantine would die in 337, the year after Arius, at about the age of sixty-five and in the thirty-first year of his reign; he was preparing an offensive in the East to defend the Christian Armenians against the Persians. He fell gravely ill and convalesced in Nicomedia. Sensing that he would not recover, he determined at last to be baptized. According to Eusebius of Caesarea, he explained that he had delayed so long because he had wanted to be baptized in the river Jordan, as had Jesus. Now, though, after preparation and acknowledgment of his sins, he was baptized by Eusebius of Nicomedia at a villa in the suburbs of Nicomedia.

His statues were frequently the target of the disgruntled Roman citizenry. But whether this colossal figure of Constantine fell to local or invading vandals is unknown. The statue's various body parts are lined up, to the delight of tourists, in the courtyard of the Conservatori Museum, Rome.

Constantine had long delayed his baptism, perhaps in the commonly held belief that sins committed after baptism could not be forgiven. Now, near the end of his life, he is helped into the font to complete the journey to faith he had begun years ago when he saw in the sky the sign that directed him to Christ's cause.

Soon thereafter, while still wearing baptismal white rather than imperial purple, Constantine died. He was placed in a coffin of gold; his body was reverently carried from Nicomedia to Constantinople, where it was entombed in the mausoleum of the Church of the Holy Apostles.[7]

Like Arius, Constantine has remained controversial over the centuries. The historian Henri Daniel-Rops assesses him as a brooding soul, struggling toward enlightenment, "a man perpetually torn by conflicting elements in his nature, obsessed by superstitious fears, desiring what was good even while doing what

---

7. Constantine's tomb was removed from the Church of the Holy Apostles a few years after his death. It was placed in the nearby Church of St. Acacius the Martyr. It then disappears from history.

was evil, disturbed in the deepest depths of his nature by inherited contradictions." His impact upon the Christians was profound—he freed them from the persecution they had endured from the beginning; he largely established Christianity as the faith of the Roman Empire; and by founding Constantinople, he focused the empire and the church eastward. "But for the chance of Constantine's conversion," writes the historian A. H. M. Jones, "Christianity might have remained a minority sect." That view is not universally shared. "A movement so expansive that an emperor could embrace it without serious political cost," observes the church historian David Priestley, "cannot have had such a pathetic future."

To some, particularly to many Protestant Christians, Constantine's purposeful mingling of church and state was a catastrophe that would result in unforeseen horrors in centuries to come. Others say that either Christianity will inform public policy or suffer under it, and that the final choice will, in the end, always lie between a Constantine and a Diocletian.

Whatever the view, nearly all agree that the palace murders of his son, nephew and wife remain deeds defensible on no possible grounds, creating the imponderable mystery of why he committed them. Perhaps it's fitting therefore that a twentieth-century mystery writer should tie all the baffling pieces of the puzzle together.

Classics scholar and Christian apologist Dorothy L. Sayers, the British detective story author, in her play *Constantine*, advances the theory that Fausta, Constantine's wife, plots with his nephew the execution of Crispus, the beloved son by his first wife, by fabricating the story that Crispus had seduced her. Infuriated, Constantine orders the young man's execution. Then, discovering too late that his son was absolutely innocent, he must execute his nephew and wife as well. All this he confesses before his baptism. He has committed a sin so grievous, he says, that nothing and no one could possibly atone for it. Then a light dawns within him. God, his Creator, could atone for it. At last he sees the point that Athanasius and Alexander had fought so hard to preserve. If Christ were merely God's creature, there could be no absolution for Constantine or for anyone else. Thus is he baptized in the faith of Christ. In the church of the East, not the West, he is recognized as a saint.

Athanasius, in the meantime, remained in comfortable exile at Trier, close to the German tribes, who were ready at any moment to burst through the frontier and despoil the whole civilized world. Christians were by now active among them, and when they came, every one of them would be Arian. ∎

Constantine's bridge on the Danube was an awesome engineering feat, stretching nearly a mile and a half across the great river. The emperor saw it as a means of subduing the unruly inhabitants of Dacia (today's Romania). But the Goths warily surveying the bridge's construction, probably view it as an opportunity for easier raiding.

CHAPTER 10

Those hideous people from the dark forests

The barbarians strike ever deeper into the empire, looting towns, bashing down the aged and infants, and seizing hosts of citizens for slavery and misery

To the peoples who populated the Roman towns and cities behind the broad arc of the empire's northern frontier, Constantine's greatest merit had little to do with his legislative program, his unifying of the imperial administration, or his dalliance (as many saw it) with Christianity. What mattered above all else was a single accomplishment. He stopped for more than thirty years the indescribably horrible phenomenon of the barbarian raid. Indescribable, that is, in the sense that it was hardly ever described. The records give it little more than bare mention. This or that town was raided by the Alamanni. Sometimes it would be sizable cities, Athens or Ephesus, struck by the Visigoths.

It is not by mere chance that little if any detail was added. After all, security against attack was supposedly guaranteed by the *Pax Romana* (the peace that had been brought by the Roman empire). Keeping the enemy from the gates was the emperor's first responsibility. Every raid represented an imperial failure. "Where were the legions?" people would understandably ask. Furthermore, any realistic account might well occasion widespread panic. Finally, in the aftermath of such a raid, who was left to write about it? Most survivors were trudging north with their captors into a lifetime of certain slavery and probable misery. Historians, therefore, have been left to reconstruct such incidents out of their known effects.

The raid would almost certainly occur at night, when the approach of the marauders was least detectable. The target town, chosen for its known affluence and unprepared because it would expect closer communities to be hit first, might be many miles from the Rhine or Danube frontier.

People would have serenely retired on a certain pleasant summer evening. Lamps were blown out, families in bed. The baths would have closed at dusk, the many inns near midnight. The night watchmen, when there were such, would be on the lookout for petty thieves or burglars. If the town had walls, they were probably neglected and crumbling at many points. It might have a little garrison

RUSH

of sleepy soldiers, a small contingent of a legion whose main force was many miles away, often fighting in a distant country.

Suddenly, perhaps about two in the morning, the sleeper would be awakened by shouts in the street. Leaping from his bed, he peers from his doorway. Neighbors are doing the same. A din and clatter is coming from the big houses in the wealthy part of town, up on the hill. The clamor grows nearer and louder. There comes the smell of smoke. The householder rouses his wife and his children.

Something terrible must be happening. A barbarian raid? Surely not—the frontier is a hundred or more miles distant. But the streets are crowded now,

The Goths became unlikely protectors of the culture of Athens even as they sacked and burned the great city. The leader of this devastating raid instructed his warriors not to burn the books and scrolls, reasoning that the more time the Greeks wasted on reading, the less time they would have to prepare an army of resistance.

stark terror written on every face. Babies cry. Women scream. "Run!" people shout. "It's the tribes! The German tribes! They've broken through!" But run where? Hide where? Now the noise and screaming is coming from every direction. What to do?

Then they appear—huge, bearded, filthy men, some in rough armor, some in reeking animal skins, some spattered with human blood! They're shouting, bellowing, some actually seem to be singing. They had moved first on those big houses, seizing the occupants, rolling wagons up to the doorways, lugging out the contents. Everything that seems of value is being seized, while the occupants are dragged or kicked outside onto the street. There, a careful assessment goes on. The aged and infirm are run through or bashed over the head, to lie gasping out the last of their lives. Men who try to resist are clubbed down, then dragged to their feet—blood streaming down their faces—and bound.

If these men live they may make good farm laborers or domestic servants, possibly even clerks. The market for educated slaves is always excellent. Children, wide-eyed and struck dumb with terror, face a chancy future. If they look capable of walking back to the border, they are bound. If not, they are hit over the head while their mothers shriek wildly. Many women are similarly tied. They may at least serve for household labor, and attractive ones can be sold to the brothels. Girls, younger women and pretty boys are treated more gently; they must not be damaged. Virgins command the best prices of all.

By morning, the remaining citizens have been assembled in the public square, dazed and traumatized, their town burning around them. They are experiencing a living nightmare. They may never see their loved ones again, even if they happen

to be still alive. The life they have known heretofore is over. The long trek north is about to begin. It may last for weeks. Those too sick or frail to continue will be left to die or summarily murdered.

When the records laconically note that the barbarians raided into Thrace or Bithynia or Gaul or northern Italy, this is the sort of thing they are referring to. This is the horror that Constantine was able to halt for three decades or more, which may be why he was known at the time and ever after as Constantine the Great. What enabled him to do so was his profound understanding of the people with whom he was dealing, that myriad assortment of tribes who lived north of the Danube and east of the Rhine, all known collectively as "the Germans."

Roman citizens had long been aware of these Germani, denizens of the immense unknown territory beyond the frontier, where thousands of square miles of dark, deep forest and dank, miasmic marshland stretched toward the frigid northern seas. This was a country they considered unhealthy in every sense. The Roman historian Gaius Cornelius Tacitus, writing about A.D. 90, speculated in his *Germania* that its inhabitants must certainly have originated there. Why would anyone fortunate enough to be born elsewhere, he reasoned, ever want to move to such a place?

Current ethnographers disagree with Tacitus. They say the ancestors of the Germani actually came from still farther north, from the Scandinavian peninsula; traces of agriculture in southern Scandinavia have been dated to neolithic times, circa 3,000 B.C. Forming into larger tribes and warrior bands, they may gradually have worked their way south, clearing spaces in the forests to plant crops and raise livestock. According to one Greek source now lost, around 200 B.C. two confederations of Germanic tribes, the Cimbri and the Teutones, embarked upon a mass migration southeastward through what would one day become Bohemia, Slovenia and Croatia, then west again. Along the way, they smashed three Roman armies; only in southern Gaul were they finally stopped.

Such exploits built the Germani a formidable reputation for strength, courage and—above all—savagery. When Julius Caesar defeated several contingents of them in eastern Gaul between 58 and 55 B.C., this was the word he used to describe his beaten enemies: *feri*, savages. He considered the Germani subhuman, so irredeemably barbaric that they could never be civilized by contact with Rome, as the Celts had been. This claim, however, would prove untrue. As Caesar must have known even then, some Germani had already managed to find their way into Gaul and were learning quickly.[1]

Over the next several centuries, many more would legitimately join them, to render notable service, particularly in the army. That their brethren beyond the Rhine and the Danube were savage and dangerous to the peace of the empire, however, probably no one knew better than these immigrants. Besides, the barbarian depredations were impossible to predict accurately. "Germani" (which roughly means "having the same parents") was simply a Roman name for the entire lot. The reality, as the Romans well knew, was a shifting conglomeration of separate groups, which, given favorable conditions, could coalesce into formidable and menacing federations.

Broadly speaking, ethnographers classify the Germani as Western Teutonic (which includes such peoples as the Franks, Alamanni, Carpi and Saxons) and Eastern Teutonic (chiefly the Goths, Vandals and Heruli). Such knowledge would have brought no comfort, however, to the victims of their devastating raids across the Rhine-Danube frontier, which increased and intensified in the third century. Terrified citizens of the provinces saw these large-skulled, strong-limbed warriors as veritable giants. (They did in fact top the average height of the Romans by several inches.)

Heavy gold rings emphasized thick necks and bulging biceps. Tacitus describes their fierce eyes of piercing blue, luxuriant mustaches and wild, flowing hair—yellow to flaming red. (They greased it with rancid, stinking butter and were known to dye it even redder.) They attacked in a disorderly but furious rush, like wild beasts or demons, shrieking battle cries and brandishing great iron-pointed spears.

However, the Romans did admire some Germanic traits, which they considered reminiscent of their own revered ancestors, the honorable and upright

The use of both porphyry and white marble in these two statues of barbarians gives them a unique, lifelike appearance. Carved in the second century for a villa near Rome, the statues now stand in the Louvre in Paris.

THE BARBARIANS AT THE DOO
TEUTONIC TRIBES OF THE FOURTH CENTUR

founders of the Roman republic. They were hardy, bold, courageous and independent, according to Tacitus, in tune with the forces of nature, devoted to their families and moral in sexual matters. They set great store by chastity, he writes, which would be in marked contrast to the profligate habits by then typical of decadent Roman society. Germani warriors were raiders but apparently not known as rapists. They married late, usually not until the early twenties, and may have been expected to remain chaste until then—possibly to safeguard their strength.

Germanic women would seem to have lived a life of daunting drudgery, having responsibility for all the domestic work, child care and farm work, while their husbands concentrated on hunting and war. Nevertheless, man and wife appear to have been in some sense partners. Concubinage was reportedly rare, and the historian Harry Elmer Barnes observes in *The History of Western Civilization* that the Germans "seem to have given women greater consideration than did many barbarous peoples." Tacitus approvingly reported that adultery was strictly forbidden among them, especially for women. An adulterous wife would have her head shaven and be driven from the community, or even put to death.

Mute evidence of this may be a pitiful corpse discovered in a Danish peat bog: a young girl, blindfolded and bound, with the blond hair on half her skull shaven, and on the other half cut to two inches. She might have been executed for some other crime, however. These northern peat bogs, a rich source of marvelously preserved bodies and artifacts, seem to have been used at times to drown criminals, but they were usually penned in wicker cages. Or possibly she was a sacrifice.

The peat bogs were almost certainly used for another kind of sacrifice, one which sheds a very interesting light on Germanic mores. Booty of every sort—captured gold and silver, armor, weapons, harnesses, even horses—was thrown into them (and also into rivers) as offerings of thanks for victory to the god of war, Tyr perhaps, or later Odin (sometimes called Wodan). Some tribes, with similar intent, hanged selected prisoners from trees. In a variation of this latter practice the Cimbri reportedly suspended prisoners above brass water pots. The priestesses would slit their throats and discern auguries according to the patterns formed by the blood on the water.

Such may at times have been the fate of defeated Roman legionaries, but the barbarian warriors did not discriminate. They treated their own kind just the same. Tacitus tells how two

---

1. The historian Herwig Wolfram, in *The Roman Empire and Its Germanic Peoples*, discerns a political motive for Julius Caesar's depiction of the German peoples as animals rather than humans, whereas Caesar portrays the Gauls as fully human and capable of becoming civilized. The fact, says Wolfram, is that Caesar knew he could not conquer Germania as he had conquered Gaul, and therefore offered its loathsome sub-human condition as an explanation.

peoples in west-central Europe, the Chatti and the Hurmunduri, went to war over disputed territory. Each tribe petitioned the war gods for victory, vowing in return to sacrifice the enemy and their equipment. The Hurmunduri won, and scrupulously honored their vow. As the ancient authors agree, the Germani generally exhibited—for better or for worse—all the typical traits of the barbarian: bravery and cruelty; hospitality and treachery; individualism, yet intense devotion to the family and kinship ties upon which their societies, and their lives, depended.

They were fond of carousing, gambling and contests of strength. In wartime,

The days of paganism

The Christian East succeeded in converting the days of the week, but in the West pagan names like Sun's Day and Thor's Day survive

While Constantine's ascendancy marked the triumph of Christianity over paganism, in one respect paganism won—in the West, anyway. That was in the naming of the days of the week.

In the Romance languages for example, the old Roman practice of naming the days of the week after the heavenly bodies, which in turn were named after the pagan gods, continued into the Christian era in northern Europe. Thus the Romans had Sun's Day, Moon's Day, Mars's Day (Tuesday), Mercury's Day (Wednesday), Jupiter's Day (Thursday), Venus's Day (Friday), and Saturn's Day (Saturday).

When these were carried into French and Spanish, a couple of changes were made because of Christian influence. Saturn's Day became *sabado* in Spanish and *samedi* in French, from the Latin *sabbati dies* meaning the Sabbath Day. Sun's Day turned into *domingo* in Spanish and *dimanche* in French, from the Latin *dies dominica*, the Lord's Day.

When the German Saxons fell under Roman influence, they exchanged some of the Roman gods for their own in the names of their days. Hence, while Sun's Day, Moon's Day and Saturn's Day were retained as what became Sunday, Monday and Saturday, Mars's Day (*martes* in Spanish, *mardi* in French) became in English *Tiwesdag*, because of similarities between *Tiw*,

oldest of the German gods, and Mars, the Roman god of war. Similarly, Mercury's Day (*miercoles* in Spanish, *mercredi* in French) became Woden's Day in English (Wednesday) after the supreme Norse-German god Woden.

Jupiter's Day (*jueves* in Spanish, *jeudi* in French) became in English Thor's Day after Thor, the god of thunder, while Venus's Day (*viernes* in Spanish, *vendredi* in French) became in English Frey's Day, after Frey, the Norse-German fertility god.

The evangelists of the Eastern church made better progress. There, the old pagan names were abolished. In Greek, Friday became Preparation Day, Saturday became Sabbath Day, Sunday became Lord's Day or Resurrection Day. Other days of the week were simply numbered, following an old Jewish practice. This is also the liturgical practice of the Catholic Church. ■

Thor, god of thunder, holds the symbol of his power, a stylized hammer.

they would usually obey their elected chiefs, who probably were chosen for military prowess by councils of fighting men. However, their individualism strongly inclined them towards a rudimentary form of democracy; important decisions were made by "the whole people"—although by this was probably meant the assembly of warriors. (That the term included women, for example, is highly unlikely.) But the glory of war remained the dominant theme in Germanic life, either from necessity (quest for land, pressure from other tribes, need for trade or booty), or from choice. How else

Some episodes of German heroic myths are said to have taken place in the hills and forests of the Teutoburg district, east of Münster. The towering Externsteine rocks, in particular, were a place of pilgrimage for pagan Celts and Germanic tribes until the eighth century, when Charlemagne cut down the sacred tree at the heart of the shrine.

were the restless young warriors to perfect their craft and prove their mettle?

The glittering wealth of the Roman Empire was a powerful lure for warrior bands, and knowledge of it spread far and wide. By A.D. 200, Germani of one sort or another were situated all along the right bank of the Rhine, a region of forests, villages and isolated farmsteads. On the Roman side, not far beyond the frontier, were cities with comfortable houses, elegant inns, public baths and amphitheaters. Tales of cities yet more magnificent were carried deep into the barbarian lands by intrepid merchants trading wine and silver drinking cups for amber, furs and blond-haired slaves. Also known to the tribes in those years was the fact that the Romans, custodians of all this wealth, were fighting among themselves, so that the legions were often diverted from the border to fight for rival caesars.

Moreover, certain West German tribes were forming larger, more permanent and therefore more dangerous federations—in particular, the Alamanni and the Franks. The word Alamanni, which means simply "all the men," has survived into modern times as "Allemagne," the French name for Germany. Coming from the Elbe River region, they decisively entered the historic record in 213 in an encounter with the emperor Caracalla, who inflicted upon them a massive, but not fatal, defeat. They were soon back at the border in force to raid the provinces of Germania Prima and Raetia.

Meanwhile, other Germani calling themselves *Franks*, were massing against the lower Rhine frontier between Cologne and the river mouth. The name meant "free," in the sense that they were a newly formed federation of tribes not subject to Rome. The Salii and Chatti were major components of the alliance, which also seems to have included such other tribes as the Bructeri, Chamavi and Sugambri. In medieval times, the descendants of this Frankish conglomerate would control an empire covering present-day France and western Germany, lay much of the foundation of Western culture,

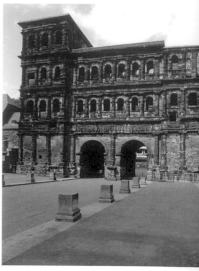

and bequeath their name to modern France.

Eastward, a yet greater menace was poised to strike, however, in the form of another Germanic people, who would carve their name deeply into seven hundred years of European history: the Goths. According to their legends, wrote the sixth-century Gothic historian Jordanes in his *Getica*, they too had originated in Scandinavia. Led by a king named Berig, they crossed in three ships to the southern Baltic coast, naming their landing place *Gothiscandza*, the Gothic Shore. This was likely the estuary of the Vistula, where the Goths proceeded to drive out the inhabitants, probably the Vandals and Burgundians. Later, they fought their way south by stages along the east bank of the river, and by 200 had succeeded in occupying a large territory north of the Black Sea, between the Don River on the east, and the Roman frontier on the west.

It was not immediately obvious to contemporaries just who these well-armed migrants were. The Romans thought at first they might be one or more known tribes, like the Gotones, Taifali or Gepidae. The Goths probably had incorporated significant elements of other peoples as they journeyed, and according to Jordanes, the Gepidae actually figured in the Gothic legend. The name Gepidae implied "slow" or "lazy," Jordanes explained, and they were so called because they had sailed in the third ship from Scandinavia and arrived last. The Greeks thought the newcomers must be Scythians, and so called them for years, although the Scythians were long gone from that region.[2]

In their new home on the Black Sea, the Goths divided into two sections, those east of the Dniester River, the area of present-day Ukraine, eventually becoming known as the Ostrogoths (eastern Goths), and those west of the Dniester, modern Romania, as the Visigoths (western Goths). They came most

---

2. The plains region north of the Black Sea, where the Gothic horde from the Baltic probably arrived about 100, was by no means empty but it, too, was in transition. The Scythians, originating in central Asia, had long controlled a vast kingdom in what would one day become Ukraine. In the first century B.C., however, the Scythian kingdom began to weaken, and in the first century A.D., was almost entirely overrun by the Sarmatians, another central Asian people. It was the nomadic but not uncultured Sarmatians whom the Gothic tribes now proceeded to evict, with characteristic dispatch, from most of their European territory.

forcibly to Roman attention early in the third century, when unknown and particularly ferocious raiders from the north destroyed the towns of Olbia and Tyras on the Black Sea coast. Well before the end of the century, their raiding parties had reached Greece and Asia Minor.

Other Germanic peoples were moving in beside the Goths: the Taifali (although they too may have been part of the Goth migration), the Heruli, the Urugundi, the Borani. All these, plus earlier inhabitants such as the Carpi, the Bastarnae and the Vandals, also proved happy to take part in joint raiding ventures.

What made the Goths such extremely effective fighters has long intrigued historians. They seemingly surpassed most of their Germanic cousins in the making and maintaining of effective military alliances, and rapidly developed an impressive number of non-military skills and trades. In *The Early Empires of Central Asia*, the renowned twentieth-century ethnologist William Montgomery McGovern surmises that the Goths absorbed into their society many of the Sarmatians they supplanted, thereby absorbing certain aspects of Scythian and Sarmatian culture.

Later Gothic art is practically indistinguishable from Sarmatian, says McGovern, and it in turn influenced other Germanic art. The Goths also adopted such aspects of the semi-nomadic Scythian-Sarmatian culture as living in tent-wagons, and acquired some of their predecessors' knowledge of, and fascination with, horses. But even the Ostrogoths never did abandon farming for a purely pastoral economy. Fifth-century Roman accounts describe them as prosperous farmers, not nomads, who raised cattle but lived in villages and also planted crops. Several Latin authors refer to the Visigoths as "plowmen."

By 300, some of the Visigoths had become proficient carpenters, potters, smiths and workers in precious metals. They learned shipbuilding as well, probably from the Greco-Roman colonies on the Black Sea, and developed a small harbor near the mouth of the Danube. With customary speed, they added this technology to their fighting technique, but likely took up fishing as well. Some became merchants, competing with Roman traders in grain, wine, cloth, luxury items like glassware, and slaves. And they enlisted in the imperial forces where some learned a great deal before returning home.

Fighting remained the chief business of barbarians, and their pressure right along the Roman frontier rarely relaxed, east or west. "The history of the third century," wrote Herwig Wolfram in *The Roman Empire and its Germanic Peoples*, "unfolded with dreadful monotony: usurpations at home, Germanic attacks in the West, Gothic advances in the East, and all this punctuated by the never-ending Persian wars."

On the upper Rhine frontier, the increasingly

Not only did the barbarians besiege the bulwarks of frontier cities, but they frequently had the audacity to assault the walls of the great cities of the south, including Rome. In the mid-third century the emperor Aurelian was sufficiently worried about marauding Germanic bands that he ordered construction of the huge walls at Rome that bear his name.

The Elbe River winds its way through the Saxony region of Germany. The general north-south orientation of the Elbe and nearly all other rivers in the region provided the Goths with natural highways for raiding and ultimately for relocation, farther south.

powerful Alamannic confederacy, probably enhanced by strays from the Marcomanni wars, was twice defeated in the first half of the century. But about 258, returning in force, they broke through the border fortifications between the Main and Danube, overpowering the Roman garrisons. This time they stayed, settling in the lands they had conquered, which left the province of Raetia open to their further raiding. What frightened the Romans much more, however, was that another immense horde of Alamanni almost simultaneously crossed the Alps into Italy, and part of it actually reached Rome. The Senate quickly assembled a makeshift force to defend the city, at which point Gallienus arrived with several legions and routed the barbarians near Milan. But that section of the frontier was obviously no longer secure; Italy itself lay open to the raiders.

Meanwhile, the Frankish confederacy was making repeated assaults on the lower Rhine frontier. For five years, from 253 to 258, Gallienus defeated them time and again, but lacked sufficient military strength to consolidate his victories. Then he was called away to deal with further Alamanni attacks, leaving his son Cornelius in charge. All might yet have been well if Cassianus Postumus, another ambitious general, had not assassinated Cornelius and been proclaimed emperor by his troops. This put the legions holding the Rhine and Danube segments of the frontier into turmoil—and the Franks poured through the gap, raiding their way almost unhindered right through Gaul and into Spain.

That was a feat quite typical of barbarian hordes; the distances they could travel, and the pace, roused awe and fear in their enemies. Furthermore, some had now taken to the seas, greatly increasing their range. The Saxons, a Germanic tribe from the southwest Baltic, began raiding the coasts of Gaul and Britannia, and the Franks shortly did likewise.[3] In the East, the Goths assembled fleets that enabled them to visit wholesale destruction on the cities of Asia Minor and Greece.

Such terror did these raiders inspire, writes nineteenth-century historian

3. Marcus Aurelius Maus Carausius, from the Menapii tribe, appointed in 286 to guard Britain from marauding Franks and Saxons, was sentenced to death for embezzling some of the loot he had recovered from the Frankish and Saxon raiders. Instead, he seized Britain, declared himself emperor, and held the island for seven years, until a colleague killed him. Not for another ten years would Rome repossess the island.

Henry Bradley, that these cities, although many were fortified and garrisoned, hardly attempted to defend themselves. They had doubtlessly heard of the fate of Philippopolis in Thrace, which tried to resist a siege by the legendary Gothic king Kniva in 250. When the emperor Decius failed to relieve the city, the Thracian governor Titus Julius Priscus declared himself emperor and tried to join the Goths. Whereupon the attackers sacked the town, killed thousands of its citizens, murdered Priscus, and made off with their customary huge masses of booty and prisoners.

The Visigoths now seemed practically unstoppable, on land or on sea. The rich city of Chalcedon on the Bosporus fell before their first major combined sea and land operation in 256. On the same trip, they immediately moved on to pillage Nicomedia, Nicea and Prusa. Resuming their maritime raids a decade later in 267, they again hit Chalcedon and Nicomedia, burned to the ground the Temple of Diana at Ephesus (one of the Seven Wonders of the Ancient World), and spread havoc through Cappadocia and Galatia.[4] By the time they were driven away by Odenath, king of the Roman colony of Palmyra, the raiders already had hundreds of prisoners aboard their ships—very possibly including the grandparents of one Ulfila, a name that would later resonate in Gothia.

One year later another and bigger fleet of Herul and Visigoth ships, said to number between five hundred and two thousand, sailed down the coast of Greece, and with a land army (minimally estimated, according to the records, at 320,000 Goths, Bastarnae and other tribes) rampaged south as far as Sparta. Having subdued Athens, Bradley wrote, they emptied the extensive libraries of that city and prepared to burn great heaps of manuscripts. The story goes that one old chief stopped them, saying "Let the Greeks have their books, for so long as they spend their days with these idle toys, we need never fear they will give us trouble in war."

However, Bradley added, one educated Greek—the historian Dexippus—was just then leading a band of citizens in setting fire to some of the Goth ships in the Athenian harbor of Piraeus. A Roman fleet had also arrived at this point to challenge the Goth fleet. So had the emperor Gallienus, at the head of an army that repeatedly engaged the Visigoth hosts as they headed north, killing a reported fifty thousand of them. But Roman victories were hard-won and far-between in

The crafts and arts of the Goths and pre-Viking tribes are distinctive for their style and for the predominance of the color red. (Above) An early Viking monument depicts Odin astride his eight-legged steed Sleipnir, while Valkyries guard the gates of Valhalla. (Below) The swirls and highly stylized animals on this memorial stone from Gotland are mirrored in folk art as far away as Ukraine, testifying to the reach of the territories that the Goths controlled in the fourth century.

---

4. The magnificent Temple of Artemis or Diana at Ephesus, described in detail in another volume of this series (*The Veil Is Torn*, page 155), was three times as big as the Parthenon at Athens, and one of the Seven Wonders of the Ancient World. That it should be destroyed in a single barbarian raid gives evidence of the depredation that the third-century barbarians were wreaking on the Roman Empire.

that era. In fact, says *The Cambridge Ancient History Vol. XII*, the fate of the provinces beyond the Rhine-Danube border had been sealed in June 251.

That was when the canny strategist Kniva trapped the emperor's army on marshy ground and nearly annihilated it, killing both Decius and his son Herennius Etruscus. Both men died bravely, but their defeat was disastrous for the Romans. Gallus, succeeding Decius as emperor, had to agree to let Kniva and his still considerable host carry home all their plunder and prisoners. He was also forced to offer them a heavy annual subsidy to dissuade them from further depredations. The remainder of the third century became one continuous struggle against attacks by the Goths and their allies. All the Danube provinces suffered terribly, especially Dacia, the most exposed. Thus, in 271, the Emperor Aurelian, hard-pressed on other fronts, decided that Dacia was no longer defensible. He ordered all Roman settlers back south of the Danube, where reinforcements were needed, in any event, to replace lost population and

Then they appear—huge, bearded, filthy men, some in rough armor or reeking animal skins, some spattered with human blood, some shouting, even singing

repair the barbarian devastation. The Dacian legions he transferred to Moesia, to defend the new frontier. The Visigoths promptly moved in, and the former Dacia got a new name: Gothia.

By the fourth century, the subsidies Rome was paying to assorted barbarian confederacies (which besides coin and gold might include shiploads of grain, clothing and other commodities) were a ruinous drain on the economy. (One cynic reportedly suggested that an occasional raid might be preferable, at any rate in financial terms.) With or without a subsidy, sometimes Rome could negotiate a *foedus*, a treaty involving such things as mutual defense and trade concessions, with a more amiably inclined neighbor. Peoples covered by such treaties were called *federates*, and these arrangements met with varying degrees of success.

Trading across the border was carefully regulated, writes historian E. A. Thompson. Germanic merchants had to enter at certain checkpoints, pay a toll, turn over their weapons, and travel with a military escort. Any export to a possible enemy of such items as weapons, armor, horses, other beasts of burden, iron and bronze was strictly forbidden, and at times punishable by death. The Romans also jealously guarded the technology, both industrial and military, which initially so awed the wide-eyed barbarians, and the technicians who built and operated these things.[5] Commodities proved easier to restrict than human beings, however, what with prisoners of war, deserting soldiers and increasing numbers of barbarians within the Roman army.

A certain "barbarization," most notably in the provinces and the army, was in fact going on. A barbarian could become a citizen if he formally surrendered, and many did. In any case, Rome had to keep importing Germani as farmers to restore agricultural production in lands left desolate by barbarian raids. It became standard practice to recruit them both for the regular army and as auxiliary units. Moreover, they rose to ever higher ranks; in 268, for example, Gallienus bestowed a consulship on the Herulean chief Naulobatus.

That was at the height of the barbarian incursions, when the legions were repeatedly withdrawn from the frontier to champion the cause of one Roman general against another, when twenty-two out of twenty-six emperors were killed by Roman troops over the space of about two-score years, when the hideous phenomenon of the raid kept every settlement within a hundred miles and more of the northern frontier in a state of terror, when good farms everywhere lay burnt and abandoned, when food production fell, and when depopulation was the empire's most grievous economic problem.

By ending dynastic turmoil, Diocletian was able to bring the frontier under control. However, with his retirement in 305, instability returned, and the conflict between Constantine and his rivals in the early fourth century was taken by the Franks as opportune for a massive assault into Gaul. In response, Constantine loosed against the Franks a vicious attack over the Rhine and into their territories, in which tens of thousands of them perished. Two of their senior chiefs were taken prisoner and then literally, as well as theatrically, fed to the lions in an exhibition calculated to impress the barbarian mind. The Franks pleaded for peace and signed a treaty that appointed them the imperial policemen on the lower Rhine, and Gaul was left alone for the next thirty or more years.

Against the Alamanni, Constantine bridged the Rhine near Cologne, giving him a path directly into their heartland. He stationed a legion there that could use the bridge, and opened a big fort on the right bank at Divitia. However, his toughest problem, and he knew it, was the people known as the Visigoths, who threatened the empire along the Danube. These celebrated the outbreak of the final showdown between Constantine and Licinius by launching a major raid over the river in 323 into the Roman provinces of Scythia, Thrace and Moesia. They were repulsed with very heavy losses.[6]

But Constantine was by no means persuaded that the Visigoths had been subdued, and five years later he bridged the Danube and its marshlands about four miles southwest of the city of Corabia in Romania with what was, at eight thousand feet, the longest bridge in the Roman world. He then drove a road

Amid a swirl of battling Romans and barbarians elsewhere on this sarcophagus, the sculptor has placed a tragic barbarian couple gazing tenderly at one another as they face death.

---

5. Roman military technology never ceased to impress and sometimes horrify the barbarians. The historian E. A. Thompson, in his *Romans and Barbarians*, describes the mixture of fascination and dread with which the first-century Batavians, recruited into the Roman forces, beheld a huge timber which the Romans could work along the top of the wall of a town under siege. Driven through the end of the timber was an enormous spike that protruded, giving the effect of an immense bird with a hideous beak. The timber was mounted like a windmill arm, so that it could sweep down the edge of the wall, skewer anyone trying to mount it, and then thrust him high into the air. If his body was not thrown clear, it would be pried off the spike by the defenders, who then launched the apparatus again to pick off another attacker. Imagining this fate befalling themselves or one of their relatives tended to discourage the barbarian yen to attack, but rarely for very long.

6. Constantine's biographers note that his son, also Constantine, accompanied the troops assigned to put an end to Visigoth raiding in 323. The boy was eight years old at the time, and destined fourteen years later to become Constantine II. His father kept him at the command center in the victorious barbarian war that followed. When he was ten, he was put in nominal command of Gaul.

north from the bridge deep into Visigoth territory. In so doing, he reoccupied the old province of Dacia, which the emperor Trajan had created in the third century and the emperor Aurelian had abandoned as untenable in the fourth. Constantine's revival of a Roman settlement there was, however, to prove very short-lived.

His suppression of the Goths began in 332. The Visigoths were by then engaged in a war with the neighboring Sarmatians. These, getting the worst of it, pleaded for help from Rome. Constantine, doubtless using the bridge, threw Roman forces in on the Sarmatian side, cutting the Visigoths off from behind, and so isolated them, say the Roman records, that his troops watched a hundred thousand of them starve to death. Then the Visigoths sued for peace and meant it. As usual, Constantine's terms were generous, and the Visigoths left the settlements alone for the next thirty years.

Meanwhile, the Sarmatians, finally rid of the Visigoth menace, themselves began raiding the imperial towns. But this time, Constantine scarcely needed to intervene. In their desperate war with the Visigoths, the Sarmatians had made the mistake of arming their slaves. These now rose in revolt from behind them, while the Visigoths attacked them from the other side. In the end, the slaughter was so terrible that Constantine effectually rescued three hundred thousand Sarmatians and resettled them in the frontier provinces, now enjoying a period of peace.

It's typical that the Visigoths should remember Constantine and his era fondly, though he thrashed them more soundly than any previous emperor. They remembered him as "Gothicus," the title he bestowed upon himself in 315. His son, Constantine II, became "Alamannicus" for his subsequent role in keeping them under control. Constantine himself maintained a Gothic bodyguard, established Gothic legions, instituted what were known as the "Gothic Games," made the first treaty ever with the Goths, and made peace with the Goths a cornerstone of his northern policy.

The pagan Romans, however, did not remember fondly Constantine's record on the northern frontier. Because of the spreading barbarian settlements in the Roman territory, the historian Zosimus describes Roman life in the late empire as "an island of survivors in a sea of barbarism," and blames Constantine's policy for hastening the fall of the empire. True, says Constantine's twentieth-century biographer Michael Grant (*The Emperor Constantine*), his resettlement policy helped repopulate deserted areas, immobilized potential enemies, strengthened depleted army garrisons, and increased agricultural production. Nevertheless, these huge barbarian settlements did not become Roman, but preserved their own culture at a critical

This argenteus comes from the early years of Constantine's career, when he was still caesar (junior emperor). The design on the reverse shows the gate of a Roman military camp, symbol of the security that Constantine brought to the imperial frontiers. When it came time to build the arch celebrating his victory over Maxentius (top), Constantine included barbarian figures that he had pillaged from other emperors' monuments, indicating that he had dealt with internal turmoils of the empire as well as the barbarian threat.

moment when Rome itself was increasingly uncertain of its identity.

In another respect, however, both Rome and the barbarians were acquiring an altogether new culture. All through the era of the raids, Christianity had been filtering in among the dreaded Goths themselves. Although the process is impossible to trace in detail, some fourth- or fifth-century historians provide intriguing glimpses, and occasionally there emerges from the mists of time and political-religious controversy an individual who unquestionably played a major role—sometimes in full public view, sometimes secretly in the background. Just such a fascinating tale concerns the life of one Ulfila (or Urfila or Ulfilas or Wulfilas; the name is spelled in at least four ways), the Apostle to the Visigoths, about whom modern secular historians still carry on lively dispute.

The story begins in Cappadocia, one of the provinces along the northern coast of Asia Minor. When the Visigoth raiders began pillaging forays into these parts after 256, they penetrated Rome's most thoroughly Christianized regions. Many of the captives they carried back across the Danube to Gothia were strong Christians, and literate as well. Among these captives, says the fifth-century Christian historian Philostorgius, was a couple from a Cappadocian village near the city of Parnassus, who would figure in the ancestry of Ulfila either as parents or possibly grandparents.

Thus Ulfila was born in a Gothic village in Dacia in 310 or 311, into a family that was likely mixed Goth and Greek. He was given a Gothic name, but raised a Christian. There were significant numbers of Christians scattered through Dacia, historians agree; some were of slave descent like Ulfila, and others were Goths whom the captives had persuaded and baptized. The historian Socrates (c. 380–450) wrote that in youth, Ulfila was a disciple of a Gothic bishop named Theophilus (who incidentally is known to have attended the Council of Nicea in 325) and became a lector (reader) in his church.

Unquestionably Ulfila was well educated. Besides speaking his native Gothic,

The confrontation between Christian and pagan influences among the Goths and other Germanic tribes was symbolically resolved at the Externsteine monoliths (see also page 267). Christian themes, in this case the descent from the cross (left of the left-hand doorway), were carved into the rock faces of the pagan sacred site.

he was fluent in Latin and Greek and could read and write both these languages. No one could then read or write Gothic because it had no alphabet, so Ulfila later invented one, using Greek characters and some Latin ones. Then he proceeded to translate the entire Bible into Gothic, with one omission. He left out the Book of Kings, Philostorgius explains, because it was "a mere narrative of military exploits, and the Gothic tribes were especially fond of war, and were more in need of restraints to check their military passions than of spurs to urge them on to deeds of war."

Of the rest of Ulfila's Old Testament translation, the only surviving fragment is the Book of Nehemiah, but his Gothic language New Testament fared better. Most of the Gospels and the Pauline letters can still be seen, preserved at Uppsala University in Sweden. They are fragments of a sixth-century Ostrogothic copy, called the *Codex Argenteus* because it is written with silver ink on purple parchment (*argentum* is the Latin word for "silver").[7]

Ulfila certainly recorded the Gothic liturgies on parchment as well, and he is known to have published polemical and didactic treatises in all three languages. But all this was merely one of his activities. According to a memoir written by Auxentius of Durostorum, a pupil of Ulfila's and later bishop of Silistria, he early began to function both as an active evangelist and as a key diplomat between the Romans and the rulers of the Visigoths.

Philostorgius also backs this claim. In 336 or 337, he wrote, Ulfila was included in a diplomatic mission dispatched to Constantinople by an unnamed Visigothic chieftain, for a purpose also unspecified. Such approaches by the Visigoths to Roman authorities were customary in times of crisis or governmental change, when they needed to test the waters or ensure that their treaties still held. Constantine died May 22, 337, and the succession was in grave doubt. Who would be emperor, and would he confirm the *foedus*, or treaty, which Constantine had signed with the Visigoths in 332?

Auxentius and Philostorgius further agree that on the same trip, the influential Bishop Eusebius of Nicomedia consecrated the young Ulfila as bishop to the

Appointed bishop to the Visigoths, Ulfila (below) bends over his most enduring legacy, a translation of the Bible into Gothic for which he created a special alphabet. However, it would have one major shortcoming. In his translation, Ulfila omitted the Book of Kings, fearful that reading its battle stories might inflame his flock's predisposition to make war, not peace. Several centuries later, the New Testament portion of Ulfila's Bible would be reproduced on purple vellum in letters of silver in the famous "Codex Argenteus" (now faded to red as depicted in this illustration).

STIRNWEIS

Goths. This claim has been the subject of considerable controversy; some ancient chroniclers omit mention of it. But the Visigoths were already known on occasion to include a Christian priest in their deputations to the Christian emperors. What could be more natural than for that anonymous chief to believe that a promising young ecclesiastic like Ulfila might be able to gain the ear of the powerful Bishop Eusebius of Nicomedia?

The testimony of Auxentius and Philostorgius certainly implies that a deal was made in which Ulfila gained a bishopric and Eusebius gained an effective evangelist to a barbarian nation; already some imperial authorities may have regarded the converting of pagans to Christianity as sound policy for Rome. As for the anxieties of that anonymous chieftain, in 337 the emperor Constantine passed beyond earthly concerns. But his son, Constantius II, who was his leading successor and was also much influenced by Eusebius of Nicomedia, did in due course reaffirm the treaty of 332.

Furthermore, another logical component to this deal suggests itself—one that would go far to explain why Ulfila, throughout most of his life, almost certainly

When his torturers awoke, they found Saba helping a village woman with her chores. They wanted to release him. 'Do your duty,' he said. So they did.

embraced Arianism, and why the Visigoths as a nation would tenaciously do likewise. In view of his ancestry, and of the fact that his mentor Bishop Theophilus stood against the Arians at Nicea, Ulfila likely began as an orthodox Christian. But Bishop Eusebius was an Arian, as were many other bishops of that era, and several emperors. Thus acceptance of Arianism may have been part of the price of Ulfila's episcopacy.[8]

In any event, after his consecration, he returned to Dacia, and for the next seven years, vigorously preached Christianity with notable success, since relations between Goths and Romans were relatively peaceful at this time. The number of Christians among the Visigothic tribes, both orthodox and Arian, had undoubtedly grown, both by natural increase, and because

7. The sixth-century *Codex Argenteus* is all that remains of Ulfila's Gothic Bible. It is also the sole surviving manuscript in the vanished Gothic language, and has a curious history. It came to light in the seventeenth century in a monastery near Essen, says historian E. A. Thompson in *The Visigoths in the Time of Ulfila*, and somehow got to Prague. There, it was seized in the 1648 Swedish invasion. Used to pay some of the debts of Queen Christina of Sweden in 1654, it reached Holland, where a copy was printed in 1665. A Swedish nobleman, Count Magus Gabriel De la Gardie, had already bought it back, however, and presented it in 1669 to the University of Uppsala, where it remains.

8. Historians tend to divide along sectarian lines on Ulfila; both Arian and orthodox wanted to claim him as their own. On the Arian side, writes Hagith Sivan of the University of Kansas, Ulfila's pupil Auxentius (350–400) presented his master as a lifelong Arian saint. So did Philostorgius (368–425). By contrast, the orthodox Christian historian Socrates (380–450) insisted that Ulfila was an orthodox believer until his middle years. Sozomen (late fourth and early fifth century), also orthodox, said he converted only about 376, to get Arian support for his hard-pressed Goths. Ulfila died in 382 or 383, after the First Council of Constantinople in 381 had rejected Arianism and opted for the Nicene formula.

some missionaries are known to have been working among them; but there was yet no hint whatsoever, says *The Cambridge Medieval History*, "of a conversion of the nation. . . . Their conversion only begins with the appearance of Ulfila."[9]

Pagan Goths seem to have cheerfully accepted the Christians who lived among them and for a time, all went well. However, twice in Ulfila's lifetime Christians in Gothia suffered persecution, separated by two decades: in 348 and from 369 to 372. It is believed that the chief Visigoth leader, Athanaric, a strong traditionalist who refused ever to be called "king," decided that these Christians, by undermining the ancestral Gothic faith, were putting at risk the unity, morale and very existence of his people. However the order came about, the persecution was so severe that Ulfila and most of his followers fled into Roman-controlled Moesia, where Emperor Constantius II allowed them to settle near Nicopolis ad Istrum (modern Trnovo in Bulgaria).

Ulfila was never again to live in Gothia, but his settlement was just inside the Danubian border. Socrates for one claimed that he continued to send missionaries both to the followers of his own subchief Fritigern, the Visigoth leader second in importance to Athanaric, with whom he presumably had influence, and also to Athanaric's people. This very possibly was an important factor in the outbreak of the second persecution of Christians, which took place about 370. It can hardly be coincidental, however, that between 367 and 369, the emperor Valens was conducting punitive attacks on the Visigoths, and severely beating them. And because Valens had also cut off their trading privileges, they were running short of food.

This second purge was far worse than the first, the Gothic records attest; at one point a whole group of Christians were burned in their church. But the hostility seems to have come from the Visigoth leadership, not from the population of the villages. In one account, *The Life of St. Saba*, a Christian openly defies the orders of a Visigoth chief, winning great sympathy from his pagan neighbors. Saba (or Sabas) had been a fervent believer since childhood, a hardworking and clearly well-liked villager, who lived simply and witnessed to his faith. When the order came down in 372 that everyone must prove his loyalty by eating meat sacrificed to the tribal idols, Saba's neighbors proposed to secretly substitute unsacrificed meat. On principle, he simply refused. So they had to drive him out of the village. However, they soon let him back. In a subsequent outburst of persecution, they all (including the Christians among them)

---

9. Not only were there growing numbers of orthodox and Arian Christians among the Visigothic tribes by 350, according to the historian Epiphanius of Salamis, there was a third kind as well. These were the Audians, who preached a formula intended to promote a compromise between the other two. They were followers of a teacher named Audius who was banished for heresy to Visigothic territory about this time, and promptly began to proselytize.

resolved to swear there were no Christians in their village. Not Saba. "Let no one swear on my behalf," said he, "for I am a Christian."

So they expelled him once again, and again let him back. Finally, just after Easter in 372, there came henchmen from one of the tribal chiefs. They strung out Saba between two wagon ends and tortured him all day, but could make no mark on him. Tired out, they fell asleep. Next morning, a village woman, up early to prepare the family breakfast, untied him. When his torturers awoke, there was the saint, helping the woman with her work. Finally, they carried him away to the river Musaeus (the modern Buzau) to drown him, and there (safely out of sight of their chief) they too wanted to release him. But Saba would allow no such thing. "Do your duty," he sternly admonished them. So they finally drowned him.

Though Saba perished, along with many others, the Visigoth nation was nevertheless reaching a religious turning point, and a major secular turning point as well. Fearful worldly events would now engulf them, and in the next six decades crucially affect many of Europe's other Germanic peoples. As to their faith,

exactly why it so quickly and radically changed is probably impossible to discover, but within the next two decades, the Visigoths would suddenly be known far and wide as an Arian Christian people.

Socrates recounts a mass conversion of Fritigern's followers in 369. This date is dismissed by most other historians, past and present, who prefer 376 at the earliest. Nor does anyone else speak in terms of a simultaneous adoption of the new faith by all of Fritigern's people. Any description of a massive communal baptism in the Danube is also notably lacking, but that something of the sort happened, either about 376 or very soon afterward, can hardly be doubted.

It would not be out of love for Rome, however, that Fritigern and his followers took such a step. The Visigoths are said to have retained deep regard for the emperor

Nearing the end of its long journey across Europe, the Danube meanders toward its delta in Romania. On the left the river passes what would have been lands of the Roman empire, with barbarian Dacia on the right.

Constantine, and admiration for his military prowess. After a passage of years, his successors also inflicted upon them punishing military defeats, in retaliation for their resumed raiding activities. But the cancellation of their trading privileges by Valens had also brought them close to starvation. Such bitterness ensued that in 369, when Athanaric had to acquiesce in a disadvantageous peace treaty with Valens, the chief refused to set foot on Roman soil. It was forbidden, he declared, by his father's orders and a terrible oath of his own. Since the emperor after that could hardly go into Gothia and maintain any semblance of dignity, the two had to meet on a boat in the middle of the Danube.

Seven years later, however, the proud Visigoths had suddenly changed their tune. From Fritigern came urgent pleas to Valens, begging the emperor to allow the whole Visigothic people to cross the Danube onto Roman soil. All of them who were left, that is. They were fleeing a new and hideous menace, he said, an enemy more terrible, more horrifying, more powerful than any they had ever met, nor even heard of in their tribal memories. Some warriors, led by Athanaric, had elected to fight. The rest were sure this enemy could not be beaten. In the event, Athanaric and his men soon fled as well.

This was the first reported arrival in Europe of the nomadic warriors known as the Huns. The sheer terror which they visited upon the peoples whom they attacked is difficult to exaggerate. The Visigoths saw them as inhuman monsters, devils and demons. These fear-

By the late fourth century, the cross had triumphed as the preeminent symbol of Christians and was becoming central in piety and prayer. A terra-cotta plaque in the Museum of Macedonia, at Skopje, invokes the cross of Christ to bring victory to all who hope in it.

some creatures, writes Jordanes, "made their foes flee in horror . . . because they had a sort of shapeless lump, not a head, with pinholes rather than eyes." Earlier descriptions credited them with possessing "red hair, green eyes and white faces." Gothic legend told of their ancestry, how an early Gothic king had expelled from the tribe certain witches, driving them into the Scythian desert, where they mated with evil spirits and brought forth this race of ferocious quasi-men.

However fanciful these claims may have been, the people so described unquestionably ranked among the world's most powerful warriors. Intrepid and indefatigable horsemen, whether descended from demons or not, they could ride like demons and shoot like them too. By the end of the fourth century they had wiped out the Sarmatians and conquered the Ostrogoths and their allies to the east, and virtually all the Germani of Europe were fleeing in terror before them.

Strangely, Valens acceded to Fritigern's request for safe passage. Thus, in the spring of 376, panicked Visigoths crossed the river in the thousands, on boats and rafts and hollowed tree trunks. So numerous was this host, recounts the *Cambridge Medieval History*, that it covered the country on the Roman side "like the rain of ashes from an eruption of Etna." Not only were they allowed to enter Roman territory; even less explicably, they were given land in adjoining Thrace and granted the right to maintain their own laws and customs. They also kept their weapons. This was contrary to established policy and entirely without precedent. No barbarian group had ever before been permitted to settle as a separate people inside Rome's boundaries.

Historians of the time agree that this is when the reception of Christianity by the Visigoth nation most likely occurred—or at the least was dramatically inaugurated—and probably by Fritigern. They do not suggest whether Fritigern's old friend Ulfila, now in his early sixties and presumably watching affairs from his own Moesian settlement, may have played any part in this momentous development. But some speak of a priest who decisively intervened, circa 370, in negotiations between Valens and Fritigern. And to believe that Fritigern's decision finally to embrace Christianity was made solely on the spur of the moment stretches credulity.

Whether Bishop Ulfila, Apostle to the Goths, played a role in such a finale, he had already fully earned his title. By providing his people with an alphabet (and he must have taught at least some of them to use it as well), he made them literate. They could read, and what they read first was the Bible. The Bible would ultimately lead them to Christ, and Christ would lead them to civilization and the concept of law. In the coming centuries, this same path would be followed by peoples all over the world.

But that massive crossing of the Danube by the Visigoths in 376 creates a yet more indelible line in human history. It is exactly here that the classical ages are demarked from the Middle Ages. As this polyglot horde of terrified humanity traverses the river, ancient history comes to an end and Medieval History begins. ∎

CONTRIBUTORS TO THIS VOLUME

THE WRITERS

CHARLOTTE ALLEN, a Washington, D.C. journalist and author, has written for many publications, including the *Atlantic Monthly*, the *Washington Post* and the *New Republic*.

VIRGINIA BYFIELD has spent more than forty years in the Canadian news media, most recently as a senior editor of the *Report* newsmagazines. She met her husband, Ted Byfield, editor of this series, when both were reporters on the *Ottawa Journal* in the late 1940s. After raising six children, she covered politics, education and religion in western Canada for some thirty years.

VINCENT CARROLL of Denver, a journalist and author, is editor of the editorial pages for the *Rocky Mountain News* in Denver and co-author (with David Shiflett, also a contributor to this series) of *Christianity on Trial: Arguments Against Anti-Religious Bigotry*.

MARK GALLI of Wheaton, Illinois, is managing editor of *Christianity Today* magazine. He is the author of *Francis of Assisi and His World*, and editor or co-author of a number of other books including *The Story of Christianity, 131 Christians Everyone Should Know* and *The Complete Idiot's Guide to Prayer*.

ELEANOR GASPARIK of Edmonton has worked as editor of *Cooking at Home* magazine, and has written for *Template* magazine, *Alberta Woman* magazine, *Western Living* and the *Alberta in the 20th Century* history series.

Dr. IAN HUNTER, who holds degrees in law and political science from the University of Toronto, has taught at several Canadian universities and has been a visiting scholar at Cambridge University. He is a columnist for *Report Newsmagazine* and a frequent contributor to the *Globe and Mail* and the *National Post*. His most recent book is entitled *Brief Lives: Heroes, Mountebanks and Lawyers*.

EDDIE KEEN of Smoky Lake, Alberta, was for seventeen years a reporter and editor at the *Edmonton Journal*, and then for twenty years a highly popular commentator on CHED radio in Edmonton, during which time he also wrote a column for the *Edmonton Sun*.

FREDERICA MATHEWES-GREEN of Linthicum, Maryland, is a columnist for *Christianity Today*, a contributor to *Touchstone* magazine, the author of several Christian books and a commentator on National Public Radio.

JOHN MUGGERIDGE is a spare-time journalist and retired college professor of English and history, living in Toronto. He is married to the Catholic writer Anne Roche. The son of the English journalist and author Malcolm Muggeridge, he has five children and twelve grandchildren.

JOHN DAVID POWELL of Houston, Texas, a former print and broadcast journalist and former public radio network commentator, is an executive speechwriter and an award-winning Internet columnist.

DAVE SHIFLETT of Midlothian, Virginia, has written for the *Wall Street Journal, Reader's Digest, Los Angeles Times, Manchester Guardian* and other publications. The author of *The America We Deserve* (with Donald Trump) and co-author (with Vincent Carroll) of *Christianity on Trial*, he has also worked as a columnist and editor at the *Rocky Mountain News* in Denver and on the editorial page of *The Washington Times*.

PAUL SULLIVAN is a columnist for the *Globe and Mail* in Toronto, and former managing editor of the *Vancouver Sun*. He is also former morning show host for CBC Radio in Vancouver, and he now runs an Internet development company in Vancouver.

STEVE WEATHERBE of Victoria, British Columbia, who is a columnist for the Sterling News Service and works for the B.C. government, is a former teacher and a former staffer of *The Report* newsmagazine.

JOE WOODARD, religion editor for the *Calgary Herald*, has taught politics and philosophy at universities in Canada and the U.S. and has researched social policy for both the Canadian and American governments.

THE ACADEMIC CONSULTANTS

Dr. CARNEGIE SAMUEL CALIAN is president and professor of theology at Pittsburgh Theological Seminary.

Dr. KIMBERLY GEORGEDES is associate professor of history at Franciscan University, Steubenville, Ohio.

Father BRIAN HUBKA is a priest of the Roman Catholic Diocese of Calgary (Alberta).

Dr. JOSEPH H. LYNCH is Distinguished University Professor and Joe R. Engle Designated Professor of the History of Christianity at Ohio State University, specializing in medieval social and religious history.

Dr. WILLIAM McDONALD is assistant professor of religion and philosophy, and chaplain at Tennessee Wesleyan College, Athens, Tennessee.

Dr. DAVID T. PRIESTLEY is professor of historical theology at Taylor Seminary, Edmonton.

Dr. DOUGLAS SWEENEY is assistant professor of church history and the history of Christian thought, Trinity Evangelical Divinity School, Deerfield, Illinois.

Dr. EUGENE TESELLE is emeritus professor of church history and theology, Vanderbilt University, Nashville, Tennessee.

THE ILLUSTRATORS

RICHARD CONNOR of Edmonton, a graduate of Alberta College of Art and Design, has worked as an illustrator and designer in a number of art studios in England and Canada, and is now a freelance architectural illustrator for companies across Western Canada.

As a fine artist, CARLO COSENTINO, a native of Montreal, paints mostly with oil on canvas. As an illustrator, he produces artwork for clients including IBM, Seagram's, Pepsi-Cola, Toshiba, Canon and Toyota. His poster art has been used to promote jazz festivals in Montreal, Toronto, Vancouver, Edmonton and Winnipeg.

BOB CROFUT of Richfield, Connecticut, is an illustrator whose clients include Doubleday, Prentice-Hall, NBC, MGM, Ford, *Reader's Digest* and IBM.

MICHAEL DUDASH of Moreton, Vermont, is an illustrator for *Reader's Digest* Books, Twentieth Century Fox, Universal Studios, Simon and Schuster, Random House, and McGraw-Hill.

GLENN HARRINGTON of Pipersville, Pennsylvania, is an illustrator whose clients include Macmillan Books, Bantam-Doubleday-Dell, and Paramount Pictures.

JAMIE HOLLOWAY of Edmonton, whose pen-and-ink character sketches of Saint Paul and other figures grace the margins of books in this series, has worked as an illustrator for Alberta advertising and government agencies.

TOM McNEELEY, who lives and works in Toronto, has won awards from the Society of Illustrators, the Art Directors Clubs of New York and Toronto, and *Communication Arts* magazine; and a Lifetime Achievement Award from the Canadian Association of Photographers and Illustrators in Communications. His clients include publishers, theater and opera companies, and major corporations.

ALEXIS REITER of Edmonton is an artist and calligrapher who has taught both those subjects and who heads up her own company, Alexis Design.

JOHN RUSH of Evanston, Ill., is an artist, illustrator and printmaker with a special interest in Roman history. His clients include Time-Life, *The National Geographic*, and the National Parks Service.

JOHN SMITH of Edmonton is a graduate of Alberta College of Art and Design and a senior illustrator, designer and art director in his own firm, Artsmith Communications, with major government, institutional and commercial clients. He is also a design instructor at Grant MacEwan Community College, Edmonton.

RICHARD SPARKS of Norwalk, Connecticut, is an illustrator whose clients include Exxon, *Sports Illustrated*, *Time*, Doubleday and Simon and Schuster.

SHANNON STIRNWEIS of New Ipswitch, New Hampshire, a founder of the Society of Illustrators, has provided illustrations for the Department of the Interior, the U.S. Air Force Museum and the Coast Guard.

ROB WOOD, GREG HARLIN and MATTHEW FREY are illustrators in the studio of WOOD RONSAVILLE HARLIN Inc. of Annapolis, Maryland. All three are contributors to *National Geographic*, the *Reader's Digest*, the *Smithsonian Magazine* and many other publications.

BIBLIOGRAPHY

General Reading

Barnes, Harry Elmer, *The History of Western Civilization*, 2 vols (New York: Harcourt Brace, 1935); Brown, Peter, *The World of Late Antiquity: From Marcus Aurelius to Muhammad* (London: Thames and Hudson, 1971); Cook, S. A. et al., *Cambridge Ancient History*, rev. Vol. 12, *The Imperial Crisis and Recovery* (Cambridge: University Press, 1956); Fox, Robin Lane, *Pagans and Christians* (New York: Knopf, 1987); Garraty, John A., and Peter Gay, eds., *Columbia History of the World*, 2nd ed. (New York: Dorset, 1981); Gwatkin, H. M., ed., *The Cambridge Medieval History*, Vol. 1, *The Christian Roman Empire and the Foundation of the Teutonic Kingdoms* (Cambridge: University Press, 1911); Jones, A. H. M., *The Decline of the Ancient World* (London: Longmans Green, 1966).

Reference Material

Bartholomew, John C., et al., eds., *Times Atlas of the World*, 7th comprehensive ed. (New York: Random House, 1985); Cross, F. L., *Oxford Dictionary of the Christian Church*, 2nd ed. (London: Oxford University Press, 1974); Dowling, Timothy, ed., *Eerdman's Handbook to the History of Christianity*, 1st American ed. (Grand Rapids, MI: Eerdmans, 1977); Farmer, David Hugh, *The Oxford Dictionary of Saints*, 4th ed. (Oxford: University Press, 1997); Freedman, D. N., ed., *Anchor Bible Dictionary* (New York: Doubleday, 1992); Herbermann, Charles G., ed., *Catholic Encyclopedia: An International Work of Reference on the Constitution, Doctrine, Discipline, and History of the Catholic Church* (New York: Appleton, 1907-1910); Kelly, Joseph F., *The Concise Dictionary of Early Christianity* (Collegeville, MN: Liturgical Press, 1992); MacMullen, Ramsay, and Eugene N. Lane, eds., *Paganism and Christianity, 100-425 C.E.: A Sourcebook* (Minneapolis, MN: Fortress, 1992); Robinson, Thomas A., *The Early Church: An Annotated Bibliography of Literature in English* ([Philadelphia]: American Theological Library Association; Metuchen, NJ: Scarecrow, 1993); Smith, William *A Dictionary of Greek and Roman Antiquities* (London: John Murray, 1995) (retrieved November 27, 2002, from http://www.ukans.edu/history/index/europe/ancient_rome/E/Roman/Texts/secondary/SMIGRA*/home*.html).

Modern Christian Apologetic Works

Chesterton, Gilbert K., *The Everlasting Man* (Garden City, NY: Image Books, 1974 [Original work published in 1925]); Gore, Charles, *The Reconstruction of Belief*, new ed. (London: J. Murray, 1930); Lewis, C. S., *Mere Christianity* (New York: Macmillan, 1952); Sayers, Dorothy L., *Creed or Chaos?*, 1st American ed. (New York: Harcourt Brace, 1949); *The Emperor Constantine: A Chronicle* (New York: Harper, 1951)

Bible Commentary and Formation

Bruce, F. F., *The Canon of Scripture* (Downers Grove, IL: Inter-Varsity, 1988); Campenhausen, Hans von, *The Formation of the Christian Bible* (Philadelphia: Fortress, 1972); Evans, C. F., "The New Testament in the Making," in P. R. Ackroyd and C. F. Evans, eds., *The Cambridge History of the Bible*, Vol. 1, *From the Beginnings to Jerome* (Cambridge: University Press, 1970); Grant, Robert M., "The New Testament Canon," in P. R. Ackroyd and C. F. Evans, eds., *The Cambridge History of the Bible*, Vol. 1, *From the Beginnings to Jerome* (Cambridge: University Press, 1970); Lightfoot, J. B., *On a Fresh Revision of the English New Testament*, 2nd ed. (London: Macmillan, 1872); Patzia, Arthur G., *The Making of the New Testament: Origin, Collection, Text and Canon* (Downers Grove, IL: Inter-Varsity, 1995); Westcott, Brooke Foss, *A General Survey of the History of the Canon of the New Testament*, 7th ed. (London: Macmillan, 1896); Williams, C. S. C., "The History of the Text and Canon of the New Testament to Jerome," in G. W. H. Lampe, ed., *The Cambridge History of the Bible*, Vol. 2, *The West from the Fathers to the Reformation* (Cambridge: University Press, 1969).

Christian Biography

Benedictine Monks of St. Augustine's Abbey, Ramsgate, *The Book of Saints: A Dictionary of Servants of God*, 6th ed. rev. (Wilton, CT: Morehouse, 1989); Brown, Peter, *The Cult of the Saints: Its Rise and Function in Latin Christianity* (Chicago: University Press, 1981); Butler, Alban, *Butler's Lives of the Saints* ed., rev., and suppl. by Herbert Thurston and Donald Attwater (Westminster, MD: Christian Classics, 1981); Catholic Information Network, *Saints, Martyrs and Other Holy Persons* (retrieved November 27, 2002, from http://www.cin.org/saintsa.html); De Clercq, Victor C., *Ossius of Cordova: A Contribution to the History of the Constantinian Period* (Washington, DC: Catholic University of America Press, 1954); Deferrari, Roy J., *Early Christian Biographies* (Washington, DC: Catholic University of America Press, 1952); Grant, Robert M., *Eusebius as Church Historian* (Oxford: Clarendon, 1980); Gregory of Nyssa, *The Life of Gregory the Wonderworker* (retrieved November 27, 2002, from http://www.sp.uconn.edu/~salomon/nyssa/thaum.htm); Petersen, William L., "Eusebius and the Paschal Controversy," in Harold W. Attridge and Gohei Hata, *Eusebius, Christianity, and Judaism*, pp. 311-325 (New York: E. J. Brill, 1992); Sellers, R. V., *Eustathius of Antioch and His Place in the Early History of Christian Doctrine* (Cambridge: University Press, 1928); Smith, William and Henry Wace, *Dictionary of Christian Biography, Literature, Sects, and Doctrines*, 4 vols (London: J. Murray, 1877-1887); Walsh, William Thomas, *Saints in Action* (Garden City, NY: Hanover House, 1961).

Athanasius, Bishop of Alexandria

Arnold, Duane Wade-Hampton, *The Early Episcopal Career of Athanasius of Alexandria* (Notre Dame, IN: University Press, 1991); Bush, R. Wheler, *St. Athanasius: His Life and Times* (New York: E. & J. B. Young, 1888); Pettersen, Alvyn, *Athanasius* (London: Chapman, 1996).

Constantine, Emperor

Baker, G. P., *Constantine the Great and the Christian Revolution* (New York: Barnes and Noble, 1930); Elliott, T. G., *The Christianity of Constantine the Great* (Bronx, NY: Fordham University Press, 1996); Grant, Michael, *The Emperor Constantine* (London: Weidenfeld & Nicolson, 1993); Holsapple, Lloyd, *Constantine the Great* (New York: Sheed & Ward, 1942); Jones, A. H. M., *Constantine and the Conversion of Europe* (London: Hodder & Stoughton for the English Universities Press, 1948); Pohlsander, Hans A., *The Emperor Constantine* (New York: Routledge, 1996); Smith, John Holland, *Constantine the Great* (London: Hamish Hamilton, 1971).

Cyprian, Bishop of Carthage

Benson, Edward White, *Cyprian: His Life, His Times, His Work* (London: Macmillan, 1897); Burns, J. Patout, Jr., *Cyprian the Bishop* (New York: Routledge, 2002); Hinchliff, Peter, *Cyprian of Carthage and the Unity of the Christian Church* (London: G. Chapman, 1974); Poole, George Ayliffe, *The Life and Times of Saint Cyprian* (Oxford: John Henry Parker, 1840); Sage, Michael M., *Cyprian* (Cambridge, MA: Philadelphia Patristic Foundation, 1975).

George, Saint and Martyr

Catholic Community Forum, *George* (retrieved November 27, 2002, from http://www.catholic-forum.com/saints/saintg05.htm); Fochios, Michael James, "Saint George, the Great Martyr," in Aristides Isidoros Cederakis, *A History of Eastern Orthodox Saints* (retrieved November 27, 2002, from http://home.att.net/~stgeorgeweb/aboutstgeorge.htm); Fox, David Scott, *Saint George: The Saint with Three Faces* (Windsor: Kensal, 1983); Kiefer, James, *George, Soldier and Martyr* (retrieved November 27, 2002, from http://elvis.rowan.edu/~kilroy/JEK/04/23b.html); Orthodox Church in America, "Holy Greatmartyr George the Victory-Bearer," in *Lives of the Saints* (retrieved November 27, 2002, from http://www.oca.org/pages/orth_chri/feasts-and-saints/april/apr-23.html#george).

Helena, Mother of Constantine

Bodden, Mary-Catherine, ed. and trans., *The Old English Finding of the True Cross* (Wolfeboro, NH: D. S. Brewer, 1987); Drijvers, Jan Willem, *Helena Augusta: The Mother of Constantine the Great and the Legend of Her Finding of the True Cross* (New York: E. J. Brill, 1992); Pohlsander, Hans A. *Helena: Empress and Saint* (Chicago: Ares, 1995).

Maurice, Saint

Woods, David, "The Origin of the Legend of Maurice and the Theban Legend" (*Journal of Ecclesiastical History*, 1994, 45: 385-395); O'Reilly, D. F., "The Theban Legion of St. Maurice" (*Vigiliae Christianae*, 1978, 32: 195-207); Saint Maurice and the Theban Legion (retrieved November 27, 2002, from http://pharos.bu.edu/cn/synexarion/MauriceOfTheba.txt).

Nicholas, Saint

Ebon, Martin, *Saint Nicholas: Life and Legend* (New York: Harper & Row, 1975); Jones, Charles W., *Saint Nicholas of Myra, Bari, and Manhattan: Biography of a Legend* (Chicago: University Press, 1978); Orthodox Church in America, "Saint Nicholas, the Wonderworker and Archbishop of Myra in Lycia," in *Lives of the Saints* (retrieved November 27, 2002, from http://www.oca.org/pages/orth_chri/Feasts-and-Saints/December/Dec-06.html).

Valentine, Saint

Kelly, Henry Ansgar, *Chaucer and the Cult of Saint Valentine* (Davis: University of California, 1986); Orthodox Church in America, "PriestMartyr Bishop Valentine [Valentinus or Valentinos] and his Three Disciples, the Holy Martyrs Proculus, Ephibius and Apollonius, and Righteous Avundius," in *Lives of the Saints* (retrieved November 27, 2002, from http://www.oca.org/pages/orth_chri/feasts-and-saints/july/jul-30.html#valentine).

Christian History

Brown, Peter, *The Rise of Western Christendom: Triumph and Diversity, a.d. 200-1000* (Cambridge, MA: Blackwell, 1996); *The Body and Society: Men, Women and Sexual Renunciation in Early Christianity* (New York: Columbia University Press, 1988); Carroll, Warren H., *The Founding of Christendom*, Vol. 1. (Front Royal, VA: Christendom Press, 1985); Chadwick, Henry, *The Church in Ancient Society: From Galilee to Gregory the Great* (New York: Oxford University Press, 2001); "The Early Christian Community," in John McManners, ed., *The Oxford Illustrated History of Christianity* (New York: Oxford University Press, 1990); *The Pelican History of the Church* (Harmondsworth: Penguin, 1967); Daniel-Rops, Henri, *The Church of Apostles and Martyrs*, 2 vols (Garden City, NY: Doubleday, 1962); Duchesne, Louis, *The Early History of the Christian Church*, 3 vols (London: J. Murray, 1909-1924); Frend, W. H. C., *The Early Church* (Philadelphia, PA: Lippincott, 1966); *The Rise of Christianity* (Philadelphia, PA: Fortress, 1984); *Town and Country in the Early Christian Centuries* (London: Variorum, 1980); Grant, Robert M., *Augustus to Constantine: The Rise and Triumph of Christianity in the Roman World* (San Francisco: Harper & Row, 1990); Johnson, Paul, *The History of Christianity* (New York: Atheneum, 1977); Lebreton, Jules, and Jacques Zeiller, *The History of the Primitive Church*, 2 vols (New York: Macmillan, 1873-1956); MacMullen, Ramsay, *Christianizing the Roman Empire: A.D. 100-400* (New Haven, CT: Yale University Press, 1984); Palanque, J. R., *The Church in the Christian Roman Empire* (New York: Macmillan, 1949); Stanley, Arthur Penrhyn, *Lectures on the History of the Eastern Church* (New York: Scribner, 1862); Thaninayagam, Rev. Father Xavier Stanislaus, *The Carthaginian Clergy: During the Episcopate of Saint Cyprian* (Colombo: Ceylon Printers, 1947).

Councils of the Church

Hefele, Charles J., *A History of the Christian Councils*, 5 vols (Edinburgh: T. & T. Clark, 1894); L'Huillier, Peter, *The Church of the Ancient Councils: The Disciplinary Work of the First Four Ecumenical Councils* (Crestwood, NY: St. Vladimir's Seminary Press, 1996);

Luibheid, Colm, The Alleged Second Session of the Council of Nicaea, *Journal of Ecclesiastical History*, April 1983, *34*(2): 165-174.

Arius and Arianism

Hanson, Richard P. C., *The Search for the Christian Doctrine of God: The Arian Controversy 318-381.* (Edinburgh: T. & T. Clark, 1988); Kannengiesser, Charles, *Arius and Athanasius: Two Alexandrian Theologians* (Brookfield, VT: Gower, 1991); Norderval, Æyvind, *The Emperor Constantine and Arius: Unity in the Church and Unity in the Empire.* *Studia Theologica* 42 (1988) pp. 113-150.

Donatism, Donatists

Frend, W. H. C., *The Donatist Church: A Movement of Protest in Roman North Africa* (Oxford: Clarendon, 1952); Tilley, Maureen A., *Donatist Martyr Stories: The Church in Conflict in Roman North Africa* (Liverpool: University Press, 1996).

Geographical References/Local Churches

Bede, the Venerable, *Bede's Ecclesiastical History of the English Nation* (New York: E. P. Dutton, 1910); Downey, Glanville, *A History of Antioch in Syria From Seleucus to the Arab Conquest* (Princeton, NJ: Princeton University Press, 1961); Griggs, C. Wilfred, *Early Egyptian Christianity From Its Origins to 451 C.E.* (New York: E. J. Brill, 1990); Livermore, H. V., *The Origins of Spain and Portugal* (London: Allen and Unwin, 1971); Moffett, Samuel Hugh, *A History of Christianity in Asia*, Vol. 1, *Beginnings to 1500* (San Francisco: HarperSanFrancisco, 1992); Salisbury, Joyce E, *Iberian Popular Religion, 600 B.C. to 700 A.D.: Celts, Romans, and Visigoths*; Thomas, Charles, *Christianity in Roman Britain to AD 500* (Berkeley: University of California Press, 1981); Toumanoff, Cyril, *Studies in Christian Caucasian History* (Washington, DC: Georgetown University Press, 1963); Trimingham, J. Spencer, *Christianity among the Arabs in Pre-Islamic Times* (New York: Longman, 1979).

Armenia

Agathangelos, *History of the Armenians*, trans. and comment. R. W. Thomson (Albany: State University of New York Press, 1976); Baynes, Norman H., Rome and Armenia in the Fourth Century, *English Historical Review*, 1910, *25*: 625-643; Lang, David Marsh, *Armenia, Cradle of Civilization*, 2nd ed. corr. (Boston: Allen & Unwin, 1978).

Germanic People/Barbarians

Bradley, Henry, *The story of the Goths, from the Earliest Times to the End of the Gothic Dominion in Spain* (New York: G. P. Putnam, 1888); Heather, Peter, The Crossing of the Danube and the Gothic Conversion, *Greek, Roman, and Byzantine Studies* 27(3): pp. 289-318; *The Goths* (Oxford: Blackwell, 1988); Jordanes, *The Origins and Deeds of the Goths* trans. Charles C. Mierow (retrieved November 27, 2002, from http://www.ucalgary.ca/~vandersp/Courses/texts/jordgeti.htm); Julius Caesar, On the Germans, in *The Gallic Wars* (retrieved November 26, 2002, from http://www2.norwich.edu/stuart/ww/caesar420.html); Lenski, Noel, The Gothic Civil War and the Date of the Gothic Conversion, *Greek, Roman, and Byzantine Studies* 36(1): 51-87; McGovern, William Montgomery, *The Early Empires of Central Asia: A study of the Scythians and the Huns and the Part They Played in World History, with Special Reference to the Chinese Sources* (Chapel Hill: University of North Carolina Press, 1939); Sivan, Hagith, Ulfila's own conversion, *Harvard Theological Review*, 1996, 89(4): 373-386; Thompson, E. A., *The Early Germans* (Oxford: Clarendon, 1965); *A History of Attila and the Huns* (Oxford: Clarendon, 1948); *Romans and Barbarians: The Decline of the Western Empire* (Madison: University of Wisconsin Press, 1982); *The Visigoths in the Time of Ulfila* (Oxford: Clarendon, 1966); Williams, Stephen, and Friell, Gerard, *Theodosius: The Empire at Bay* (London: B. T. Batsford, 1994); Wolfram, Herwig, *History of the Goths*, rev. ed. (Berkeley: University of California Press, 1988); *The Roman Empire and its Germanic Peoples* (Berkeley, CA: University of California Press, 1997).

Catacombs and Christian Art

Milburn, Robert, *Early Christian Art and Architecture* (Berkeley: University of California Press, 1988); Rutgers, L. V., *Subterranean Rome: In Search of the Roots of Christianity in the Catacombs of the Eternal City* (Leuven, Belgium: Peeters, 2000); Stevenson, J., *The Catacombs: Life and Death in Early Christianity* (Nashville: T. Nelson, 1985), (Original work published 1978).

Judaism and Jewish Religion

Johnson, Paul, *A History of the Jews* (London: Weidenfeld and Nicolson, 1987); Neusner, Jacob, *Judaism and Christianity in the Age of Constantine: History, Messiah, Israel, and the Initial Confrontation* (Chicago: University Press, 1987); Reuther, Rosemary Radford, *Faith and Fratricide: The Theological Roots of Anti-Semitism* (New York: Seabury Press, 1974).

Persecution of Christians

Frend, W. H. C., *Martyrdom and Persecution in the Early Church: A Study of a Conflict from the Maccabees to Donatus* (Oxford: Blackwell, 1965); Gregg, John A. F., *The Decian Persecution* (Edinburgh: Blackwood, 1897); Gustafson, Mark, Condemnation to the Mines in the Later Roman Empire, *Harvard Theological Review*, 1994, *87*, pp.42-133; Healy, Patrick J. *The Valerian Persecution* (Boston: B. Franklin, 1905); Ricciotti, Giuseppe, *Age of Martyrs: Christianity from Diocletian to Constantine*, trans. Anthony Bull (Milwaukee, WI: Bruce, 1959); Sordi, Marta, *The Christians and the Roman Empire* (Norman: University of Oklahoma Press, 1986).

Rome and the Empire

Brauer, George C., *The Age of the Soldier Emperors: Imperial Rome, 244-284* (Park Ridge, NJ: Noyes Press, 1975); Cameron, Averil, *The Late Roman Empire, A.D. 284-430* (Cambridge, MA: Harvard University Press, 1993); Jones, A. H. M., *The Decline of the Ancient World* (London: Longmans, Green, 1966); *The Later Roman Empire, 284-602*, 3 vols (Baltimore, MD: Johns Hopkins University Press, 1986); Millar, Fergus, *The Emperor in the Roman World: 31 B.C.-A.D. 337* (London: Duckworth, 1977); Sextus Aurelius Victor, *Liber de Caesaribus of Sextus Aurelius Victor*, trans. H. W. Bird (Liverpool: University Press, 1994); Williams, Stephen, *Diocletian and the Roman Recovery* (New York: Methuen, 1985).

Early Christian Writers and Writings

There are many widely available translations of the writings of the early Christian writers and historians. In addition to those cited below, the 1885 "Edinburgh" series, including *The Ante-Nicene Fathers*, edited by Alexander Roberts and James Donaldson, and *The Nicene and Post-Nicene Fathers*, edited by Philip Schaff and Henry Wace, has been reprinted by Eerdmans (Grand Rapids, MI, 1986) and is available online at www.ccel.org.; Athanasius, Bishop of Alexandria, *Selected Treatises of St. Athanasius in Controversy with the Arians*, trans. John Henry Newman (London: Longmans Green, 1911); Cyprian of Carthage, *Letters (1-81)*, trans. Sr Rose Bernard Donna (Washington, DC: Catholic University of America Press, 1964); Dionysius of Alexandria, *Letters and Treatises*, ed. Charles Lett Feltoe (London: S.P.C.K., 1918); Eusebius of Caesarea, *A History of the Church from Christ to Constantine*, trans. G. A. Williamson (New York: Dorset, 1966); Eusebius of Caesarea, *Life of Constantine by Eusebius*, trans. Averil Cameron and Stuart G. Hall (Oxford: Clarendon, 1999); Optatus, Bishop of Mileve, *Against the Donatists*, trans. and ed. Mark Edwards (Liverpool: Liverpool University Press, 1997); Prudentius Clemens, Aurelius, *Prudentius*, trans. H. J. Thomson, 2 vols (Cambridge, MA: Harvard University Press, 1949); *Poems of Prudentius*, trans. Sister M. Clement Eagen, 2 vols (Washington, DC: Catholic University of America Press, 1962-1965); Rufinus of Aquileia, *The Church History of Rufinus of Aquileia*, trans. Philip R. Amidon (New York: Oxford University Press, 1997); Sozomen, *The ecclesiastical history of Sozomen: Comprising a history of the church from A. D. 324 to A. D. 440 / translated from the Greek, with a memoir of the author; also, The ecclesiastical history of Philostorgius, as epitomised by Photius Patriarch of Constantinople*, trans. Edward Walford (London: Bohn, 1855); Stevenson, J., ed., *A New Eusebius: Documents Illustrating the History of the Church to A.D. 337, Based on the Collection of the Late B. J. Kidd* (New York: Macmillan, 1957); Theodoret, *History of the Church from A.D. 322 to the Death of Theodore of Mopsuestia, A.D. 427* (London: Henry G. Bohn, 1854); Zosimus, *A New History*, trans. Ronald T. Ridley (Sydney: Australian Association for Byzantine Studies, 1982).

PHOTOGRAPHIC CREDITS

INDEX